USE THIS BOOK WITH CAUTION!

Armed with the advanced concepts of poker that this book teaches, you know how to play good poker—and how to force others into playing poor poker. You know when to bet, raise and bluff—how to elicit bets, raises and bluffs from those you have to beat. You know how to read the hands and intentions of opponents, how to extract the maximum money from them—how to bankrupt them. You are in control of the game and its players. You can lure them into following their emotions, into losing control of themselves, into disorienting their psyches . . . even into destroying themselves.

HOW FAR CAN YOU GO WITH POKER?

Let your conscience and your goals be your guide.

Special Features!

- A complete glossary, bibliography and history of poker.
- The only accurately defined table of odds ever published.

POKER

A GUARANTEED INCOME FOR LIFE

---

by using the

Advanced Concepts of Poker

BY

FRANK R. WALLACE

WARNER BOOKS

A Warner Communications Company

Dedicated to
John Finn

WARNER BOOKS EDITION

Copyright © 1968, 1972, 1976, 1977 by Frank R. Wallace

Library of Congress Catalog Card Number: 76-30703

ISBN 0-446-81369-9

Cover design by Gene Light

Cover photo by Mort Engel

This Warner Books Edition is published by
arrangement with Crown Publishers, Inc.

Warner Books, Inc., 75 Rockefeller Plaza, New York, N.Y. 10019

A Warner Communications Company

Printed in the United States of America

Not associated with Warner Press, Inc., of Anderson, Indiana

First Printing: March, 1978

10 9 8 7 6 5 4 3 2

PREFACE

You can earn $50,000 a year by playing poker . . . yes, even more if you want to. Any man or woman can get rich by applying the "Advanced Concepts of Poker".

This book is for the penny-ante novice as well as the professional poker player; this book is for anyone who will ever pick up a poker hand. Once you are familiar with the "Advanced Concepts of Poker", your only limitation in winning money is the extent you choose to apply these concepts.

What is your goal in poker? Do you want to get rich, be the biggest winner in the game, gain confidence, punish another player, or just have more fun? Define what you want, then increasingly apply the "Advanced Concepts of Poker" until you reach your goal. How far should you go? . . . That depends on you, your conscience, and your goals.

CAUTION

The poker player armed with the "Advanced Concepts of Poker" knows how to play good poker—he also knows how to force others into playing poor poker. He knows when to bet, raise, and bluff—he also knows how to elicit bets, raises, and bluffs from those he has beat. He knows how to read the hands and intentions of opponents—he also knows how to delude opponents into misreading his hands and intentions. . . . But most importantly, the poker player armed with the "Advanced Concepts of Poker" knows how to extract maximum money from his opponents—he knows how to bankrupt them.

And most dangerously, the poker player armed with the "Advanced Concepts of Poker" knows how to control the game and its players—he knows how to control and manipulate the minds of players. He knows how to lure players into following their emotions, into losing control of themselves, into disorienting their psyches . . . even into destroying themselves.

INTRODUCTION

Every week millions of poker players lose more money than many nations spend in a year.* Around the world, billions of dollars await those knowing more than the basic concepts and techniques of poker. . . . The opportunities for the good player are great.

From 1850 to 1977, over one-hundred and fifty books have been published about poker—none focus on the concept of extracting maximum money from a poker game. This book reveals methods to win maximum money from *any* game. This book also describes methods to generate more money by quickening the betting pace, raising the stakes, expanding the game, creating new games, and finding bigger games. . . . This book shows how amateurs and professionals alike can win a guaranteed income from poker—in private games or in public casinos.

The player who knows and applies the "Advanced Concepts of Poker" is a rare person . . . few have ever played against him. He can win money so fast that he could bankrupt most games at will. But he controls his winnings and preserves the game in order to extract maximum money from his opponents. He camouflages his poker skill; his opponents seldom realize that he is taking all their money.

* *A LIFE magazine article (August 16, 1968) about poker reported that 47,000,000 poker players in the United States wager 45 billion dollars annually. . . . Most poker players are poor players who lose both their time and their money in poker. The good players win all the money the poor players lose.*

Once familiar with the "Advanced Concepts of Poker", any player can—

- recognize the good player
- guard against the good player
- develop into a good player.

The "Advanced Concepts of Poker" are objective and realistic. Many involve deception. Some are ruthless. A few are immoral.* Know them and be wiser. Apply them and get richer.**

* None of the "Advanced Concepts of Poker" employ cheating, but a few are immoral because they involve deception outside the poker game. The good player, however, does not need to use a single immoral concept to achieve his goals. So why include immoral concepts? This book is a definitive treatment of poker and, therefore, all concepts are included. Also, by identifying the immoral concepts, the reader can recognize them and take defensive measures when such concepts are used against him.

** This Manual identifies the true nature of winning poker as a highly profitable but a time-consuming, nonproductive activity that requires bringing out the worst in each opponent. In certain cases, therefore, poker can work against the good player's self-esteem and happiness no matter how much he wins.

CONTENTS

(*Number in parentheses indicates concept number)

PART THREE
STRATEGIES

PART SIX
PROFESSIONALS

PART SEVEN
POKER NOTES

The
Advanced Concepts
of Poker

How much money can you win at poker? It makes no difference if you are a professional poker player, a novice, or have never played poker before* . . . the following 142 "Advanced Concepts of Poker" can guide any man or woman to unlimited winnings. How much you win depends on how *fully* and how *many* of these concepts you choose to apply.

---

* Complete Beginners: *The basic rules and concepts of poker are simple and can be learned after a few hours exposure to any poker game.*

PART ONE

DEFINITIONS

Definitions of the broadest aspects of poker (i.e., the game, odds, betting, players, emotions, and concepts) are given in the following pages as contextual descriptions.*

---

* *Definitions of specific words or phrases used in poker are given in the Glossary in Appendix C.*

I
GAME OF POKER (1)*

The object of poker is to win maximum money.
Poker is not a card game; it is a game of money management. Cards are merely the tools for manipulating
money. From the smallest penny-ante game to the
largest table-stake game, all money eventually goes to
the good player. His key weapons are his mind and a
license to use unlimited deception.

Poker is unique among money-making situations. In
business, for example, opportunities to apply the
proper business concepts are limited in number. The
financial outcome, therefore, cannot be certain. But in
poker, while chance may influence each separate hand,
the opportunities (hands) are so numerous that
"luck"** becomes insignificant. Application of the
proper poker concepts assures financial success.

**Poker concepts are best illustrated by players in
actual game situations. The following players are the
nucleus of a weekly, Monday night game:**

Sid Bennett
Ted Fehr
John Finn
Quintin Merck
Scotty Nichols

**Although other men play in this game from time to
time, most of the poker situations in this book are
illustrated with these five players.**

**"Four in the morning," Quintin Merck grunts at the
dark-whiskered men still sitting around the rectangular
poker table. It is not a real poker table, not the kind
with trays for money and a green felt top . . . it is the
dining room table at Scotty Nichols' house. They have
played here every Monday night for the past six years.**

---

*   *The 142 "Advanced Concepts of Poker" are listed in order
by numbers in parentheses following each concept heading.*
** *Luck is a mystical illusion that does not exist in reality
(see Concept 11).*

Rising layers of gray smoke mushroom around the overhead cluster of electric bulbs that push light down to a leather table mat covered with ten and twenty dollar bills. The largest pile of money is in front of John Finn, a twenty-eight-year-old social worker.

In the sticky summer heat, the men slouch in squeaking wooden chairs. Only John Finn appears alert. The tall, black-haired man slips on his glasses and hooks the gold rims around his ears. His dark eyes move from player to player.

On his left sits Sid Bennett, a thirty-five-year-old paving contractor. His large smiling head flops in a semicircle as straight yellow hair falls over his forehead and nearly touches his faded blue eyes. He's in a daze, John says to himself. Look at him grin.

On John's right sits Ted Fehr, a thirty-year-old gambler and restaurant owner. He coils a fifty dollar bill around his skinny fingers while waiting for the next hand. Under bristly red hair, his freckled face wrinkles. His sagging, bloodshot eyes watch John Finn's arm hook around the huge pot. "The biggest pot of the night," he moans, "and look who wins it. You . . ."

John interrupts, "Wake up, Professor, it's your deal."

With a growling noise, Professor Merck deals. John watches the deck and sees the bottom card plus two other cards flash. He then studies Quintin Merck's green eyes . . . they are watering from the cigarette smoke curling over his mustache and into his leathery face. Wearing a sweaty beret and an opened polo shirt, the wiry fifty-five-year-old college professor hunches over the table. Suddenly he looks up and frowns at John Finn.

Without flinching, John refocuses his eyes and looks into the kitchen. Then his eyes return to the game . . . he studies Scotty Nichols. The plump forty-two-year-old stockbroker slumps half dozing in his chair. His mouth droops open to expose a cluster of gold-capped teeth. His thick glasses magnify his eyes into brown globes that float in circles between each squeezing blink. A tie droops from the frayed collar of his scorched white shirt.

20

They're all valuable to me, John Finn tells
himself as his eyes draw into narrow slits.

II
ODDS (2)

Three types of odds are important in poker. Most
players are familiar with the *card* odds, and most players base their playing and betting decisions on them.
The card odds, however, can be meaningless unless the
investment odds are also considered. Another type of
odds is the *edge* odds, which evaluate the relative performance of each player. These three types of odds are
described below.

1. Card Odds (3)

The card odds are the probabilities of being dealt or
drawing to various hands. These odds are reviewed in
most books about poker. The following table is based
on the card odds and shows the statistical frequency
that different poker hands occur.

High Hands	Approximate Deals per Pat Hand	Hands Possible
Total hands	1	2,598,960
No pair	2	1,302,540
One pair	2.5	1,098,240
Two pair	20	123,552
Three of a kind	50	54,912
Straight	250	10,200
Flush	500	5,108
Full house	700	3,744
Four of a kind	4,000	624
Straight flush	70,000	36
Royal straight flush	650,000	4
Five aces (with joker)*	3,000,000	1

---

* *A 53-card deck with the joker has 2,869,685 possible hands.*

Low Hands	*Approximate Deals per Pat Hand*	*Hands Possible*
Ace high (+)	5	502,860
King high (+)	8	335,580
Queen high (+)	12	213,180
Jack high (+)	20	127,500
Ten high (+)	37	70,360
Nine high (+ +)	36	71,860
Eight high (+ +)	70	35,840
Seven high (+ +)	170	15,360
Six high (+ +)	500	5,120
Five high (+ +)	2,500	1,024

(+) No straights or flushes. Ace is high.
(+ +) Including straights and flushes. Ace is low.

There are 2,598,960 different poker hands in a fifty-two card deck. If a player is dealt 100,000 hands in his lifetime, he will never hold (on his first five cards) more than four percent of all the possible hands.

Other poker probabilities based on the card odds are tabulated in Appendix D.

The card odds can reveal interesting information. For example, how many pat straight flushes will Sid Bennett get during his lifetime? To figure this, the expected number of hands that will be dealt to him during his life is estimated by the following calculation:

10 hands/hr.×5 hrs./game×50 games/yr. ×40 yrs./poker life=100,000 hands/poker life

From this estimation, the number of pat (on the first five cards) poker hands that Sid should get during his lifetime is calculated from the card odds and tabulated below:

	Approximate Number of Pat Hands in a Lifetime
No pair	50,000
One pair	40,000
Two pair	5,000
Three of a kind	2,000

Straight	400
Flush	200
Full house	170
Four of a kind	25
Straight flush	1.4
Royal straight flush	0.15

So statistically, Sid should get a pat straight flush on his first five cards once or twice during his life. He will, of course, catch straight flushes more frequently on the draw and in seven-card stud.

. . . Sid wins a big pot with a full house. He throws back his massive head and shouts, "I'm on a spinner! I'm going to break this game!" His head drops; he shakes his finger at the players and continues, "Just watch my luck. I'm getting a whole round of pat flushes . . . starting next deal."

"That won't happen till the sun burns out," Quintin Merck snorts.

Statistically, Quintin is right. Sid will be dealt five consecutive straight flushes once in every 1.7×10^{24} deals, or once in every 700,000,000,000,000,000,000 years. Yet his five consecutive straight flushes could start coming with the next deal.

Let him hope, John Finn says to himself.

2. Investment Odds (4)

Investment odds are the estimated returns on money that is bet. These odds are approximated by the following formula:*

$$\frac{\text{(potential size of pot, \$) (probability of winning pot)}}{\text{potential loss, \$}} = \text{Investment Odds}$$

* If you are a beginner or are not mathematically inclined, do not be discouraged or get bogged down by this formula. Forget the formula for now and read on. With experience, you will realize that accurate estimations of investment odds are achieved by the proper thinking methods and not by mathematical problem-solving. This formula is merely a shorthand expression of the thought process required for properly evaluating a bet.

For example, if a player estimates that a $40 potential pot would require a $10 betting investment (his potential loss), and if he estimates that his probability of winning that pot is .4 (40%)*, then his investment odds would be calculated as follows:

$$\frac{(40)\,(.4)}{10} = 1.6$$

When the investment odds are greater than 1.0, the play is favorable and should be made.

Investment odds are important for making correct betting and playing decisions. Most players rely only on card odds, which often lead to wrong decisions. For example, investment odds sometimes favor drawing to an inside straight. At other times, investment odds favor folding three aces before the draw. In both cases, the wrong play may have resulted if the decisions were based on the card odds.

Determination of investment odds is not a mathematical problem. Numbers plugged into the formula on page 23 are quick estimations or guesses derived by gathering together and then objectively evaluating the facts of the game, players, and situation. These estimations become more valid with increased thinking effort and experience. While the good player may never actually use or even think about this formula, it does express his thought process for evaluating bets.

Quintin, Ted and Scotty each draw one card. John Finn holds two low pair, tens and fours. What does he do? He considers the card odds, the past betting, probable future betting, his observations (e.g., of flashed cards), and his reading of each opponent . . . he then estimates the following investment odds:

* How does a player estimate the probability of winning a pot? He does this by assessing his own hand and position against the behavior and betting of his opponents. Initially, these estimates may be little more than guesses. Accuracy will improve with practice, experience and application of the various concepts described in this book.

Draw one card to his two pair . . .

$$\frac{(\$200)(.2)}{\$60} = .66 = \text{fold}$$

Draw three cards to his pair of fours . . .

$$\frac{(\$300)(.1)}{\$20} = 1.5 = \text{play}$$

So instead of folding his two pair (and often the investment odds favor folding the two small pair), he breaks up his hand and draws to the pair of fours at favorable investment odds. The low $20 estimate of his potential loss is the key to making this play favorable. John figures his chances for catching and having to call the last bet are small.* When the high probability of a no-bet or a folded hand (zero dollars) is averaged into the numerator, the potential loss becomes relatively small—even though the last round bet may be large if he improves his hand. In other words, he will fold with no additional cost unless he catches three of a kind or better, which would let him bet heavily with a good possibility of winning.

In another hand, Sid and Ted draw three cards. Again John has two low pair. After objectively weighing all factors within the framework of the investment odds formula, he estimates his most favorable play is to stay pat and then bet the last round as if he had a straight or a flush:

Play pat . . .

$$\frac{(\$100)(.8)}{\$60} = 1.33 = \text{play}$$

The advantages of this play are: If either Sid or Ted catches two pair or even trips, he may fold and let

* *The weakness of hands such as small pairs, four flushes and four-card straights after the draw increases the investment odds because failure to improve these hands causes an immediate fold, thereby reducing the potential loss.*

John win on a pat bluff. If either catches a strong
hand and shows any betting strength, John folds with
no additional cost. Also, neither will try to bluff into
John's pat hand. And finally if Sid and Ted do not
improve, John Finn wins additional money if either
one calls.

3. Edge Odds or Edge Percentages (5)

Edge odds indicate the relative performance of a
player in a poker game. These odds are calculated by
the following formula:

$$\frac{\text{average winnings (or losses) of player, \$}}{\text{average winnings of the biggest winner, \$}} \times 100\% = \text{Edge Odds } \%*$$

For example, if the biggest winner of *each* game
averages plus $150, and if a player averages plus $75
per game, then the edge odds for this player are $+75/150 \times 100\% = +50\%$. The more games used to calculate edge odds, the more significant they become.
Edge odds based on ten or more games should reflect
the relative performance of a player fairly accurately.
The good poker player usually maintains edge odds
ranging from 25% to 65% depending on the game
and abilities of the other players. An approximate
performance grading of poker players based on the
edge odds is tabulated below:

Grading	Edge Odds† in Games Without A Good Player		Edge Odds† in Games With A Good Player	
Good Player	—		25 —	65
Sound Player	10 —	25	5 —	20
Average Player	0 —	15	(−5)—	10
Weak Player	(−10)—	5	(−15)—	0
Poor Player	(−20)—(−5)		(−65)—(−10)	

† *These edge odds are estimated for an average, seven-man game.*

* *If you are not mathematically inclined and do not understand this or other formulae and ratios presented in this
chapter, do not worry, just skip over these formulae and read
on, for these formulae are not necessary to understand and
utilize the concepts identified in this book.*

The good player is a very expensive person to have in a poker game as indicated above by the sharp decreases in everyone's edge odds when he plays.

In a black leather notebook, John Finn keeps records of every player. After each game, he estimates their winnings and losses. After every ten games, he calculates their edge odds as shown below.

Ten-Game Average Edge Odds, %

Player	Estimated Average Win or Loss per Game, $	Edge Odds,† %	Grading
John Finn	+262	+59	Good
Quintin Merck	+ 45	+10	Sound
Scotty Nichols	− 10	− 2	Average
Sid Bennett	− 95	−21	Poor
Ted Fehr	−100	−22	Poor
Other Players	−135	−30	Poor

†The biggest winner for each game averaged +$445.

By reviewing his long-term edge odds data (shown below), John notices slow changes in the players . . . Quintin is gradually improving, Scotty and Ted are deteriorating, while Sid remains stable.

Ten-Game-Average Edge Odds, % (1961–1962)

Ten-game period #	1	2	3	4	5	6	7
John Finn	+61	+53	+62	+59	+55	+60	+56
Quintin Merck	− 2	+ 2	− 5	+10	+ 8	+12	+15
Scotty Nichols	+ 4	+ 7	+ 6	− 2	+ 1	−10	−18
Sid Bennett	−22	−20	−23	−21	−20	−18	−12
Ted Fehr	−18	−20	−19	−22	−28	−30	−31
Other Players	−23	−24	−26	−30	−25	−22	−20
Average biggest winner, +$	295	315	430	445	570	650	630

The steady increase in profit for the biggest winner also reflects John Finn's progress in driving up the betting stakes and pace.

III
BETTING (6)

Few players differentiate between the betting stakes and the betting pace. The betting *stakes* are the size of bets and raises permitted. The stakes are established by the house rules. The betting *pace* is the tempo or frequency of bets and raises. The pace depends on the games played and the willingness of players to bet. Both the stakes and pace determine how expensive the game is . . . or how much money can be won or lost.

The good player is seldom characterized as a tight player. His betting pattern is generally (but not always) aggressive*, and often lopsidedly aggressive. Pushing hard whenever he has an advantage (i.e., at favorable investment odds) and quickly dropping against stronger hands lets him maximize his wins and minimize his losses.

When the good player bets, he generally bets aggressively. For the good player, increased aggressiveness advantageously quickens the betting pace, while lopsided aggressiveness advantageously creates confusion and fear in his opponents.

As the stakes increase with each round of betting, the losses of the poor players will increase faster than the *potential* losses of the good player. Indeed, the investment-odds formula on page 23 suggests that a steeper and steeper betting progression within a hand (causing the numerator to increase more rapidly than the denominator) permits greater and greater betting aggressiveness, which in turn allows the good player to bet with poorer and poorer hands. In other words, the good player not only tries to drive up the betting stakes

---

* *Good players are confident in their betting and generally play aggressively. Poor players are either too loose or too tight in their betting and seldom play aggressively.*

and betting pace within a game, but also tries to create a steeper betting progression within a hand.

1. Betting Stakes (7)
Most players think only of the betting stakes when they consider the size of the game.

The betting stakes in John Finn's Monday night games are as follows: In draw, $25 is the maximum bet or raise on the first round of betting. This maximum increases to $50 in subsequent rounds of betting. In stud, the maximum bet is $5 on the first up card. The bet then increases in $5 increments on each subsequent round of betting to $10, $15, $20 and so on. Only three raises are allowed except when only two players remain, and then raises are unlimited. Check raising is permitted.

2. Betting Pace (8)
The betting pace is often more significant than the betting stakes in determining the size of the game. The good player knows the betting pace of both the game and of each individual hand. The betting pace of the *game* (game pace) is determined by comparing the betting done on various hands to the betting normally done on these hands. The pace may differ markedly among different poker games. In a fast-paced game, for example, two pair after the draw may be worth two raises. In a slow-paced game, these same two pair may be worth not even a small bet.

The betting pace of each *hand* (hand pace) is determined by comparing the extent of betting, calling, raising, and bluffing to the size of the pot. Often this pace is too slow during certain phases of a hand and too fast during other phases. The good player controls his offensive and defensive game by altering his betting pace at various phases of a poker hand. The ratios shown on the following page reflect the betting pace during the various phases of a poker hand.

Phase	Ratio*	Increasing Ratio ⟶
Open	$\dfrac{\text{(opening bet,\$) (\# callers)}}{\text{pot, \$}}$	Slow Pace→Fast Pace
Raise	$\dfrac{\text{(raise bet, \$) (\# callers)}}{\text{pot, \$}}$	Slow Pace→Fast Pace
Final Bet	$\dfrac{\text{(last bet, \$) (\# callers)}}{\text{pot, \$}}$	Slow Pace→Fast Pace
Bluff	$\dfrac{\text{(\# bluffs) (average \# final callers)}}{\text{\# hands played}}$	Slow Pace→Fast Pace

Few hands are played at the optimum betting pace.
And if, for example, the betting pace is relatively slow,
the optimum pace will be somewhat faster. A person
increases his investment and edge odds by playing
closer to the optimum pace.

In the Monday night game, John realizes that the
betting in seven-card stud moves at a fast pace during
the early rounds, but slows considerably in the late
rounds of big bets. He takes advantage of this im-
balance by laying back during the early rounds as
players get drawn in and disclose their betting tendencies. Then in the later rounds, he quickens the
pace by betting aggressively. But while playing closer
to the optimum pace himself, John is careful not to
correct the imbalanced pace of other players.

The following ratios illustrate how John Finn estimates and influences the hand pace of the Monday
night, seven-card stud game.

---

* If you are not mathematically inclined and do not understand this or other formulae and ratios presented in this chapter,
do not worry, just skip over these formulae and read on, for
these formulae are not necessary to understand and utilize
the concepts identified in this book.

Phase	Without John Finn		With John Finn
	Estimated Ratios	*Pace*	*Estimated Ratios*
Open	$\dfrac{\$4 \times 4}{\$23} = .70$	Too fast	$\dfrac{\$3 \times 5}{\$22} = .68$
Raise (first round)	$\dfrac{\$5 \times 3}{\$38} = .40$		$\dfrac{\$5 \times 4}{\$42} = .48$
Final Bet	$\dfrac{\$20 \times 2}{\$198} = .20$	Too slow	$\dfrac{\$25 \times 3}{\$297} = .25$
Final Raise	Best hand should raise, but often does not		John Finn often makes final raise

IV
POKER PLAYERS (9)

There are good poker players and poor poker players. Most players fall in between these two extremes. The good player works hard to maintain maximum edge odds . . . he never compromises his advantage for the sake of others. He shares his abilities or earnings with no one. The poor player displays laziness and a lack of discipline. Unlike those in the non-poker world, the poor poker player cannot sponge off of the advantages or earnings of others.

1. Good Player (10)
The good player plays solely for his own benefit. He is *not* a gambler* because he bets only when the odds are favorable. (Gamblers bet money at unfavorable odds and eventually lose all the money they risk.) The good poker player cannot lose; he eventually wins all the money that gambling players will risk.

* *See the footnote in Concept 81 for a definition of gambling.*

31

Ability to play good poker does not correlate with intelligence or ability to play games such as bridge or chess. What makes a good poker player? ... The good player can subjugate his impulses and motivate all his actions toward meeting the objective of poker, which is to win maximum money. He never gives anything away or helps others without the motive of eventual profit. The good player thinks ahead and plans his moves in advance. He disciplines himself and maintains an emotional consistency. He objectively analyzes the game as well as each invidual player, hand, and bet; he then adapts to any situation. The good player continuously expands his skill by soaking up the experience of every play made by each player.

Good poker players are rare, and their paths seldom cross. In fact, most players have never encountered a good player. In the rare event that two good players are in the same game, their effective control is diluted and their edge odds are reduced by each other's presence. A good player searches for weaknesses in his opponents, but two good players will not waste time in trying to analyze each other. They direct their mental effort more profitably toward studying the game and the other players.

When involved in a hand against the good player, meaningful investment odds can be difficult to estimate, and card odds may be the best basis for a decision. The strategy of the good player often depends on creating impulse reactions in his opponents. The proper move, therefore, can sometimes be made against a good player by acting oppositely to one's initial impulse. For example, when undecided about calling a good player and the impulse is to fold, the best move may be to call or even raise.

John Finn is the only good player in the Monday night game. He works hard, thinks objectively, and adapts to any situation. By applying the "Advanced Concepts of Poker," he wins maximum money from the game.

To overcome mental laziness and restrictive thinking, he forces himself to think constantly and imaginatively about the game. This lets him make more

profitable plays. For example, he breaks up a pat full house* to triple the size of the pot while decreasing his chances of winning only slightly (from 98% down to 85%). But this play increases his estimated investment odds from

$$\frac{(100)\ (.98)}{\$20} = 4.9 \qquad \text{up to} \quad \frac{(300)\ (.85)}{\$40} = 6.4.$$

John wins consistently, but still his opponents refuse to realize that they are paying him thousands of dollars every year to play in their game.

2. Other Players (11)

The other players supply income to the good player. They are working for him and are his assets. He treats them with care and respect. He plans his actions to extract maximum money from them.

The differences in attitude between the good player and other players are listed on the next two pages.

The major enemy of poker players is their rationalization for their failure to think. They continually find excuses for their self-imposed weaknesses and their lack of self-control. Their losses are directly proportional to their mental laziness. The poor player evades thinking by letting his mind sink into irrational fogs. His belief in luck short-circuits his mind by excusing him from the responsibility to think. Belief in luck is a great mystical rationalization for the refusal to think. . . . In method of thought, good players are right and poor players are wrong.

John Finn uses the mystical attitudes of his opponents to extract more money from them. In his black

---

* *The opportunity to profitably break a full house by drawing to three of a kind rarely occurs. The above case results when several players with weak hands would fold if the full house were played pat, but would call if a draw were made. Also, the full house would be broken to draw to four of a kind if sufficient evidence existed that the full house was not the best hand.*

notebook, he has a table that summarizes everyone's attitude:

Situation	Mystical Attitude	Objective Attitude
Evaluation of a play	Quintin, Scotty, Sid, Ted	John
Winner or loser	Scotty, Sid, Ted	John, Quintin
Streaks of luck	Scotty, Sid, Ted	John, Quintin
Wild games	Quintin, Scotty, Ted	John, Sid
Play past time limit	Scotty, Sid	John, Quintin, Ted
Violation of rules	Quintin, Ted	John, Sid, Scotty
Cheaters	Scotty, Ted	John, Quintin, Sid

Situation	Mystical Feelings of Many Players	Objective Attitude of Good Player
Poker game	A relaxing mental diversion to escape reality.	A mental discipline requiring full focus on reality.
Evaluation of a play	Winning the pot is most important.	Playing the hand properly is most important.
Winner or loser	Play according to winnings or losses.	Never be influenced by winnings or losses.
Streaks of luck	Chances or odds are influenced by previous events. Luck runs in cycles.	Past means nothing, except for the psychological effects it has on other players.
Wild games	Such games are not real poker and require less skill. "Good" poker players will not play these games.	Complex or wild games require more skill and offer greater advantages to the good player.

34

Situation	Mystical Feelings of Many Players	Objective Attitude of Good Player
Ante Increase	Attitudes are mixed.	A bigger ante encourages looser play and decreases any advantage of a tight player.
Table stakes	Winner has an advantage when he takes money off the table.	The good player has more advantage with maximum money on the table.
Play past time limit	Chances of winning decrease.	Advantages for the good player increase as opponents get tired and think less.
Violation of rules	Enforce rules equally.	*Apply* rules rigidly to better players and more liberally to weaker players. *Interpret* rules consistently and equitably.
Change in sequence of cards while dealing.	The run of cards is broken . . . misdeal.	Makes no difference . . . keep on playing.
Playing errors such as betting out of turn	Scold or penalize the culprit.	Usually benefits the good player. Encourage sloppy play.
Cheater	Throw him out of game.	If he is a loser, say nothing and let him play.

V
EMOTIONS (12)

Money affects emotions, and emotions control most players. Poker involves the winning and losing of money. Common emotions of anger, excitement, greed, masochism, sadism, and self-pity often take control of players during the action. Most players fail to recognize or are unable to suppress these emotional influences that decrease their objectivity and poker ability. The good player recognizes his own emotions and prevents them from influencing his actions. . . . He avoids acting on his whims and feelings.

Players respond emotionally to various experiences during the game. The good player uses these emotional reactions to his financial advantage. Some typical reactions and their causes are listed on the opposite page.

Emotional Reactions	*Causes of Reactions*
Playing loose to recover losses Playing tight to minimize losses	A losing streak
Playing loose to push good luck Playing tight to protect winnings	A winning streak
Extending good luck by playing recklessly	Winning a big hand or several consecutive hands
Playing poorly to avenge a loss or to retaliate for injured feelings	Losing a big hand or having feelings hurt
Acting comical or silly	Fear, nervousness, lack of confidence, or desire for diversion
Becoming prone to impulsive actions and mistakes	Fear, nervousness, or desperation
Losing concentration and decreasing awareness of situation	Laziness, other thoughts, fatigue

Recognition and control of one's own emotions are difficult and require thinking effort. This is one reason why good poker players are rare.

The good player directs his actions to produce desirable emotions (e.g., pleasure and self-esteem); the poor player lets his emotions produce undesirable actions.

Poker is a unique medium for studying people. Where else can one stare at and intensely observe another person for hours every week?

The opportunity to study players, often in highly emotional situations, is probably better than most psychoanalysts get to analyze their patients. The observant, good player will soon understand his opponents better than their own families do.

Poker players are often fatigued and under emotional stresses that expose their characters. On another page in John's notebook, he summarizes the emotional characteristics of his opponents:

Player	Emotional Characteristics
Quintin Merck	Fairly stable and objective. Can be roused by insulting or humiliating, then his playing disintegrates. Becomes less objective during late hours as he fatigues.
Scotty Nichols	Has inferiority complex and lack of confidence. Plays extremely tight if winning. He loosens up and plays recklessly after suffering a heavy loss or after losing several consecutive hands.
Sid Bennett	Hides his lack of confidence with silly behavior. Humor him and keep atmosphere relaxed to bring out his worst. Be careful not to hurt his feelings, or he will sulk and play tight. Goes wild when winning.
Ted Fehr	A compulsive gambler. Wants to punish himself. Wants to lose. Deteriorates easily into a desperate condition. Insensitive to insults. Low level of pride.

VI
POKER CONCEPTS (13)

Ideas on how to play poker can be assembled into concepts. The normal concepts described in most poker books are popular ideas based on a combination of common sense and generalizations. These concepts can help some poor players improve their game. But good poker requires a much sharper definition of the problems followed by actions based on more sophisticated and advanced concepts. The "Advanced Concepts of Poker" offer objective approaches to each aspect of the game and are designed for winning maximum money.

1. Common Concepts (14)

The most common concept for winning at poker has always been to play conservatively (tight) and to play according to the card odds. Most books on poker stress this concept. They usually include some basic techniques as well as some rules for betting, raising, and bluffing. They also present some common ideas about strategy and psychology. . . . But none of these books offer a maximum-win approach to poker. (Appendix B lists all the known books about poker published since 1872.)

The following summary pages identify and analyze the fallacies of many common concepts presented in the well-known and classic books on poker.

By applying the *common* concepts of poker, one can win moderately in small-stake games that consist mainly of poor players. But in regular high-stake games, continual losses force most poor players to quit or to improve. High-stake games, therefore, often consist of experienced poker players advanced beyond these common concepts.

When a player using the common concepts enters a high-stake game, he usually feels confident that by playing tight he will eventually win over his looser-playing opponents. Bewilderment gradually replaces

EXAMPLES OF COMMON CONCEPTS IN POKER LITERATURE

Book	Concept	Failure of Concept
Abbott, J.—1881 Jack Pot Poker	Never lend or borrow money.	Credit is necessary to keep most private, high-stake games going week after week.
Allen, G. W.—1895 Poker Rules in Rhyme	"It's the game the boys like best Two or three times a week, One man often beats the rest With nothing else but cheek."	Action on objectively thought-out plans (not cheek) is needed to win consistently.
Blackbridge, J.—1880 The Complete Poker Player	To play for a minimum loss or gain is what a gentleman should hope for.	To play for maximum gain is what the good player strives for.
Cady, Alice H.—1895 Poker	Bluffing should be shunned, for only an old player can experiment in this.	Only the weakest players will shun bluffing.

Book	Concept	Failure of Concept
Coffin, G. S.—1949 Fortune Poker	Shrewd players in bad luck should call for a new deck of cards to break the cycle.	A sign of a poor player is one who calls for a new deck of cards to break his "bad luck" . . . he fails to understand poker.
Crawford, J. R.—1953 How to be a Consistent Winner	Treat every bet as though it were your first one. Forget the money already in the pot.	Must consider the money in the pot to estimate the potential return on the present bet (investment odds).
Culbertson, E.—1950 Culbertson's Hoyle	Never raise early unless the purpose is to drive out players.	Raise early to start bluffs, build pots, control betting, keep players in, drop players out—depending on the situation.
Curtis, D. A.—1901 The Science of Draw Poker	New-fangled, high-low poker is mental weakness and should soon die out, even among the feeble-minded.	High-low poker requires more skill and offers greater advantages to the good player than does straight poker.
Dowling, A. H.—1940 Confessions of a Poker Player	Players acting out of turn should be penalized.	Players acting out of turn benefit the good player.

Book	Concept	Failure of Concept
Encyclopaedia Britannica—1965 Poker	In high-low seven-card stud, never play for high unless first three cards are trips.	When to play depends on the investment odds, not on fixed dogma.
Florence, W. J.—1891 Handbook on Poker	A good player will at times purposely play poorly to vary his game.	The good player never purposely plays poorly. With thinking, he finds infinite ways to vary his game at favorable investment odds.
Foster, R. F.—1904 Practical Poker	The compulsory ante is not based on judgment and has been the ruin of the scientific poker player.	The ante helps the loose player and usually benefits the good player.
Frey, R. L.—1947 The Complete Hoyle	Never open unless the probability is that you hold the highest hand.	Open without best hand to establish betting position, to defend against a larger bet, or to set up a play at favorable investment odds.

Book	Concept	Failure of Concept
Henry, J. R.—1890 Poker Boiled Down	Elements of poker success are good luck, good cards, cheek, good temper and patience.	"Good luck" and good cards have no bearing on poker success . . all players eventually get the same "luck" and cards.
Jacoby, O.—1947 Oswald Jacoby on Poker	The most successful bluffs are likely to be the innocent ones.	The most successful bluffs are likely to be the well-thought-out and properly executed ones.
Keller, J. W.—1887 Draw Poker	Playing poker without money is really an intellectual and scientific game. Playing poker with money becomes mere gambling.	Poker is a game of money management, not a card game.
Morehead, A. H.—1956 New Complete Hoyle	The most widespread mistake is to play long hours in a futile losers' game.	The greatest advantages occur in a game consisting of tired losers . . . they are usually the poor players at their poorest. Also, the losers' game will usually move at a faster pace and with sloppier play.

Book	Concept	Failure of Concept
Morehead, A. H.—1967 The Complete Guide to Winning Poker	Many of the finest poker exploits are inspirational and intuitional.	The only fine poker exploits are the ones consciously thought out.
Moss, J.—1955 How to Win at Poker	Beware of poor players. Stay out of games in which there are fish.	Poor players are the most profitable opponents. Seek poor players and games in which there are fish.
Ostrow, A. A.—1945 The Complete Card Player	Seven-stud, wild-card, and high-low poker increase the element of luck so greatly that rules for improving one's play cannot be set down.	The more complex the poker variations, the less the element of "luck" affects the outcome.
Philips, H.—1960 Profitable Poker	No sillier resolution is uttered than, "Well, I must see it through."	If the pot is large and the final bet is small, the investment odds may heavily favor "seeing it through."
Radner, S. H.—1957 The Key to Playing Poker	To assure a night's winnings, sit to the left of loose bettors and to the right of tight players.	The good player usually sits to the right of loose bettors and to the left of tight players.

44

Book	Concept	Failure of Concept
Reese, T. and Watkins, A. T.—1964 Secret of Modern Poker	To win consistently, you must play tight.	To win consistently, you must adapt to the game pace.
Rottenberg, I.—1965 Friday Night Poker	High-stake games are played by grim, salty players.	High-stake games are played by all types of players.
Scarne, J.—1965 Scarne on Cards	Do not lend money. It often comes back to break you.	The good player lends money in order to win more money.
Schenick, R. C.—1872 Rules for Playing Poker	The dealer has no special advantage.	The dealer has an advantage in draw games . . . and a large advantage in low-ball and twist stud games.
Smith, R. A.—1925 Poker to Win	The yellowest, most contemptible form of cheating is welching.	The welcher has lost his money in the game before borrowing; therefore, he has been an asset.
Steig, I.—1959 Poker for Fun and Profit	When someone says, "There isn't much to poker," walk away from him; he is a lout.	When someone says, "There isn't much to poker," get him in the game; he will be a valuable loser.

45

Book	Concept	Failure of Concept
Wickstead, J. M.—1938 How to Win at Stud Poker	In poker, fortune favors the brave.	In poker, the objective thinker makes fortune favor him.
Winterblossom, H. T.—1875 Draw Poker	The bluffing element in draw poker is fictitious.	The importance of bluffing depends on the stakes, not on the type of game.
Yardley, H. O.—1957 Education of a Poker Player	In all my life, I've never lost at over three consecutive sittings.	A good player at theoretical maximum edge odds (an impossible situation) will lose about once every four sessions . . . or lose in four consecutive sittings about once every 250 sessions. Also, the good player never brags about his success—he tries to conceal it.
General Advice in most poker books from 1872 to 1968	Keep stakes down, hold to a rigid quitting time, play tight and according to the card odds.	The good player drives the stakes up, usually avoids a rigid quitting time, and plays according to the investment odds.

46

confidence as he continually loses against players whom he considers inferior competition.

> Scotty Nichols usually plays sensibly . . . he bets only good hands and is the tightest player in the game. He has studied many books about poker and faithfully follows their techniques and strategy. According to these books, he should be a consistent winner, particularly in this game with its loose and wild players. Why is he a loser? John Finn knows the answer . . . Scotty plays too tight. The pots he wins are usually small, and the pots he loses are often large. Why? Whenever Scotty shows betting strength or even stays in a hand, the other players either fold or stop betting. When he wins, therefore, the pots are smaller than normal. When players do bet against him to make a large pot, they usually hold powerful enough hands to beat him. In other words, Scotty is a tight player who, like the wild player, has not adjusted to the game pace.

2 Advanced Concepts (15)

A player extracts maximum money from a poker game by using the "Advanced Concepts of Poker." Use of these concepts involves—

- opponents who do not fully understand poker

- ownerless pots that separate players from their money*

- interactions among a good player, other players, and pots.

By using the "Advanced Concepts of Poker", the good player eventually wins all the money that his opponents are willing to lose.

---

* Unattached money in a pot belongs to no one and can be ethically won by any deceptive means, except cheating. But poker-like deception used to take money directly from an individual (rather than from an ownerless poker pot) would be dishonest or fraudulent.

Objective, planned deception is the strategic basis for the "Advanced Concepts of Poker." Unlimited deception is accepted and ethical in poker. John Finn makes full use of this unique license and will do anything (except cheat) that brings him an advantage.

The other players in the Monday night game believe they are deceptive. Their deception, however, is generally unimaginative and repetitive . . . it seldom fools John Finn. He eventually wins all of their money.

The techniques for applying the "Advanced Concepts of Poker" are described in Part Two of this book.

PART TWO

TECHNIQUES

(DTC METHOD)

Discipline, Thought, and Control are the techniques of good poker. The DTC method is the application of these three techniques.

VII
DISCIPLINE (16)

Discipline is the mechanism of good poker. Self-control develops through discipline. Self-control is necessary to—

- prevent emotions from affecting actions
- allow total concentration to focus on the game
- permit continuous objective thinking in order to analyze past action, to carry out present action, and to plan future action.

Self-control develops by practicing the following disciplines during the game:

Discipline Practiced	Self-Control Developed
Consume no food or beverage	Awareness
Do not swear or display feelings	Emotional control
Maintain good posture—sit straight and keep both feet flat on the floor	Alertness
Memorize important hands played and the performance of each opponent	Concentration
Mentally review and criticize each play	Objectivity

The good player increases his advantage as the game grinds into late hours. His disciplines become more nagging and thus more effective for maintaining self-control. At the same time, the concentration and playing ability of his tired opponents decrease. Also, as his opponents develop into big winners or big losers for the evening, they become less objective and respond more to their feelings.

A decrease in discipline has a cumulative effect that can cause even a sound player to deteriorate into a poor player. For example, if a loss in discipline generates a breakdown in self-control, then a process of deterioration starts. Deterioration may be only temporary . . . but it can be permanent, especially with compulsive gamblers.

Deterioration can start spontaneously or can be induced by—

- a long losing or winning streak
- entering a higher-stake or a lower-stake game
- a close loss of a big hand
- a bad play or bet
- an upsetting remark
- a personal problem.

The good player recognizes any loss of discipline during the game. He adopts the following attitudes to prevent deterioration of his own discipline and play:

—Actual winning or losing of a pot is not important.

—Each well-played hand, won or lost, is a victory.

—Each poorly-played hand is a defeat (even if the pot is won).

—Each move or action lacking discipline can eventually cost much more money than is in any pot.

Consistent, tight discipline can build momentum toward a continuous string of flawless plays. If a bad play spoils this momentum, the resulting loss of self-control can lead to poorer quality poker. A bad play to a good poker player can be as a cigarette is to an ex-smoker . . . one slip (betrayal of one's self) breaks the momentum of discipline and can bring disaster.*

A few minutes of post-game discipline are necessary to record valuable information and data about the

---

* The good player does not consider an honest error in judgment as a flaw. To him, the flaw is the failure to think and act rationally. The flawless play, therefore, is not based on omniscience or perfect judgment, but is based on full rational thought.

game. In addition to his notes written after each game, the good player periodically re-evaluates the game and its players. These evaluations point out slow changes occurring in the game and often suggest changes in strategy necessary to maintain optimum edge odds.

John Finn uses convenient, mimeographed outlines as shown below and on pages 54, 56 and periodically fills them out as shown on pages 53, 55, 57. These outlines provide him with consistent, up-to-date information on the game and its players.

A few minutes of pre-game discipline is needed to review past notes. Also, a nap before the game improves discipline and thought. A bath and a shave before the game help retain the freshness necessary to sustain peak performance throughout an all-night session.

WEEKLY GAME NOTES*
GAME —
DATE —

Highlights —
Evaluation of game —
Evaluation of own performance —

(a) errors —	(b) unusual plays —
(c) number of wins —	(d) calculated edge odds —

Information on opponents

(a) observations	(b) performance
(c) winnings, losses, and debts,$	(d) bluffs, tried/called —

Statistics

(a) number of hands played —	(b) starting and quitting time —
(c) maximum win —	(d) maximum loss —

Miscellaneous —

* *Collecting and remembering the data for these Weekly Game Notes require discipline and concentration. Indeed, the chief value in acquiring these notes is not the data themselves, but is the forced mental attention on the game that is required to collect these data.*

WEEKLY GAME NOTES
GAME — *Monday, weekly*
DATE — *9/10/62*

Highlights —

Sid cheats Quintin out of $700 pot. Have talk with Quintin. Everything okay. . . . New player Jeff Klien is a good addition. Will be permanent loser. . . . Ted absent. Broke from playing horses. . . . Sid plays wildly and poorly, but won big.

Evaluation of game —

Continues at fast pace. Near optimum stakes for now. Only Charlie appears in financial trouble. Scotty is starting to hurt.

Evaluation of own performance — *$550 win*

(a) **errors** — *2*
   (details in black book, pg. 52)

(b) **unusual plays** — *3*
   (details in black book, pg. 78)

(c) **number of wins** — *12*
   (7 full, 5 split)

(d) **calculated edge odds —**
   550/650x100=85%

Information on opponents

(a) **observations**

Jeff blinks eyes when a bet is made against his weak hand. Keeps eyes open wide when he has a strong hand.

(b) **performance**

Aaron - *fair*	Jeff - *fair*
Quintin - *good to fair*	Mike - *fair*
	Sid - *poor*
Scotty - *fair to poor*	John - *good*
Charlie - *very poor*	

(c) **winnings, losses, and debts,$**

Sid - +650	Aaron - —250
John - +550	Scotty - —300
Mike - +400	Quintin -
Jeff - +200	—350
	Charlie -
	—900
	(borrows $300)

(d) **bluffs, tried/ called** — *30/19*

Aaron - 3/2	Jeff - 1/1
Quintin - 1/0	Mike - 0
Scotty - 0	Sid - 15/10
Charlie - 6/5	John - 4/1

Statistics

(a) number of hands
played — *108*
(*%won=12/108=*
11%)

(b) starting and quitting
time —
8:15 PM - 5:00 AM

(c) maximum win —
+$650 (Sid)

(d) maximum loss —
−$900 (Charlie)

Miscellaneous —

- *Need another regular player.*

- *Everyone absorbing losses okay, except Charlie who is getting desperate.*

- *Problem about Ted's debts and bounced checks.*

SEMI-ANNUAL
GAME PROFILE
GAME —
PERIOD —

Pace and Stakes —

Average maximum win —

Average maximum loss —

Performance of opponents —

Regular players —

New or occasional players —

Games played —

Ante per player —

Betting —

Raising —

Attitudes —

Personal performance —

Miscellaneous —

GAME — *Monday, weekly*
PERIOD — *1/8/62 - 6/4/62*

Pace and Stakes — *Fast pace is near maximum. Pressure for higher stakes.*

Average maximum win — *+$550*

Average maximum loss — *-$450*

Performance of opponents — *Average and fairly stable. Quintin is improving. Scotty, Aaron, and Ted are deteriorating.*

Regular players — *John Finn, Quintin Merck, Sid Bennett, Ted Fehr, Scotty Nichols.*

New or occasional players — *Aaron Smith, Mike Bell, Charlie Holland, Mac Zimmerman, Jim Todd, Jake Fehr, Lee Pennock, Jeff Klien.*

Games played — *Draw and stud with twists, high-low and qualifiers. Occasionally use wild cards and the Bug.*

Ante per player — *$1.00 for stud. $5.00 for draw.*

Betting — *In draw, $25 open then $50 in subsequent rounds. In stud, $5 first card then increase by $5 for each additional card. Twists are free. . . . 80% of bets are at the maximum.*

Raising — *Right to bet rule. Normally three raises. With only two players, raises are unlimited. Check raises okay.*

Attitudes — *Generally good. Sid continues to cheat without problems. No one resentful or in danger of quitting.*

Personal performance — *Good, but leveling off in effort. Areas to improve - Increase focus on broader aspects of the game. Increase flexibility in style during early rounds.*

Miscellaneous — *Stakes are ready to move up to next level. Try doubling stakes for the last round in the next few games.*

SEMI-ANNUAL
PLAYER PROFILE
NAME —
PERIOD —

Classification —

Motive —

Attitude —

Performance —

Average won or lost/game —

Edge odds —

Behavior

   Open —

   Bet —

   Call —

   Raise —

   Last bet —

   Bluff —

   Fold —

Weaknesses —

Strengths —

Changes —

Miscellaneous —

SEMI-ANNUAL
PLAYER PROFILE

NAME — *Quintin Merck*
PERIOD — *1/8/62 - 6/4/62*

Classification — *Sound player and improving.*

Motive — *Pass time. Satisfy ego. . . . Shifting to motive of making money.*

Attitude — *Grouchy but improving.*

Performance — *Above average.*

Average won or lost/game — *+$50 and increasing.*

Edge odds — *+10% and increasing.*

Behavior

Open — *When under the gun, he holds back good hands. When dealing, he will almost always open.*

Bet — *Bets too light in early rounds. Same give-away habits (listed in black book, pg. 17).*

Call — *Calls with much weaker hands than he is willing to bet.*

Raise — *Too conservative. Seldom raises a good winning hand if it is of low value.*

Last bet — *Bets only when sure, but calls with weak hands.*

Bluff — *Seldom. Averages once every two sessions. Same give-away habits (listed in black book, pg. 17).*

Fold — *Folds too easily early in hand and too hard late in hand.*

Weaknesses — *Play deteriorates when he gets angry from personal insults or from humiliating losses. Betting is out of proportion. Too conservative, but tires in late hours then plays too loose.*

Strengths — *Fairly objective. Conservative. Tries to concentrate.*

Changes — *Improving and becoming more objective. Making conscious effort to improve. Better control over emotions.*

Miscellaneous — *He becomes less valuable as he improves. If improvement and winnings continue, he will be a liability. May have to eliminate him from the game.*

How valuable is discipline? Obviously it is important in poker. But, how valuable is discipline to the extent of not eating refreshments? Did you ever eat a $600 sandwich? Well, such costly sandwiches are sometimes eaten in John Finn's game.

Consider Scotty Nichols who tries hard to play a good game. . . . Sid deals draw poker. Scotty seems nervous, as if desperate to win a pot. He opens for $25 with a pair of aces. Sid raises to $50. Now Scotty is sucked in and calls. Nervous hunger seizes him. He rushes to the food table and rapidly piles many slabs of ham and cheese into a giant sandwich. In the meantime, Ted Fehr draws a card and carelessly flashes it—the ace of diamonds. Then the dealer, waving the deck around, exposes the bottom card for all to see—except for Scotty who is laying pickles on his sandwich. The bottom card? It is the ace of clubs.

Now it is Scotty's turn to draw. Hurrying back to the table, he smiles at his sandwich. Then with a yawning mouth, his teeth chomp into the pile of food. Beads of mustard ooze over the crust and drip onto his slacks. Then with mustard-covered fingers, Scotty picks up his cards . . . John Finn watches him play. Yes, the pair of aces are still there. But wait . . . he also has four spades. Scotty wonders what to do. Staring at his sandwich, he continues to eat.

"Come on," Quintin grunts. "Speed up the game."

"Got to go with my best hand," Scotty finally blurts. He draws three cards to his pair of aces and then jams the rest of the sandwich into his mouth. The first card off the deck is the king of spades . . . his flush card. So what — he still catches another king to give him two pair, aces and kings . . . a pretty good hand.

This pretty good hand is enough to keep him in for a $50 bet plus a $50 raise. Quintin Merck wins with a queen high flush.

"What rotten luck," Scotty whines as he grabs an overflowing handful of potato chips. His words are followed by a slobbering crunch.

Rotten luck? If Scotty had stayed at the table, he would have seen the two flashed aces and drawn to his four flush to win the $600 pot. Instead he loses $150. That ham and cheese sandwich cost him $600! . . . Also, John Finn uses the mustard stains on Scotty's cards to identify them in future hands.

VIII
THOUGHT (17)

Thought is the labor of good poker. Objectivity and steady concentration are needed to think properly. This requires discipline. *Analytical* thinking is necessary to understand and predict the actions of opponents. *Objective* thinking is necessary to plan the proper action.

The good player continually thinks about poker during the game. He looks at his cards quickly to allow maximum time for observation and thought. He never wastes precious time by slowly looking at or squeezing open his cards. When involved in a hand, his thoughts concentrate on strategy. The good player gains a major advantage over other players by thinking ahead and forming several strategical plans based on anticipated hands. When an anticipated hand develops, he can make quicker and more accurate playing decisions.

. . . When not involved in a hand, the good player studies the game, gathers data, and plans future strategy. Between hands, he analyzes the action of each concluded hand.

Intensive thought and concentration also help to overcome nervousness, which even a good player may experience when playing in a strange, an unfriendly, or a high-stake game.

Since thinking is the labor of poker, maximum effort should yield maximum returns. How much is this effort worth in dollars? When a player wins an average of $40 per game, his winning rate is equivalent to a job paying $15,200 per year*. Average winnings of $150 per game is equivalent to a $57,000 per year job.*

Compare the effort in poker to the effort required in a job yielding similar earnings. For example, a winning rate of $5 per game is equivalent to a job paying only $1,900 per year*; such pay would not be worth the effort needed to play good poker.

Let us see how thinking pays off. John Finn is under the gun in draw poker. He has a four flush in hearts and checks. Next is Sid Bennett, who opens for $25. John check-raises to $50. Sid and Scotty call the raise. Now John draws and immediately looks at his card . . . he misses his flush. Does he give up? No . . . by paying attention and thinking, there is still a chance to win that $250 pot. John stays alert, and this is what he sees and hears:

Sid Bennett draws one card, sticks it in the center of his hand, then quickly looks at it. Is he drawing a flush, a straight, or two pair? Probably two pair, because when he draws one card to the flush or straight he places the draw card at the back end of his hand and then looks at the card very slowly. This along with his betting pattern (opens then reluctantly calls a raise) suggests that Sid has two pair.

* *Calculated for a five-hour weekly game . . . and 1900 hours of actual work per year (estimated from data in the U. S. Government Bulletin, "Employment, Earnings and Monthly Report on the Labor Force", volume 12, number 10, April, 1966).*

Ted Fehr flashes a black picture card when dealing Scotty's draw card. While ruffling the cards through his chubby fingers, Scotty exposes the deuce of hearts. Therefore, if he were going for the flush or straight, he missed it. Scotty slowly squeezes his cards open to look at his new card, then gives a blowing exhale. He usually inhales when he sees a good draw card.

Now John has a good view of the situation. The opener (Sid with two pair) looks weak with respect to the two one-card draw hands behind him . . . especially after John raised the first-round bet. Knowing that Scotty has a busted hand, John sits in a position of strength, despite his worthless hand. He has the last bet, and the other players respect his hand because of his first-round raise followed by his single-card draw. John has an excellent chance of buying the $250 pot with a bluff.

If Sid and Scotty check and John bets $50, Sid would probably drop his winning hand because he would also have to contend with Scotty's one-card draw as well as John's one-card draw. If Sid folds, Scotty would then fold his busted hand leaving John the pot. John figures his chances of a successful bluff under the circumstances are better than 1 to 2. The return for winning the pot would be about 5 to 1. He estimates his investment odds at $250 \times 0.3/\$50$ $= 1.5$ . . . these are good odds.

What if Sid bets his two pair? Does John fold his hand or does he still bluff by raising back? He would probably fold for the following reasons:

— After already betting $50, Sid would probably call John's raise—out of pseudo pride if for no other reason.

— Sid's bet would drive out Scotty, thus eliminating a big factor needed to bluff Sid out. John's chances of a successful bluff would decrease sharply.

— John would have to risk $100 for a $300 pot—a 3 to 1 return on his bluff play rather than the 5 to 1 return if Sid does not bet. His investment odds would fall to $\$450 \times 0.1/100 = 0.45$ . . . a very unfavorable level.

What actually happens? Well, things turn out better than John hoped. Sid checks. Scotty hesitates and then suddenly bets $50. This is his normal pattern when bluffing—hesitate and then bet fast. Scotty's obvious bluff attempt makes John's bluff even easier. He casually raises to $100. Sid and Scotty fold immediately. . . . John wins a $300 pot with a worthless hands plus a little thinking.

Incidentally, in 1965 John Finn earns $42,000 while playing 400 hours in the Monday night game. This equals $105 per hour, which is equivalent to a job yielding $200,000 per year. . . . A job paying that much is worth a concentrated thinking effort.

IX
CONTROL (18)

Control is the result of good poker. When the good player achieves self-control through discipline and understands his opponents through thinking, he then can seize control of the game. When in control, he becomes the center of attention. His opponents spend a major portion of their time and effort trying to figure out his moves and then adjusting to them . . . they play according to his moves and actions. From this controlling position he can—

- influence the betting, raising, and bluffing of his opponents

- force opponents into traps and wrong moves

- dilute opponents' attention toward one another so he can play them off against each other.

The player who continually strives for maximum *investment* odds cannot control the game. Always making the play that yields the maximum return reduces the flexibility needed to control the players and to achieve maximum *edge* odds. The good player, therefore, chooses from a wide variety of plays available at slightly less favorable odds. For example, by backing away from the maximum investment odds, the good player increases his flexibility in play-making so greatly that he can produce almost any desired effect. Also, by under-betting a hand and then over-betting a subsequent similar hand (with only occasional bets made at maximum investment odds), he makes his betting unpredictable. This flexibility and this unpredictability allow the good player to control the betting.

Money flows toward the player who controls the betting. The best time to get this control is early in the hand while the bets are still small. The good player often gains control by unexpected or unusual bets (such as a raise into obvious strength of an opponent), by larger than usual first-round bets, or by weird bets (such as a four-dollar bet instead of the usual five-dollar bet). He then makes subsequent offensive or defensive betting manipulations designed to influence the big, last-round bets and raises.

Offensive manipulations designed to maximize a potential win are done by altering (increasing or decreasing) the betting pace in order to—

- build pots

- encourage players to stay for the large, last-round bets

- set up bluffs

- induce opponents to bluff.

Defensive manipulations designed to minimize a potential loss are done by altering (increasing or decreasing) the betting pace in order to—

- suppress bets or raises

- prevent bluffs

- drive out or keep in players in order to create favorable odds for drawing to a potential hand such as a four flush or two pair.

Confusion and fear decrease the ability of players to

think objectively and to play their hands properly. Most players fear the confusing play and unpredictable betting of the good player. By making spectacular shock plays, he further increases their fear of him. Many opportunities occur where investment odds actually favor spectacular maneuvers such as—

- holding a high pair pat in draw poker
- breaking up a full house to draw to three of a kind
- raising and then dropping out on the next bet
- making a colorful bluff such as holding pat and betting four kings in a lowball game
- raising a weak-looking stud hand in the face of strong-appearing opposition
- dropping a strong-looking stud hand in the face of weak-appearing opposition.

John Finn has a big psychological advantage over his opponents. He confuses, shocks, bullies, frightens and worries them into focusing their attention on him. They react strongly to his actions. Their moves and bets are often distorted because they base them on trivial moves by John while ignoring significant moves by other players. Knowing how they will react to his moves, John can often make them do what he wants, while he alone retains a balanced view of the game. The results? He controls the game. . . . Watch how this control works.

Immediately after bluffing Sid Bennett (on page 61), John spreads his cards face up across the table. Seeing John's four hearts with a big black club right in the middle, Sid moans and groans as the other players laugh at him. With his face blushing red, he mutters, "I'll sleep in the street before you bluff me out again."

The players are still talking about John's bluff as Scotty Nichols starts the next deal. Ted opens for $25. Sid fumbles with his money . . . an indication that he wants to raise. John has a pair of aces that could be played with good investment odds if he can gain an offensive betting position and prevent Sid's raise. This is an easy problem for John. He just throws some confusion at the players by making a weird $3 raise.

Sid drops the money he was fingering. "What's Finn up to?" he says wrinkling his nose. "He's either got nothing or a powerhouse. Uh . . . probably hoping for a raise."

Perfect. That is exactly the reaction John wanted. The silent players stare at him as they try to figure out his bet. The result? Everyone just calls and then anxiously awaits John's next move. With that three-dollar bet, John prevents any raising, gets everyone's attention, and assumes the offensive betting position.

Now the draw. John Finn takes three cards—Sid frowns at him. Immediately John looks at his draw. He catches a pair of jacks to give him aces-up two pair. His expression remains unchanged. Sid draws one card, glances at it and then grunts, "I had John beat all the time. Should've raised him out of his seat."

A convenient statement for John . . . it verifies that Sid still has two pair. Scotty also draws one card. By knowing his betting and playing habits, John reads him for two pair also. Ted draws one card; his freckled face stiffens as he slowly squeezes his cards apart. Then with a burst of swear words, he flings the cards across the table.

"Miss your flush?" Quintin Merck asks while smiling with a fluttering mustache. Ted just pouts his lip and looks at the ceiling.

John makes a nominal $1 bet. Sid, still mumbling about being bluffed out of the previous hand and then being tricked out of the first-round raise, reacts emotionally, "You ain't getting off cheap this time," he snorts. "I raise fifty bucks."

Scotty Nichols hesitates a long time before calling. This confirms he has two pair. If Scotty had three of a kind or better, he would have called without hesitation. Now John is in a strong fundamental position with his aces-up; he raises to $100. Both Sid and Scotty, having already bet their hands heavily, feel

65

compelled to call. So they do. . . . John's aces-up wins the four-hundred-dollar pot.

So with a normally unfavorable hand and position, John controls the betting and wins the pot. Also by controlling the players, he builds a potential one-hundred-dollar pot into a big, four-hundred-dollar pot by tickling Sid's emotions.

John Finn is a good player because he disciplines himself, thinks objectively, and then takes control of the game. Discipline, thought, and then control—the DTC method—is his technique for good poker.

Parts Three, Four and Five of this book show how the good player with the DTC Method achieves—

- improved edge odds (increased advantage)

- faster money flow (increased income)

- more players and games (increased future earnings).

PART THREE

STRATEGIES

With discipline and objective thinking, the good player takes control of poker games. With the proper strategy, he molds these games to his maximum advantage. His prime strategical tool is deception.

X
INGREDIENTS OF STRATEGY (19)

Proper strategy depends on the game, opponents, and the situation. Certain phases of poker remain more or less constant; other phases change from bet to bet, hand to hand, or game to game. The good player bases his long-term strategy on the more constant phases of poker and his short-term strategy on the variable phases. Good strategy contains the following ingredients:

Strategy	Principal Ingredient
Long range	Understanding of game (a constant)
Short range	Knowledge of opponents (a variable)
Immediate action	Awareness of situation (a variable)

1. Understanding Game (20)

The mechanics of poker are simple and can be learned in a few minutes. Yet, the strategy of poker has infinite possibilities. Strategy depends more on proper technique than on experience. Even a novice can acquire an immediate strategic advantage over seasoned opponents by applying the DTC technique (discipline, thought, and then control).

Long-range (general) strategy develops from an understanding of the game. The good player understands the game by knowing the—

- quality of players
- betting pace
- availability of cash
- credit situation
- general attitude and friendliness
- areas of resistance and resentment
- bluffing attitudes
- reasons for player turnover

When a player fails to appraise a game accurately, he experiences—

- decreased edge odds
- errors and missed opportunities
- less effective strategy.

The good player continually evaluates the game in order to detect changes and inaccurate appraisals.

All sorts of game and player information are in John Finn's black leather notebook. Every month he summarizes his observations in a section labeled "General Appraisal of Game and Players." Here is a typical summary:

"Monday—7/9/62. The players have stabilized over the past month, except for the gradual disintegration of Scotty, who gets desperate when losing heavily and then makes poor bets and bluffs. The betting pace is slowly increasing as wild modifications are added. The betting stakes remain stable. The cash situation is good despite heavy losses by Sid, Ted, and Scotty. But Ted is in financial trouble; he runs up large debts and then pays them off with borrowed money. He may soon go broke.

"Resentment is building between Quintin and Sid. Quintin sarcastically questions Sid's honesty. Sid shouts back angry insults about Quintin's stinginess. This quarrel must end before it hurts the game.

"The game is in good shape and yields a reliable and substantial income. No one seems about to quit, except Ted if he goes bankrupt. But the game needs one or two new players . . . Aaron Smith would be a profitable addition."

2. Knowing Opponents (21)
Short-range strategy develops from knowledge of opponents. The good player knows his opponents by appraising their—

- personalities
- weaknesses and strengths
- behavior patterns

- motives for playing
- financial status
- betting and raising tendencies
- dropping and bluffing tendencies
- areas of confusion and errors.

Classification of opponents is a major step toward understanding them. Poker players usually can be put into one of the eleven classes below:

Class of Player	Ability to Control	Ability to Read	Performance
Good	Hardest	Very difficult	Biggest
Sound		Difficult	winner
Daring and unconventional		Medium	
Loose winner		Medium	
Tight winner		Medium	Loser
Tight loser		Easy	
Loose loser		Easy	
Very tight		Easy	
Wild		Medium	
Desperate		Medium	Biggest
Suicidal	Easiest	Medium	loser

(Ability to Control: Increase ease to control. Performance: Decrease winnings / Increase losings.)

Some players are a mixture of two classes. Also, the class of a player can change from moment to moment or over the long term as shown on opposite page:

Time Span for Class Change	Reasons for Change
Over long term	Increased experience, personality changes
From game to game	Feelings, emotions, stakes, financial condition
From one type of game to another	Differences in understanding various games
From hand to hand	Winning, losing, tired, upset
During play of a hand	Erroneous perspective on different phases of betting

Bu classifies the players in his Monday night game as follows:

Player	Class	Ability to Control and Read	Performance	Changes
John Finn	Good	Very difficult	Big winner	Stable. General long-term improvement.
Quintin Merck	Sound	Hard	Winner	General long-term improvement. Some deterioration when tired or insulted.
Scotty Nichols	Very tight	Easy	Loser	Deteriorates when losing heavily or on a long losing streak, then plays loose and poorly.
Sid Bennett	Wild	Medium	Big loser	Plays wild when winning. Tightens up if feelings are hurt.
Ted Fehr	Suicidal	Easy	Big loser	Plays tight early in game and then disintegrates, especially if losing. His playing becomes even worse when on a horse-betting spree.

72

3. Situation and Position (22)

Action strategy depends on the immediate situation. This strategy involves decisions about calling, opening, betting, raising, dropping, and bluffing. In making these decisions, the good player correlates the following poker variables to the immediate situation:

1. *Estimated strength** and *statistical value ** of his own hand

2. Game
   pace
   temperament
   atmosphere
   time (such as first hand, a late hour, last hand)
   size of pot
   potential size of pot

3. Opponents
   indicated strength
   attitude
   attentiveness
   win or loss status
   effect of previous bet

4. Position
   fundamental
   technical

The good player appraises his situation from both a fundamental and a technical position. His *fundamental position* is the *estimated strength* and *statistical value* of his hand relative to the other players. His *technical position* is the strategical and psychological advantage he holds over his opponents at a given moment. An important strategical consideration is *seat position*.

---

* Estimated strength *of a hand is relative to the estimated strengths of opponents' hands.*
** Statistical value *of a hand is relative to the number of opponents. The statistical value of a hand decreases with increasing number of opponents.*

Seat position is important in nearly every decision. The good player adjusts his strategy according to his seat position relative to the dealer, opener, bettor, raiser, and the strong and weak hands. He considers his seat position in decisions about—

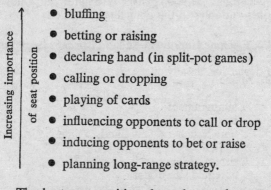

- bluffing
- betting or raising
- declaring hand (in split-pot games)
- calling or dropping
- playing of cards
- influencing opponents to call or drop
- inducing opponents to bet or raise
- planning long-range strategy.

Increasing importance of seat position

The best seat position depends on where the other players sit. The anecdote on p. 75 and several Advanced Concepts show why the good player likes to position himself as follows:

Good player prefers to bet before these types of players—	*Good player prefers to bet after these types of players—*
Weak	Strong
Wild, but readable	Impulsive, erratic, not readable or predictable
Loose, but predictable	Tight
Plays dealer-advantage games (such as twist and draw games)	Plays conventional stud games
Fast.	Slow.

The good player usually gets a desirable seat at the start of a game because his opponents seldom care where they sit. If an opponent is conscious of position, he generally tries to sit behind (bet after) the loosest or wildest player . . . the opposite position sought by the good player. A player can often pick a good position by arriving after the players are seated and then squeezing into the best seat position. (But continuous late arrival for this purpose can hurt a game.) The good player can also use the excuse of "changing his luck" to swap seats with a player in a better seat position. This ploy also gives his opponents the erroneous but advantageous impressions that he is superstitious and believes in luck.

The dealer has an advantage in draw or closed-hand poker because he bets last. When the same person always deals (e.g., a house dealer), this advantage is evenly distributed by using a marker, a button, or a buck that passes in turn to each player. Usually the player with the marker bets first, and the player to the right of marker bets last.

Most regular players get into a habit of sitting in the same position. In the Monday night game, John quietly arranges the seating to his advantage, and then game after game the players sit approximately in the same positions. He maintains this arrangement by preventing the players from realizing that they keep sitting in positions favorable to him.

Ted Fehr's betting is wild, erratic, and impulsive. While John can usually read Ted's hands, he can seldom predict his betting actions. By positioning himself so Ted bets first, John can adjust his strategy according to Ted's play. Sid Bennett's betting is even wilder, but is predictable. By betting before him, John can often check his strong hands and let Sid do the betting for him. It makes less difference to John where Quintin (a sound player) or Scotty (a tight player) sit. The ideal seating arrangement for John is illustrated below:

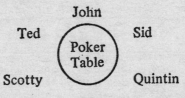

75

XI
TAILOR-MADE GAME (23)

The good player designs poker games to his maximum advantage by increasing the betting pace, the betting stakes, and his edge odds. A major step in this direction is to complicate the game by orienting the action around stud poker rather than draw poker. Stud poker offers the following advantages to the good player.

—More skill and effort are needed to assimilate the additional information and variables offered by the exposed cards.*

—Added rounds of progressively higher bets effectively increase the betting *stakes*.

—Faster and more rounds of bets effectively increase the betting *pace*.

1. Increasing the Betting Pace (24)

The good player increases the money flow in a poker game to increase his profits. But opposition to higher stakes exists in most games. Often a more subtle and effective way to increase the money flow is to increase the betting pace (rather than the betting stakes). A faster pace usually increases excitement in a way that is appealing to most players, especially weak players.

The betting pace is increased by adding modifications to the game such as listed on the next page:

---

* *The good player often adds another variable by inconspicuously altering the order of his face-up cards.*

Modification	Advantageous Effects
Twists	Provides additional large, last-round bets. Induces players to stay for twist cards. Increases confusion. Amplifies players' weaknesses.
Split pots (high-low)	Allows more bets and raises. Provides more playing opportunities. Increases confusion. Amplifies players' weaknesses.
Check raises	Allows more and larger raises.
Pick-up checks	Permits larger bets.
Right to bet	Allows more raises.
Early bet	Early buildup of pot keeps players in for large last-round bets.
Bet or get	Produces more betting.
Additional cards	Produces more calls.
Novel games	Increases confusion. Amplifies players' weaknesses.
Wild cards, freak hands	May or may not increase betting pace. Increases confusion.
Table stakes or pot limit	Allows direct control over the betting stakes.

The good player can gradually work many of these modifications into most games—even into games that are not dealer's choice. Most modifications increase the circulation of money, which lets the good player win more because the faster pace allows his opponents to lose more. The following paragraphs describe these modifications.

a. Twist (25)

The twist increases the betting pace. At the normal conclusion of a poker hand, a card or cards may be exchanged (twisted) for a new card or cards. An additional round of betting follows each twist. As players grow accustomed to this modification, they usually become addicted to it and make the twist a permanent part of the game.

A single twist played with five-card stud is the gentlest way to introduce this modification. Most players will accept a twist as a good way to convert normally dull five-card stud into a more lively "six-card" stud game. As players get accustomed to the twist, the good player can further quicken the pace by adding other twist modifications such as—

- twist in seven-card stud
- twist in draw poker
- pay for each twist (for example, an amount equal to the ante)
- double twists
- giant twist in stud (as many cards as the player desires are exchanged on each twist)
- progressive paying for unlimited twists (second twist costs twice the first twist, third twist costs twice the second, and so on).

Faster betting pace →

b. Split pot, high-low (26)

Because of the dynamic betting action between high hands and low hands, the betting pace increases markedly when pots are split between the highest hand and the lowest hand (high-low poker). Many players are initially hostile to high-low poker. Seven-card stud high-low is probably the gentlest way to introduce split-pot games. With patience and persistence, the good player can usually generate great interest in high-low poker. Again, the good player can further quicken the pace by adding other high-low modifications such as—

Faster betting pace →

- high-low five-card stud
- high-low draw
- high-low with qualifiers (minimum hands required to win, such as two pair for high and nine for low)
- high-low with a twist
- high-low with qualifiers and twists.

c. Check raise and pick-up checks (27)

Player A checks; player B bets; now player A raises . . . this is called *check raising*. Player A checks; player B checks; player C makes a bet three times larger than the maximum bet by making A's bet, B's raise, and then his own raise . . . this is called *picking-up checks*. Check raising and picking-up checks increase the betting flexibility as well as the number of large bets and raises. But if these modifications cause a defensive attitude among players, a decrease in the betting pace can occur. Also, house rules of many games prohibit check raising and picking-up checks.

d. Right to bet (28)

Every player has a chance to bet or raise during each round of betting. With this rule, a player holding a strong hand cannot be shut out of his bet or raise by three minimal raises made in front of him. Right to bet increases the betting pace, particularly in split-pot games. Players seldom object to this seemingly equitable modification.

e. Early bet (29)

An indirect method to increase the ante is to permit a small bet after dealing the first hole card in stud or the second card in draw. This early bet holds more players in the game for the later rounds of more expensive betting. But if most players stay or drop on the strength of their cards rather than on the size of the pot, this modification can drive out potential players and thus decrease the betting pace.

f. Bet or get (30)
No checking is permitted with this rule . . . each player must either bet or drop. This modification gets players involved early and keeps them in for the big, last-round bets. Most players are unaccustomed to this modification and may object vigorously to it.

g. Additional cards (31)
An additional sixth card is dealt to each draw hand. The hands are then reduced to five cards during the draw. This additional card keeps more players in the hand, particularly in lowball draw. Players seldom object when this simple modification is introduced.

h. Novel games (32)
Poorer playing normally results when a new or novel game is introduced because the players do not understand the changes in play and odds that occur. Novel games may range from simple lowball draw or hold-'em stud to a complex game such as "place-and-show-tickets-split-pot-with-twist-your-neighbor." (This game is played as follows: At the conclusion of a stud or draw game, each player draws a card from the hand of an adjacent player for use in his own hand. The pot is then split between the second and third best hands.)

A decreased betting pace may result, however, if players become frightened or excessively confused by wild games or modifications that are too extreme or are introduced too rapidly.

i. Wild cards and freak hands (33)
Wild cards can increase the betting pace and loosen up certain games. As players get accustomed to wild cards, their fear of very strong hands usually dissipates. But if so many wild cards are used that hands such as

five-of-a-kind or straight flushes become common and any betting strength suggests these maximum-value hands, the betting will dry up.

The bug card (the joker—used in low hands as a wild card . . . and used in high hands as an ace or as a wild card for completing straights and flushes) can increase the betting pace without causing fear of maximum-value hands.

The good player rarely encourages the use of freak hands such as blazes, tigers, dogs, kilters and skeets. While such hands could temporarily increase his edge odds by adding confusion, the use of freak hands may deter players from accepting other more profitable modifications such as twists and split pots.

j. Table stakes and pot limit (34)

Table stakes or pot-limit betting gives the good player direct control over the betting stakes. But such open-end stakes can slow down the betting pace and normally cannot be used with split-pot games. In many games, therefore, table stakes or pot-limit betting would actually decrease the financial opportunities for the good player.

Six years ago, Sid Bennett insisted that good poker players liked only straight draw and stud games. He claimed five-card was the greatest gambling game of all. As John Finn gradually increased the betting pace by adding one modification after another, Sid went to the other extreme as shown below:

Sid is winning; his pale lips are smiling. He grabs the deck, shoves his face over the table and announces, "New game!" He then deals two separate hole cards to everyone.

"What's this?" Quintin says with his face twisting into knotted shapes.

"Seven-stud high-low. Everyone plays two hands. You can even raise yourself," Sid says with a snorting laugh. "And the hand to the left of the highest hand wins high and the hand to the right of the lowest hand wins low."

81

"I'm going home," Quintin says as he grabs his ante from the pot and stands up to leave.

"Sit down; we aren't going to play that," John Finn says. He then turns to Sid and explains gently, "I know it's dealer's choice, but that's no poker game. You can't have hands next to the winners as winners."

"Bunch of ribbon clerks," Sid whines. "Okay, straight high-low . . . play your left hand for high and right hand for low. And you can still raise yourself."

"That's more like it," John says.

Sid's toothy grin stretches wider as he continues to deal.

2. Increasing the Betting Stakes (35)

After increasing the betting pace, the good player can often increase the betting *stakes* sharply. Most games can withstand a tenfold to even a hundredfold increase in the betting stakes. Even when the big losers seem to be at their financial limits, the stakes can usually be increased significantly.

The good player increases the stakes in carefully planned steps. Several temporary increases may be necessary before higher stakes become permanent. But in some games, stakes can be increased immediately and rapidly. Opportunities to increase the stakes occur when players want—

- a chance to get even by increasing the ante or stakes in the late hours or during the last round

- a more equitable relationship to the ante by increasing the first-round or opening bets

- a chance to protect a hand by increasing the middle-round bets

- an opportunity to bet a good hand by increasing the last-round bets.

The stakes are normally easier to increase after the betting pace increases. Opposition to higher stakes and game modifications often diminishes when the resisting player is—

- tired
- losing heavily or winning big for the evening
- on a losing or a winning streak
- upset by some occurrence during the game
- affected by personal problems
- drinking.

A good way to increase the stakes is to let those players who want to double the stakes, for example, play at double stakes whenever they are the only players left in the hand.

John Finn starts playing in the Monday night game on June 6, 1960. The game is already seven-years old, and the stakes have stabilized over the past five years. A dollar is the maximum bet, and only straight draw and stud games are allowed. . . . The following table shows how both the betting pace and stakes steadily increase after John takes control of the game:

| | | | Money Flow | | |
Date	Pace	Stakes,$	Average Big Winner,$	John Finn's Average Winnings,$	John Finn's Edge Odds,%
6/60	Straight stud and draw	0.50— 1	25	8	30
7/60		1— 2	40	14	35
8/60	Add twist		70	32	45
9/60		2— 4	100	40	40
1/61	Add high-low	5— 10	170	94	55
2/61		10— 20	210	105	50
6/61			260	130	50
12/61	Add qualifiers	25— 50	360	234	65
1/62		50—100	450	270	60
7/62		25— 50	600	210	35
8/62		50—100	550	358	65
3/64		50—100	700	350	50
6/65	Add complex and wild modifications	50—100	1400	840	60

The above data show three interesting phenomena:

1. When the stakes increase, there is not a proportional increase in the average winnings (money flow) because most players initially play tighter at higher stakes. But an increase in the pace causes looser play and a relatively large increase in the money flow.

2. John's edge odds go up when the pace increases and down when the stakes increase. This is because his opponents play more poorly as the pace increases, but more cautiously at higher stakes.

3. An increase in the pace eventually leads to higher stakes.

These data also show how the increases in stakes and pace affect John's profits. The doubling of stakes during July, 1962 causes his edge odds to drop sharply—from 60% down to 35%. At these higher stakes, he must spend a greater portion of his income to hold valuable losers in the game. On realizing this, John drops the stakes back to the previous level and brings his edge odds up to a healthy 65%. Why the big increase in John's edge odds when he lowers the stakes? After getting a taste of higher stakes, the players bet more loosely and play more carelessly when the stakes are lowered to the old level. A year and a half later, John increases the stakes again . . . and this time the increase is profitable and permanent.

John usually tries raising the stakes soon after increasing the betting pace. Under the pretense of giving the losers a break, he often increases the stakes during the last round of the game. The following round of dialog shows how he advantageously manipulates this last round.

"You're getting blasted again," Sid Bennett says to Ted Fehr. "Must be losing a grand."

"That's only four thousand hamburgers at my drive-in," Ted says smiling weakly. "Wait till I get the deal. I'm doubling the stakes like we did last week. Got to make a big comeback."

"No sir, none of that," Quintin Merck interrupts as his cigarette falls from his mouth. "Next thing you know, we'll be playing the whole game at doubled stakes."

"Quintin's right," John says trying hard to sound sincere. "If anything, we should ban double stakes even for the last round . . . it's too expensive."

"Yeah," Scotty Nichols says while counting his winnings.

. . . Two hours later, John announces the last round.

"Hey, double the stakes for the last round," Ted cries.

"Well . . . we made a rule against it," John says with a shrug. He then turns to the other players and continues, "We gave the losers a break last week. Ted is stuck bad. Let's double the ante and play a round of high-low draw—for Ted's sake."

"Yeah!" Scotty says as he checks his freshly emptied wallet.

"I'm in," Ted says throwing his double ante into the pot.

"High-low draw? That's a stiff game," Quintin grumbles while anteing slowly. "That's worse than doubling the stakes."

What does John accomplish by this? He introduces the fast pace, high-low draw game. He doubles the ante, which will make it easier to increase the stakes at a later date. He creates the images that he is both helping a loser and opposing higher stakes . . . while actually setting up conditions for both higher stakes and a faster pace.

3. Increasing the Edge Odds (36)

The good player designs a game to yield maximum edge odds. The theoretical maximum edge odds occur only when the perfect player is in the most complex game, under the most confusing circumstances against the poorest players. While the conditions for theoretical maximum edge odds can never be achieved, the good player strives to approach them. The perfect situation

THE DIAMOND

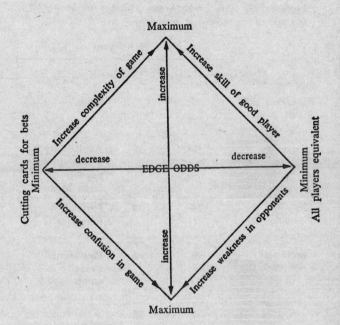

Maximum

Increase complexity of game

increase

Increase skill of good player

Cutting cards for bets
Minimum

decrease   EDGE ODDS   decrease

Minimum
All players equivalent

Increase confusion in game

increase

Increase weakness in opponents

Maximum

is represented by the completion of The Diamond shown on page 87. The Diamond measures the idealness of a poker game for the good player.

How far does John Finn go toward completing the Diamond on page 87? How much further could he increase his edge odds in the Monday night game? He makes the following estimations:

	Estimations		
Side of Diamond	% Completed	Maximum Possible %	Limitation
Increase skill of good player	95	100	None
Increase weakness in opponents	45	65	Availability of weak players capable of large losses
Increase confusion in game	70	80	Human tolerance
Increase complexity of game	90	95	Opponents' capacity to comprehend
Total (average), %	75	85	

Playing with the Diamond 75% complete, John's edge odds are about 65%. He estimates that under the best conditions, the Diamond would be 85% complete, and thus his edge odds could improve to a maximum of 74%. This estimation of maximum edge odds establishes a goal that John Finn strives for by increasing his thinking effort . . . each side of the Diamond is controlled by thinking effort.

XII
BEHAVIOR (37)

The good poker player directs his actions toward achieving maximum advantages while preventing his opponents from realizing that he is motivated entirely by self-profit. . . . He is a winner acting like a loser.

1. Systemization and Blandness (38)

To prevent opponents from reading his hand or sensing his strategy, the good player systemizes his—

- procedures for observing opponents
- physical movements
- verbal expressions
- vocal tones.

While playing his hand, the good player is seldom an actor. Instead he practices a bland behavior that—

- minimizes his readable patterns or tells
- frustrates and confuses his opponents
- allows greater concentration.

A good player never loses interest in his hand until it is his turn to fold. If opponents can sense his intentions to fold before his turn, they will become more defensive when he does hold a playable hand, thus decreasing his edge odds.

Improvised acting while playing a hand is usually ineffective because the act does not develop from a well planned basis. Yet when not involved in the action, many opportunities arise to act effectively on a carefully planned basis. Occasionally while playing in a hand, the good player deviates from his systemized behavior when he knows a certain behavior will cause an opponent to make a desired move (call, drop, bet, or raise).

"What's John doing now?" Scotty Nichols whines. He rubs his whiskered face while wondering if he should call John's $50 raise. ". . . Can't ever read him."

"That's 'cause he sits like a tree stump," Quintin Merck explains. "Gives you nothing to grab. You guys that act are easy to read."

John Finn will act, however, when he is reasonably certain of his opponents' reactions. Consider this hand where he is supposedly sitting like the tree stump:

Wanting Scotty to call, John lets his fingers creep into the pot and spread out the money. He pulls out the big bills and lays them on top. Scotty stares at the money; he is a loser, and winning that pot would make him even . . . he licks his lips and calls.

Poor Scotty never should have called. His kings-up two pair were no match for John's full house. Was John acting? Yes, because Scotty was undecided and John varied his own behavior to make him call. John also did some long-range acting toward Quintin Merck. How was this? Quintin observed John's maneuver to make Scotty call. John heard Quintin snort when Scotty fell into the trap.

The following week, John and Quintin are battling for a large pot. John raises . . . Quintin scratches his head and then starts to call. John's fingers creep into the pot and spread out the money. He pulls out the big bills and lays them on top. Quintin snorts, shows his three deuces to everyone, and then folds with a prissy smile. His smile snaps into a frown when John throws his hand face up on the table. His hand this time? . . . a four flush.

Why does Quintin fall into this trap? He forgets that John would not apply the same tactic toward a poor player like Scotty as he would toward a sound player like Quintin. John plays against the individual as well as the situation.

90

`2. Personality (39)`

The good player varies his personality to obtain the best advantage. Typical poker personalities he adopts are described below.

a. Unfriendly (40)

In public (club or casino) games or in games consisting mostly of professionals or strangers, a tough or unfriendly behavior may be best. Tough behavior makes opponents defensive . . . and defensive players are easier to control. Unfriendly behavior irritates opponents, causing them to act more emotionally and to play poorer poker.

The following unfriendly behavior can be advantageously practiced by the good player:

— Silently throw bets and raises into the pot. Give an unpleasant reply when asked about these bets or raises. Make disagreeable remarks when other players err because of silent bets.

—At the conclusion of a hand, throw cards faceup on the table without comment. Make opponents figure out the hand.

—Stage displays of bad temper.

—Delay anteing and making good on lights (money owed to the pot).

—When dealing new games, give inadequate explanations. When asked for more explanation, give details begrudgingly.

—Push rules and ethics to the limit. For example, fake moves to make the next player believe that you have dropped, called, or raised . . . then when he reveals his move (a drop, bet, or raise), remake your play accordingly.

Planned unfriendly behavior can be effective for increasing edge odds and for controlling opponents. Still the good player uses caution when being unfriendly.

He analyzes the game to determine if such behavior is advantageous from both a short-term and a long-term basis.

In some games, unfriendly behavior is tolerated if a little humor or congenial behavior is blended in. Also, the good player may adopt a split personality or may be unfriendly to certain players and congenial to others ... whatever is most advantageous.

b. Congenial (41)

Tough or unfriendly behavior is undesirable for most friendly or regular private games. Unpleasant behavior could break up the game, result in expulsion from the game, or cause valuable losers to quit. Congenial behavior is often necessary in such games. But most friendly traditions are disadvantageous to the good player, such as—

- no betting when only two remain in a hand
- no betting a lock hand (a sure winner)
- no squeeze raising when only three players are in a split-pot game.

Only an occasional but obvious display of these friendly traditions, however, will usually satisfy the other players.

Sometimes John Finn is the most congenial player in the game. At other times, he is not so congenial. He always behaves in a way that offers the greatest profit.

How can John switch his personality to fit the game? He keeps himself free from emotional ties with the game and the players. This allows him to think objectively and define what behavior offers the most advantage. For example, he will drive a good player out of the game with unfriendly behavior (see Concept 108). Why will he do this? Another good player would increase the financial strain on the losers, which would cost John more money to keep these losers in the game. In other words, a good player would cost

John money . . . so why let him play? Why not re-place him with a more profitable, poor player?

c. Introvert and extrovert (42)

The good player usually behaves oppositely to the general behavior of his opponents. For example, in a quiet game with serious players, an extrovert personality may be advantageous. In a wild or boisterous game, an introvert personality is often advantageous.

The extent of introvert or extrovert behavior that John Finn assumes depends on the game as shown below:

Game	Players' Behavior	Advantageous Behavior (John Finn's Behavior)
Monday	Mixed	Ambivert
Tuesday	Introvert	Extrovert
Thursday	Ambivert	Ambivert
Friday	Extrovert	Introvert

3. Practicing Deceit (43)

Only in poker can a man lie and practice any form of deceit, except cheating, and still remain a gentleman . . . and an honest person. The good player makes extensive use of his right to deceive. He conceals facts and lies about anything that offers him an advantage.

a. Concealing desires (44)

The good player confuses his opponents by concealing his desires in the following ways:

Desires for	*Methods to Conceal*
More weak players	Never discuss weaknesses of players.
Faster betting pace	Increase betting pace without verbally expressing a desire for a faster betting pace. Occasionally complain about the fast pace and wild modifications.
Higher stakes	Never suggest higher stakes unless chances are good for an increase, then suggest higher stakes as a way to give losers a break or to make the betting more equitable.
More games	Never reveal activities in other games. Organize games without expressing an eagerness to play.

b. Concealing facts (45)

The good player conceals the following facts to avoid arousing unfavorable suspicions:

Facts	*Methods to Conceal*
Easiness of game	Never mention the poor quality of poker played in any game. Praise skill of opponents.
Winnings	Never discuss personal winnings. After each game report less than actual winnings or more than actual losses . . . but exaggerate only to a believable extent. Never reveal long-term winnings. Conceal affluence by driving an old car to the game.
Tight play	Fold cards without comment or excuses. Make wild or loose-appearing plays whenever investment odds are favorable.
Good play	Never explain the true strategy behind a play. Instead, give erroneous reasoning for strategy. Never brag . . . downgrade own performance.
Control over game	Assume a humble attitude.

To turn attention away from his poker success, the good player praises and exaggerates the poker ability of other winners. In a verbal smoke screen, he discusses and magnifies everyone's winnings except his own. When losing, the good player complains about the tough game and exaggerates his losses. But he never mentions the losses of other players.

c. Lying (46)

Lying is a key tool of strategy. For example, when asked about his folded cards, the good player lies about them to create the impression that he plays loosely or poorly. To lie effectively, he must always lie within believable boundaries to keep others from automatically doubting him.

With careful lying and calculated deceit, John Finn builds his image as a kind-hearted, loose player who is an asset to the game. Here is an example of how he builds this advantageous image:

The game is highball draw with a twist. John starts with a pair of aces, draws three cards and ends up with two pair. During the betting, he notices Ted Fehr putting twenty-five dollars too much into the pot. John says nothing and plays his two pair pat on the twist. Sid Bennett misses his flush and folds out of turn . . . this out-of-turn fold is very helpful to John.

Now with only two remaining in the hand, Ted bets $25. John reads him for trips and reasons Ted's bet like this: Ted thinks his three of a kind are beat by John's pat hand. So if he checks, John will bet the $50 maximum, and he will have to call. By making a smaller bet, he hopes that John will only call, thus saving him twenty-five dollars. Ted's strategy backfires . . . John raises to $75.

"How many cards you draw in the first round?" Ted asks.

"One," John quickly lies.

"A one-card draw then pat on the twist . . . I can't call that," Ted sighs as he folds his cards.

John places his cards facedown next to Sid's dead hand.

"What'd you have, the straight or flush?" Ted asks.

John pulls in the pot. He then picks up Sid's cards, gives them to Ted and says in a low voice, "Don't tell anyone my hand."

"What!" Ted cries on seeing the cards. "You play a four flush pat to win a three-hundred-dollar pot?" . . . John smiles and nods. Ted slumps in his chair.

"That's what I like," Sid says. "His wild playing beats all you tight players. . . . You're great, John."

John shrugs his shoulders and then throws twenty-five dollars to Ted.

"What's this for?" Ted asks.

"Your last bet," John says. "I don't feel right about taking it."

"Merciful guy," Ted smiles. Then counting the money, he continues, "You might win all my money, but you're still a gentleman."

"That's no gift," Quintin Merck mumbles, "Ted put . . ."

"Whose deal?" John interrupts. . . . So besides winning a three-hundred-dollar pot, he did a lot of good image-building with that hand.

4. Creating an Atmosphere (47)

A carefree, relaxed, and pleasant poker atmosphere is advantageous to the good player. He creates these atmospheres in the following ways.

a. Carefree (48)

A carefree atmosphere stimulates a careless attitude about money and causes opponents to play poorer poker. A carefree atmosphere is developed by—

- increasing the betting pace

- complicating the game

- using poker chips instead of money

- appearing careless with money.

The good player himself is never carefree about poker or careless with money . . . he always respects money. His careless behavior is only a planned act.

b. Relaxed (49)

A relaxed atmosphere lulls opponents into decreased concentration, which diminishes their playing abilities and increases the readability of their hands. Contributing to a relaxed atmosphere are—

- a suitable location

- good food and beverages

- a comfortable setting with proper table, chairs, and lighting.

To maintain peak concentration, the good player denies himself the effects of comfort and relaxation.

c. *Pleasant (50)*

A pleasant atmosphere holds weak players in the game and attracts new players. The good player creates a pleasant atmosphere by—

- being congenial (when advantageous)

- preventing unpleasant remarks and unfriendliness among players

- displaying a sympathetic attitude toward losers.

Most players gain pleasure from feeling accepted or belonging to the group. But the good player gains pleasure from his ability to win money and control the game.

Whenever the Monday night game gets serious, the players think more clearly and make fewer mistakes. When serious, everyone plays tighter and is less prone to John Finn's influence. So he keeps the game carefree and careless by behavior such as described below:

A newcomer, playing in the high-stake Monday game for the first time, is nervous and is playing very tight. He shuffles . . . the cards spray from his trembling hands and scatter all over the floor. Finally he deals five-card stud. John gets a pair of aces on his first two up cards. Everyone drops out except big loser, Scotty Nichols. "Haven't won a pot all night," he says and then gulps. "I . . . I gotta win one." . . . John makes a few small bets. Scotty stays to the end and loses with his wired pair of queens The pot is small, containing perhaps thirty-five dollars.

With quivering lips, Scotty slowly turns his cards over. Suddenly John shoves the whole pot across the table and into Scotty's lap while laughing, "Don't be so miserable. It's only money. . . . Take it all."

The newcomer's mouth snaps open. "What a crazy game!" he exclaims. "I've never seen anything like that!"

Scotty grins and mumbles something about John's generous act.

"Help thy neighbor, help thy luck," John tells everyone. . . . "Nothing is cheaper than money."

That move will be remembered and discussed for a long time. The cost to John, about thirty-five dollars. The return to John, certainly many times that.

5. Observation (51)

The good player depends on his observations to plan his strategy. Observation of opponents requires an analytical technique. Observation of the cards requires a trained eye. . . . Knowing what his opponents observe and know also affects his strategy.

a. Reading opponents (52)

All players have repeating habits and nervous patterns that give away their hands. The task of the good player is to find and interpret these patterns. Most poker players offer readable patterns (tells) in their—

- initial reaction to looking at cards (freshly dealt hands, draw cards, hole cards, up cards, opponents' up cards)

- behaviors on making calls, bets and raises

- reactions to calls, bets, raises, and folds of opponents

- ways of handling and looking at cards

- ways of handling money before and during each bet

- extents and directions of interest during the action

- behaviors and remarks during each phase of action

- mumblings and spoken thoughts

- tones of voice

- reactions to comments

- responses to questions.

Questions can be very useful in reading opponents' hands. Often players reveal their hand by impulsive responses to innocuous questions as—

- how many cards did you draw?

- who made the last bet?

- how much was the last bet?

- is it your bet? (when it really is not)

- did you call the last bet?

- are you light?

The good player controls the position of his head and eyes to avoid a direct stare at those opponents who become cautious and less readable when feeling observed. He will, however, stare directly at those players who get nervous and more readable when feeling observed. In some games, especially public games, the good player may wear dark glasses to conceal his eye actions.

When involved in action, the good player reads his opponents and then makes his play accordingly. When not involved in the action, he analyzes all players for readable patterns. At the conclusion of each pot, he correlates all revealed hands to his observations. By this technique, he can discover and build an inventory of readable patterns for each opponent.

The most valuable pages in John's black leather notebook describe the readable patterns of his op-

ponents. For example, consider his notes about Scotty Nichols:

Readable Patterns of Scotty Nichols

Before hand—When winning, breaking even, or losing slightly, he plays very tight and never bluffs. Stays to end only when holding a strong hand. When losing heavily, he panics—he plays wildly while trying to bluff far too often. Once hooked in a hand, he stays to the end. Gets wide-eyed and wildly alert.

Receiving cards—Grabs for each dealt card when a good hand is developing. Casually looks at new cards when holding a hold with poor potential.

Dealing—Usually flashes bottom card when picking up the deck. Often flashes cards he deals to himself.

Looking at cards—When planning to play, he looks to his right. When planning to raise, he looks to his left. When planning to drop, he looks blankly into space.

Handling cards—Leaves cards on table when he intends to fold. If holding a playable pair, two pair, trips, or a full house, he arranges his cards and then does not disturb them. If holding a lowball hand, a bobtail straight, or a four-flush, he continuously ruffles the cards through his fingers.

Before bet—Touches his money lightly when going to call. His thumb lifts edge of money when going to raise. Picks up money when going to bluff. Does not touch money when going to fold.

Betting—Puts money in pot with a deliberate motion when not confident, with a flicking motion when confident, and with a hesitation followed by a flicking motion when sandbagging.

Raising—Cheek muscles flex when holding a sure winner. A stiffness develops around his upper lip when worried. Breathes through mouth when bluffing.

Drawing—Inserts cards randomly into his hand and then ruffles cards when drawing to a four flush or a pair. Puts cards on one end with no ruffling when drawing to a four straight or trips.

Puts card second from the end when drawing to trips with a kicker. Puts card in center of hand when drawing to two pair. With two pair, he looks at draw quickly. With all other hands, he slowly squeezes cards open. Squeezes very slowly when drawing to lowball, flush, or straight hands. Jerks hand when he misses.

Looking at draw—Exhales when he misses, and his eyes stare blankly at the table. Inhales when he catches, and his eyes glance at his opponents and then at the pot.

Stud up cards—After catching a good card, he touches it first and then reorganizes his cards. Confirms catch by looking several times at his hole cards.

Stud hole cards—When hole cards are good, he keeps them neatly organized and touches them periodically. Does not bother to organize or touch poor cards. If one fakes a move to grab his hole cards, he impulsively jumps and grabs the cards if they are good . . . does nothing if they are poor.

Last round bet—A quick call means he will call a raise. Picking up all his money when calling means he will not call a raise. Watching the next caller without looking directly at him means he is hoping for a raise.

Questions—"Do you have three tens beat?" Scotty blinks his eyes if his hand does not beat three tens . . . no blinking if it does. "How many cards did you draw?" Scotty hesitates and turns eyes up in thought if he is bluffing. Gives a casual answer if holding a normal hand. Hesitates and stares at the pot if holding a powerful hand.

After hand—He will play carelessly when sulking over losses. He will play extra tight when winning and counting his money.

With so many readable patterns, Scotty has little chance against John Finn. By putting together several of these patterns, John reads him with consistent accuracy. And Scotty's low awareness level keeps him from recognizing the habits that reveal his cards and intentions.

John also has similar dossiers on the other players and can usually read them accurately . . . even a sound player ilke Quintin Merck. Because of Quintin's greater awareness, he occasionally recognizes and eliminates a habit that tips off his hand. But John uses several habits to cross-check readable patterns and can quickly detect when anyone changes or eliminates a habit. After each game, he records in his notebook any new or changed habits. . . . John Finn knows that all players have telling habits and readable patterns that give away their hands and intentions. The task of the good player is to identify and interpret these habits and patterns so he can accurately read the hands and intentions of every opponent. This method is much more effective than using marked cards . . . and it is honest.

The question-type giveaways or tells are quite reliable and are particularly useful for pinpointing the exact value of an opponent's hand. For example, if John holds trips and reads his opponent for trips, he might use questions to find out who has the best hand. Excessive use of questions, however, can rouse suspicion and decrease the usefulness of this valuable tool.

b. Remembering exposed cards and ghost hands (53)

By remembering all exposed cards, a player increases his accuracy in estimating investment and card odds. In games with many players (eight or more), discarded and folded cards are often redealt. Knowledge of these cards can be crucial for estimating meaningful investment odds. In some games, discarded and folded cards are actually placed on the bottom of the deck without shuffling. (The good player encourages this practice.) If these cards are redealt during the late rounds, the good player will know what cards are to be dealt to whom . . . a huge advantage for the latter rounds of big bets.

With disciplined concentration and practice, any player can learn to memorize all exposed cards. From the discipline value alone, remembering exposed cards is always a worthwhile effort. But many players excuse themselves from this chore by feeling that memorizing cards dissipates their concentration on the other aspects of the game. This may be true when a player first tries to memorize cards, but a disciplined training effort toward memorizing all exposed cards will ultimately increase his concentration powers in every area of poker.

Remembering the exposed draw hands or the order of exposed stud cards from the previous deal can bring financial rewards. Old hands often reappear on the next deal (ghost hands), especially when the shuffling is incomplete (the good player encourages sloppy and incomplete shuffling). For example, a good player is sitting under the gun (on the dealer's left) and needs a king to fill his inside straight in five-card stud. But the last card dealt in that round (the dealer's card) is a king. The good player, rather than being discouraged, recalls that the winner of the previous hand held three kings. Since the deck had been poorly shuffled, the chances of the next card (his card) also being a king are good. Knowing this, he now has a strong betting advantage.

John Finn memorizes all exposed and flashed cards. He mentally organizes every exposed stud card into one of the four following categories by saying to himself, for example . . . Sid's two of hearts would help—

- my hand
- his (Sid's) hand
- another opponent's (e.g., Quintin's) hand
- no one's hand.

This association of each card with a definite hand not only organizes John's thoughts but also aids his memory.

Now if Sid folds and his two of hearts is the first card to go on the bottom of the deck, John will remember that the fifty-third card is the two of hearts. Then by mentally counting the dealt cards, John will know when and to whom the two of hearts will be redealt. By this procedure, he often knows several cards that will be redealt. For example, he may know the 53, 54, 57, 60, and 61st card. . . . The cards he knows depends on how the folded cards are put on the bottom of the deck.

c. Seeing flashed cards (54)

Many important cards are flashed during a game. Players who see flashed cards are not cheating. Cheating occurs only through a deliberate physical action to see unexposed cards. For example, a player who is dealing and purposely turns the deck to look at the bottom card is cheating. But a player who sees cards flashed by someone else violates no rules or ethics. To see the maximum number of flashed cards, one must know when and where to expect them. When the mind is alert to flashing cards, the eye can be trained to spot and identify them. Cards often flash when—

- they are dealt
- a player picks up his hand or draw cards
- a player looks at his cards or ruffles them through his fingers
- a kibitzer or peeker picks up the cards of another player (peekers are often careless about flashing other players' cards)
- a player throws in his discards or folds his hand
- cards reflect in a player's eyeglasses.

The good player occasionally tells a player to hold back his cards or warns a dealer that he is flashing cards. He does this to create an image of honesty, which keeps opponents from suspecting his constant use of flashed cards. He knows his warnings have little permanent effect on stopping players from flashing cards. In fact, warned players often become more careless about flashing because of their increased confidence in the "honesty" of the game.

Using data from one hundred games, John Finn

105

compiles the following table, which illustrates the number of flashed cards he sees in the Monday night game.

Flashed by	Average Number of Flashed Cards Identified per Hand (adjusted for a seven-man game)	
	Draw	7-Stud
Dealer*	6	2
Active Players	7	1
Kibitzers and Peekers	2	1
Folded Players	9	3
Total	24	7

Also, the bottom card of the deck is exposed 75% of the time.

These data show that in addition to seeing his own cards, John sees over half the deck in an average game of draw poker—just by keeping his eyes open. The limit he goes to see flashed cards is illustrated below:

Mike Bell is a new player. John does not yet know his habits and must rely on other tools to read him . . . such as seeing flashed cards.

The game is lowball draw with one twist. The betting is heavy, and the pot grows large. John has a fairly good hand (a seven low) and does not twist. Mike bets heavily and then draws one card. John figures he is drawing to a very good low hand, perhaps to a six low.

John bets. Ted Fehr pretends to have a good hand, but just calls—John reads him for a poor nine low. Everyone else folds except Mike Bell, who holds his cards close to his face and slowly squeezes them open; John studies Mike's face very closely. Actually he is not looking at his face, but is watching the reflection in his eyeglasses. When Mike opens his hand, John sees the scattered dots of low cards plus the massive design of a picture card reflecting in the glasses. (You never knew this? . . . Try it, especially if your spectacled victim has a strong light directly over or

106

behind his head. Occasionally a crucial card can even be identified in a player's bare eyeball.)

In trying to lure a bluff from the new player, John simply checks. Having already put $100 into the pot, Mike falls into the trap by making a $50 bluff bet. If John had not seen the reflection of a picture card in Mike's glasses, he might have folded. But now he not only calls the bluff bet with confidence, but tries a little experiment . . . he raises $1. Ted folds; and Mike, biting his lip after his bluff failure, falls into the trap again—he tries a desperate double bluff by raising $50. His error? He refuses to accept his first mistake and repeats his error. . . . Also, he holds cards too close to his glasses.

John calmly calls and raises another $1. Mike folds by ripping up his cards and throwing them all over the floor. His playing then disintegrates. What a valuable reflection, John says to himself.

[Note: Luring or eliciting bluffs and double bluffs from opponents is a major money-making strategy of the good player. In fact, in most games, he purposely lures other players into bluffing more often than he bluffs himself.]

d. Intentional flashing (55)

The good player intentionally flashes cards in his hand to cause opponents to drop, call, bet, raise, or bluff. But he uses the intentional flash with caution. If suspected, intentional flashes are less effective and can cause resentment among players.

After the final card of a seven-card stud game, John Finn holds a partly hidden flush—three clubs showing and two clubs in the hole. He also has a pair of jacks showing and a pair of sevens in the hole. Ted Fehr has the other pair of sevens showing, and John reads him for two pair—queens over sevens. Sid Bennett has aces up and makes a $1 bet. Ted, betting strong from the start, raises $25. John just calls.

"I should raise," Sid thinks out loud as he strokes his chin. "John is weak . . . probably has jacks up. But Ted might have three sevens . . . no other sevens are showing."

John picks up his hole cards, shifts his position and crosses his legs. Accidentally-on-purpose he turns his hand so Sid can see two of his hole cards . . . the pair of sevens.

"I'll raise to $50," Sid says while chuckling; he knows that John has two pair and that Ted cannot have three sevens. Never thinking that John might also have the flush, Sid looks pleased with his sharpness in spotting John's hole cards.

After Ted folds, John raises back. Sid calls and then slaps his hand against his massive forehead when John shows him a flush. He grumbles something about bad luck while never realizing the trap he was sucked into.

e. Peekers (56)

Spectators and players who have folded often peek at undealt cards or at hands of active players. Most peekers exhibit readable behavior patterns that give away the value of every card and every hand they look at. These patterns are found in their—

- levels of and changes in interest toward peeked-at hands

- timing of peeks and re-peeks

- reactions (after folding) to peeking at hands of ex-opponents

- eye movements and areas of interest immediately after peeking at cards to be dealt.

Players who allow others to peek at their hands encounter problems of—

- readable patterns given to opponents

- flashed cards

- upset strategy

- disturbed concentration

- more frequent, unsolicited peeking.

The good player carefully selects those whom he lets look at his hand. He lets certain players peek at his cards in order to—

- convey certain information to the peeker or to the other players

- advertise plays that encourage loose or poor playing by others

- create a more carefree and careless atmosphere

- upset certain players by not allowing them to peek

- encourage peekers to look at hands of other players.

The good player controls peeking by the following methods:

—He never peeks at cards of other players. This avoids any obligation to let other players peek at his cards. After dropping out of a hand, he concentrates on observation and planning strategy rather than wasting his time on peeking.

—He develops a consistent way of holding his cards to prevent unwanted peeking.

—When players ask to look at his cards, he refuses gently by a remark such as, "I'll show you later."

—Whenever possible, he buries his folded hands and dead cards before anyone can look at them. He can then advantageously lie about them.

New player, Charlie Holland, sits next to John Finn. In his first big-stake game, Charlie is nervous and impressionable. John takes full advantage of this by using his peeking strategy to throw Charlie into permanent confusion:

In a hand of lowball draw, John discards a king, and draws a seven low. Charlie holds a pat nine low. John has lured him into calling a large first-round bet and two raises. In the last round, Sid makes a defensive $25 bet; Charlie calls. John raises to $75 and everyone folds. John throws his cards on top of his discarded king and then pulls in the pot.

"What'd you have?" Charlie asks.

"A fat king," John smiles as he picks up the cards and shows him the king.

Charlie Holland groans. With a drooping face, he stares at the large pot. "I should've called," he moans as John slowly pulls in the pot while laying the larger bills on top for better viewing.

What does this have to do with peeking? Nothing yet. . . . The next hand is seven-card stud. Charlie drops out early to study John's technique. He stretches his neck to peek at John's hole cards. With an air of friendship, John Finn loops his arm around Charlie's shoulder and shows him the hole cards— John has an ace-king diamond flush.

"We'll kill 'em with this ace-king diamond flush," John says loudly.

Surprised that John announced his exact hand, Charlie looks at the cards again, then replies, "Yeah man!"

But actually, John is not confident of his flush because he reads both Ted and Quintin for two pair, and all eight of their full house cards are alive. He figures the odds are about 2 to 1 that one of them will catch a full house. He also knows that they fear his flush and will not bet unless they catch the full house.

Scotty Nichols who folded early is sitting between Quintin and Ted. With his head bobbing back and forth, he peeks at their hands as they catch new cards. Now, the last hole card is dealt. John watches Scotty . . . first his plump head points toward the highest hand—Ted's queens over jacks. He peeks at Ted's new hole card; immediately his head snaps over to check Quintin's cards. Obviously Ted's new card is not very interesting . . . he failed to catch his full house, John figures.

Now Scotty looks at Quintin's new card. He looks

again and then glances at Quintin's up cards . . . then checks the hole cards once again. Scotty does not say a word, but he may as well be yelling, "Interesting! A very interesting catch for the full house!" . . . Adjusting his thick glasses, Scotty looks at John's up cards; his eyes then dart back and forth between Quintin and John while ignoring Ted's hand.

What happens? Ted foolishly bets $25. Quintin raises $1. Scotty covers his smiling mouth with his hand. Expecting some lively action, he waits for John to get sucked into Quintin's great trap. . . . Across the table, Charlie Holland smiles; he waits for John to blast Quintin with a big raise. John Finn folds.

Charlie rises halfway out of his seat while making gurgling noises. "You . . . you know what you dropped?" he stammers.

"Yeah, a busted hand," John shrugs.

"A busted hand!" Charlie bellows. His hand shoots to the table and grabs John's folded cards. "Look, you had an ace-king diamond flush. You even announced it!"

"Oh, no! I thought it was a four flush," John lies. Quintin glowers at John's flush and then shows his winning full house. . . . Charlie sits down talking to himself.

Alert playing not only saves John money, but confuses everyone and sets up Charlie for future control.

6. *Non-Game Behavior (57)*
The good player behaves in the following ways toward non-game contacts that could influence his poker activities.

Non-Game Contact	Behavior
Friend of a player	Flatter performance of the player. Exaggerate merits of the game.
Potential player	Suggest the easiness of winning money in the game. Stress the social and pleasant aspects of the game.
Player from another game	Indicate a desire to play in his game. Extend an invitation to own game. Create an image of being a loose, sociable player.
Family of a player	Flatter poker skill of the player. If they complain about his losses, suggest that his bad luck is due to change.
Other acquaintances	Indicate a desire to play poker. Down-grade personal performance in poker . . . talk about losses.

Sometimes the good player practices contrasting *game* and *non-game* behavior. For example, if during the game he practices unfriendly behavior toward a certain opponent, he may find it advantageous to be congenial toward this same person outside of the game.

Although all poker players in the Monday night game view themselves as independent men (most habitual poker players view themselves as rugged individualists), their wives retain various degrees of control over them. John plans his behavior toward their wives according to the following notations in his notebook:

Betty Nichols	**Concerned about Scotty's losses. To calm her, recall his past winnings. She will not make him quit if reminded that poker keeps him from drinking.**
Florence Merck	**Supports Quintin's playing, especially since he is winning.**
Stephanie Bennett	**Thinks Sid is foolish for playing. Realizes he will never win and wants him to quit, but realizes she has no control over him. Also, having plenty of money, she is not too worried about his losses.**
Rita Fehr	**Does not care and makes no attempt to influence Ted, despite his suicidal losses.**

XIII
POLICIES (58)

The good player forms policies about money, credit, and rules. These policies are his guidelines for strategy and are planned to yield both short-term and long-term advantages. Proper policies result in fewer mistakes and better decisions.

1. Money (59)

Money is the rational basis for poker. To win money is the rational reason to invest time and effort in poker.

a. Maintaining proper attitude (60)

Since poker is a game of money management, the proper attitude about money is crucial. What is the good player's attitude about money? Realizing that each dollar represents an irreplaceable segment of life (the time required to earn that dollar), he respects money out of respect for himself.

b. Stimulating poor attitude in opponents (61)
A poor money attitude in opponents increases the edge odds for the good player. Since most players are influenced by the opinions of the good player, he uses this influence to stimulate poor money attitudes by advancing *erroneous* ideas such as—

- one must be dealt good cards to win
- luck is required to win
- streaks of luck run hot and cold, and cards should be played accordingly
- betting should depend on how much one is winning or losing.

The good player often encourages the use of poker chips instead of money in order to—

- decrease the sense of value for money
- stimulate looser play and a faster betting pace
- speed up the game.

In certain games, however, players will play for higher stakes when cash (rather than chips) is used.

c. Increasing money in game (62)
The good player tries to increase the cash brought to the game because more cash—

- allows the betting pace and stakes to increase more rapidly
- decreases opponents' respect for money
- makes more money available for loans.

An effective way to increase money brought to the

game is to increase the money needed to play by limiting the use of credit.

Ted Fehr has been losing heavily on the horses. His cash position is low; he is borrowing excessively to stay in the action. John is worried because now Ted brings less than a hundred dollars to the game, loses it promptly, and then borrows for the rest of the game. John figures that each player should bring at least three-hundred dollars to keep the game healthy. This is how he puts pressure on Ted to increase his cash position:

"Lend me a hundred," Ted says turning to John after losing a pot.

"It's only the third hand and you're broke?" John growls and makes no move to lend him money. "I can't lend my cash right off . . . what'd I play on?" The other players nod in agreement.

"Who'll lend me a hundred?" Ted asks as he looks around the table . . . his mouth smiles. There is no reply . . . his mouth droops.

Noticing Ted's sweaty forehead, John finally says, "Write out a check and put it in the game. Next time bring five or six hundred like everyone else does. Then if you run out, there'll be enough cash in the game to lend."

Ted's freckled face wrinkles as he pulls a blank check from his wallet. "I've lost thousands in this game," he says in a choking voice. "Can't even borrow a hundred. Isn't my credit any good?"

"Sure your credit is good," John explains as he cashes the check. "That's not the point. It's for your own protection. How can you possibly win without money to back you up? Got to have money to make money." . . . John knows this meaningless platitude will be swallowed as the truth by most players, especially gamblers like Ted.

"Got to have money to make money," Ted mumbles. "I'll bring plenty next week and overpower everyone."

During that week, Ted wins at the race track. Remembering John's advice and blaming his poker losses to a lack of cash, he brings over a thousand dollars to the next game. The excess cash clouds his sense of value for money . . . he tries to over-power everyone. His overpowering play is an exhibition of wild, reckless poker. By two in the morning, Ted is writing a check; John Finn is a very big winner.

2. Credit (63)

Credit policies can determine the health of a poker game. The proper use of credit allows a faster betting pace and higher stakes. Since the good player is the most consistent winner, he is the prime source of credit and, therefore, exercises a major influence on the credit policies. He applies the following *credit rule* to poker games:

> *All debts must be paid by the start of each game. No one may play while owing money from a previous game.*

This policy is effective in preventing bad debts that can damage or destroy a game. This credit policy also prevents a valuable loser from accumulating such a large poker debt that he might quit the game and never play again just to avoid paying the debt. But when a loser is temporarily forced out of the game by this credit policy, he usually recovers financially, repays his debts, and then returns for more losses.

The following additional advantages are offered by this credit policy:

—Provides a clear rule that forces prompt payment of poker debts.

—Forces more cash into the game, which means more cash available for the good player to win.

—Increases the willingness of players to lend money, which provides more cash for the losers.

—Detects players headed for financial trouble.

—Forces bankrupt players out of the game before serious damage is done.

116

The good player is flexible and alters any policy when beneficial. For example, he may ignore this credit policy to prevent a wealthy, heavily losing player from quitting the game. But he carefully weighs the advantages against the long-range disadvantages before making any exception to this credit policy.

By not borrowing money himself, the good player avoids obligations that could reduce his influence over the credit policies. If the good player loses his cash, he writes a check. A check puts more money into the game and sets a good example for using cash and checks instead of credit. If the good player must borrow, he does so from a player who rarely borrows himself and thus would seldom demand a reciprocating loan.

a. Extending credit (64)

The good player extends credit only for personal financial gain. He selectively extends credit for the following reasons:

- —Available credit keeps big losers in the game. Steady losers who must constantly beg to borrow may quit the game out of humiliation or injured pride. But if big losers can borrow gracefully, they usually continue playing and losing.

- —Opponents often play poorer poker after they have borrowed money.

- —The good player can exercise greater influence and control over players who are in debt to him.

To obtain maximum benefits when lending money, the good player creates impressions that he—

- is extending a favor
- gives losers a break
- lends only to his friends

- lends only when winning and then on a limited basis

- expects other players, particularly winners, to lend money.

b. *Refusing credit (65)*

Easy credit automatically extended by a winning player will make him the target for most or all loans. Automatic credit decreases the money brought to the game, which in turn decreases the betting pace. Ironically, losers often feel ungrateful, resentful, and often suspicious toward the overly willing lender.

Refusal of credit is an important tool for controlling credit policies. The good player selectively refuses credit in order to—

- prod players into bringing more money.

- force other players to lend money

- make borrowers feel more obligated and grateful

- avoid being taken for granted as an easy lender

- enhance an image of being tough (when advantageous)

- avoid poor credit risks

- upset certain players.

c. *Cashing checks (66)*

In most poker games, checks are as good as cash. The threat of legal action forces fast payment of most bounced checks. The good player likes to cash losers' checks because—

- money in the game is increased

- losers get cash without using credit

- his cash position is decreased, which puts pressure on other winners to supply credit

- losers are encouraged to write checks, particularly if resistance is offered to their borrowing, while no resistance is offered to cashing their checks.

d. Bad debts (67)

A bad poker debt is rare. Losing poker players are gamblers, and most gamblers maintain good gambling credit above all else. Some players go bankrupt, but almost all eventually pay their poker debts. When a loser stops gambling to recover financially, the best policy usually is to avoid pressuring him into paying his poker debt. Such pressure can cause increasing resentment to where he may never pay . . . or even worse, never return to the game to lose more money.

A house rule that allows bad debts to be absorbed by all players (e.g., by cutting the pot) has two advantages:

1. Lenders are protected, therefore, all players are more willing to lend money.

2. A debtor is less likely to welch against all the players than against an individual player.

Establishing a maximum bad debt that will be reimbursed by cutting pots is a wise addition to this house rule. Limiting this bad-debt insurance will—

- restrain excessive or careless lending

- provide a good excuse for not lending cash to a loser beyond this insurance level

- discourage collusion between a player and a potential welcher

- avoid any large liability against future pots that could keep players away from the game until a large bad debt were paid by cutting the pot.

A gambling debt has no legal recourse (except debts represented by bad checks). A welcher, however, will usually pay if threatened with a tattletale campaign. If

119

he still does not pay, a few telephone calls to his wife, friends, and business associates often forces payment before news of his unpaid poker debt is spread too far. The good player openly discusses any bad poker debt as a deterrent to others who might consider welching.

Handling credit is an important and delicate matter for John Finn. He must make credit available to keep the game going, but must limit the use of credit to keep cash plentiful. He must appear generous in lending his winnings while appearing tough against players abusing the use of credit. John pressures other winners into lending their money and pressures losers into writing checks. He must prevent losers from getting their feelings hurt as he enforces the credit rule (described on page 116). . . . All this requires careful thought and delicate maneuvering.

Sid Bennett is wealthy and loses many thousands of dollars every year. John takes special care of him. Usually Sid brings plenty of cash to the game, maybe five or six hundred dollars. When he loses that, John gently pressures him into writing checks. Occasionally, Sid gets upset and refuses to write any more checks. He then borrows with gusto. Sometimes when he runs out of money, he scans the table for the biggest pile of money. Then smash, his big fist descends without warning . . . he grabs the whole pile of money and peels off a couple-hundred dollars. If the victim objects, Sid just grunts and looks the other way, but keeps the money. Most players grant him this liberty because they know he is rich and will always repay them.

Occasionally, Sid gets bitter when suffering big consecutive losses and refuses to pay off his debts by the next game. John realizes that Sid might quit the game if the credit rule were applied to him. So if Sid owes him money under these conditions, John quietly lets the debt ride until the following week. But if Sid refuses to pay money he owes to another player, John pays off the debt while reminding everyone that debts cannot be carried over. Sid usually pays John later the same night or the following week. With his tantrums appeased, Sid happily goes on to lose many thousands more.

While lax with Sid, John Finn rigidly enforces the credit rule against other players. He is particularly tight about extending credit to Ted Fehr because of his poor financial condition. John often refuses him credit and makes him write checks. This tough policy forces Ted to quit when he is broke. Then when he accumulates enough money, he returns to the game, pays off his debts and then loses more.

When Ted quits for several weeks to recover financially, a losing player occasionally complains about holding one of Ted's debts or bounced checks. John offers to buy the debt or check at a twenty-five percent discount. This keeps everyone happy; it gives the loser more cash to lose, and John picks up a good profit.

At times, John Finn refuses to lend money to anyone. This forces others to lend their cash. At other times, he puts on subtle displays of generosity. For example, if players with good credit run low on money, John advantageously reduces his cash position by silently handing them loans before they even ask for one. Everyone is favorably impressed with this act of fake generosity.

In John's notebook is the following list:

Credit Rating

Quintin Merck	Best
Sid Bennett	
Scotty Nichols	↓
Ted Fehr	Worst

When a player writes a check, John usually makes a quick move to cash it. To him, checks are often better to hold than money because cash winnings are more obvious targets for loans than are check winnings.

3. *Rules* (68)

The good player shuns fixed *poker rules*. He does, however, provide equitable and consistent answers to poker problems and questions because such a policy—

- eliminates the rule problems
- increases acceptance of complex games and modifications
- increases his control over the game
- improves his image as a fair and desirable player
- increases his invitations to other games
- establishes him as judge and arbitrator over all poker problems
- increases his ability to control the *house rules*.

Poker, unlike other card games, is not subject to rigid rules. Published rules and the various "Hoyles" on poker are merely descriptions of general conventions. Strict adherence to any set of poker rules produces an array of contradictions and inequities. By avoiding reference to Hoyle or to any fixed rules and by consistently interpreting poker situations and equitably resolving poker problems, the good player gains control of the rules.

a. Modified rules (69)

Rules are found in most poker books. These rules fail to cover many situations, especially in games involving split pots, twists, and other more complex modifications. To cover the many ruleless situations, the good player equitably formulates new rules (actually, he formulates flexible guidelines rather than rules). He will then consistently follow these guidelines, even when they cost him money. But why would he do something that would cost him money? Because in the long run, this policy delivers major financial benefits by giving him control of the rules. Furthermore, he can from time to time remind everyone of the money he has lost because of his fairness . . . this reinforces everyone's confidence in him as the controller of the rules.

b. Disputed plays (70)

Because the good player interprets the rules consistently and fairly, his opponents implicitly trust him and call on him to settle disputed plays and technical problems about poker. Typical approaches he uses in settling commonly disputed plays are summarized below:

Disputed Play	*Consistent Approach*
Misdeal	Cards are never redealt because of a misdeal. Each player is responsible for his own cards. Any misdealt hand having an uncorrectable advantage must be dropped. Any misdealt hand that is correctable or left at a disadvantage can be played.
Exposed card during the deal	An exposed card can never be exchanged for a new one . . . all cards must be accepted.
Exposed card before the deal	All cards must come off in order. No one can ask for a reshuffle, a cut or a different card.
Out-of-turn betting, calling, raising or checking	Any play made out of turn (except folding) is meaningless and can be remade or changed during the player's proper turn.

[Note: These approaches are for private games. Approaches for public games (casino and club poker) may be entirely different. See Section Six for information on public poker.]

These approaches provide clear and consistent solutions to disputes that commonly occur, especially in complex games involving split pots and twists.

c. Inequitable rules (71)

The good player may favor a chronic loser with an inequitable rule interpretation in order to keep him in the game (to everyone's benefit). But he interprets a situation and applies a rule inequitably only if the financial value of the loser outweighs the financial value of a consistently equitable rule policy.

d. House rules (72)

House rules are very important to the good player. They concern betting and playing procedures plus any other rules the players wish to adopt. The house rules determine not only the game stakes, but also the game pace.

Since most players fail to differentiate between the house rules and poker rules, they often let the good player control the *house rules* because of his fairness in interpreting *poker rules*. Important house rules that he seeks to control and manipulate concern—

- stakes and antes

- games permitted

- rules for betting (e.g., betting limits for each round, table stakes, pot limit)

- rules for raising (e.g., pick-up checks, check raising)

- treatment of discards to be redealt (such as placing unshuffled discards on the bottom of the deck)

- courtesies (such as showing non-called hands and hole cards).

The good player avoids well-defined or written rules. This gives him the flexibility needed to change the rules when advantageous.

In the Monday night game, John Finn verbally insists on adhering to the rules, but he carefully avoids any reference to specific rules. Instead, he mediates all disputes fairly, even when it costs him the pot. In his black notebook, he records his rule interpretations and dispute settlements. As a book of law, he refers to these entries in settling future problems. The entries in which he loses money are marked by big stars and recorded in accurate detail. He remembers these entries, and at every appropriate opportunity he reminds everyone how his honest rule interpretations cost him money. Of course, he never mentions the interpretations that favored him.

With this policy of integrity, John wins the confidence of the players. They know he is fair . . . everyone trusts him. They ask him to settle disputes, and they abide by his decisions. They accept him as the controller of the rules. Failing to realize that the poker rules bear no relationship to the house rules, they let John's influence spill into the house rules, thereby giving him a key tool for controlling the game.

Using his influence over the rules, John slowly alters and then obliterates the original house rules. In the Monday night game, the original house rules allowed a maximum bet of one dollar and permitted only straight draw and stud games . . . fifty-dollar winners were rare. Now hundred-dollar bets are made in draw. Wild, twist, and split-pot games prevail. Thousand-dollar winners are common. After six years of controlling the rules, John increases his edge odds from 35% to 65%, and his profits soar from $2,500 to $42,000 per year.

4. Arguments and Emotional Situations (73)

The good player avoids involvement in emotional situations such as—

- disputes and arguments
- personal problems
- exposing cheaters or players who steal money.

He avoids involvement by outwardly ignoring the situation. The good player will, however, study any emotional situation in order to exploit it. He intervenes

125

only in those situations that could cost him money. For example, he steps in to prevent a loser from quitting the game because of an argument.

When the good player faces a potential argument, he controls the situation either by yielding quickly or by standing firm. He avoids taking positions that he may have to compromise or yield. He takes a firm position only when financially profitable. When in doubt about yielding or holding firm, he usually yields before a confrontation occurs.

Sid's loud mouth constantly bellows good-natured insults at the players. Professor Merck does not like Sid to tease him about his mustache, his tight playing, or his beret. He tells Sid to stop. But Sid Bennett grins and rides him even harder by calling him a dirty old man. Quintin accuses Sid of running a dishonest road-paving business and calls him a pasty-faced crook. Sid shouts back louder insults. As their bickering hurts their poker playing, John increases his winnings from the upset men. . . . But their animosity increases each week and John begins to worry. Blows are nearly exchanged when Quintin threatens to expose Sid's payola on city paving contracts. Sid threatens to sue him for slander and then calls him a queer. Squinting his green eyes, Quintin cracks the edge of his hand on the table and threatens Sid with a karate blow. Sid vibrates his big fist close to Quintin's nose, calls him a queer again, and then storms out of the house while shouting that either he or Quintin must quit the game.

Fearing that Sid may quit, John telephones both men the next day and settles their argument. He explains how their feud is hurting their playing and is costing them money. They both agree and thank him for straightening out their problem.

John made extra money from their feuding. But when it almost caused the loss of the biggest loser, he stepped in and eliminated their argument in a way that improved his image as a desirable player.

CHEATERS (74)*

The good player never cheats ... he never needs to.

In friendly and private poker games, most players consider a cheater less honorable than a thief because a thief robs from strangers, but a poker cheat robs from his friends. The normal emotional impulse is to banish the cheater from the game ... or worse.** The good poker player, however, resists acting on emotions. He views any cheating situation objectively and then acts in his best long-range financial interest.

1. Cheating (75)

Cheating involves the following manipulations of cards, money, or betting:

—Cards are covertly switched to alter the value of a hand. Cards are purposely flashed to see undealt or unexposed cards. The deck is culled and stacked to change the sequence of cards to be dealt.

—Money is stolen from the pot or from other players. Wrong change is purposely taken from the pot. Lights are purposely not paid.

—Mechanical devices such as marked cards, strippers, mirrors, and hold-out equipment, and techniques to smudge, nick, or mar cards for future identification are used.

—Furtive betting agreements or partnerships are made and then the colluding partners signal each other when to bet or raise.

* *See Concepts 128-134 for more details and information about amateur and professional cheating.*
** *Stronger emotional reactions against cheaters are common. Some reactions can result in physical violence—even stabbings or shootings.*

Honest poker allows any behavior or manipulation, no matter how deceptive, except cheating. Cheating is the only dishonest, illegal, or unethical behavior in poker. But where does cynical deception end and cheating begin? Actually, a sharp distinction exists. Poker cheating is the conjuring up of advantages unavailable to others. Poker deception is the taking advantage of situations available to all. For example, *all* cards are marked. A sharp-eyed player can find printing imperfections in honest decks of cards. Some common imperfections are printing-ink spots, inkless dots, and slightly off-centered designs on the back side of the cards. Also, the normal use of cards produces identifying smudges, nicks, scratches and creases on their backs. (Purposely marring cards for identification would, of course, be cheating.) These natural imperfections and markings that identify unexposed cards are available to any player willing to train his eye and discipline his mind. The good player willingly exerts this effort to learn and then use these natural markings. He may even increase this advantage by providing the game with cheaper (but honest) cards with less perfect printing patterns.

Sid Bennett cheats. While it is quite obvious, only John Finn fully realizes that he cheats. Quintin Merck suspects it, but never makes any direct accusations. The other players watch Sid's cheating, but refuse to suspect him. His crude cheating techniques include—

- looking through the discards to select cards for use in his hand

- culling or sorting cards prior to dealing

- peeking at cards to be dealt, especially twist cards

- stealing money from the pot when going light

- slipping a good card into the hand of a losing player (Robin Hood cheating).

John estimates that Sid cheats once in every eight or ten hands.

2. Accepting Cheaters (76)

The good player quietly accepts cheaters if they are losers. In fact, he often welcomes their cheating because they generally lose more money when cheating, particularly when cheating in complex games involving split pots and twists. . . . A player usually increases his losses when cheating because he—

- dilutes his attention toward the game by worrying about and concentrating on his cheating

- overestimates the benefits of cheating and thus plays looser and poorer poker

- makes his cards more readable.

Why does a player cheat if his cheating increases his losses? Some players cheat to satisfy emotional needs. Other players cheat out of financial desperation.

Sid cheats for emotional reasons rather than financial reasons. His cheating costs him thousands of extra dollars every year as shown by the data below. These data include a three-month period when Sid stopped his cheating because he was worried about getting caught.

| | Edge Odds for Sid Bennett | |
Period	Cheating Frequency	Average Edge Odds, %
1963	Seldom	−10
1964–1965	Regular	−23
Oct.–Dec. 1965	Seldom	−12
1966	Regular	−25

These data indicate that Sid doubles his losses when cheating. With his current losses in the Monday night game totaling $20,000 per year, his cheating costs him about $10,000 per year.

3. Rejecting Cheaters (77)

Under certain conditions, cheating by others can financially hurt the good player. For example, valuable losers might quit the game if they detected cheating. Or the game itself could be destroyed by cheating. If necessary, therefore, the good player can eliminate the cheater or his cheating in one or more of the following ways:

Time of Action	Form of Action	Results
Indirectly, during game	Make the cheater feel that he is suspected and is being watched.	Cheating stops.
Privately, outside of game	Tell the cheater that if he cheats again, he will be publicly exposed.	Cheating stops.
Privately, outside of game	Tell suspicious players about the cheater. Point out that he is a loser and the best way to penalize him is to let him play.	Cheating continues, and the players are satisfied.
Privately, outside of game	Form a conspiracy with other players to cheat collectively in order to bankrupt the cheater.	Cheater is driven from game.
Publicly, during game	Expose the cheater during the game in front of everyone.	Cheater quits the game.

The best action against a cheater depends not only on the situation, but on the attitudes of the other players. If a cheater must be eliminated, the good player assumes a righteous hero's role by exposing the "nefarious cheater." This righteous role provides the good player with the valuable image of being the most honest and trustworthy player in the game—an ideal image for manipulating his opponents.

What about stealing money from the pot? If the good player does not win the pot, he keeps quiet when losers shortchange the pot or fail to pay their lights (money owed to the pot). But if chronic stealing upsets other players enough to hurt the game, the good player stops this stealing by taking the same action used to stop cheating (as described on the previous page).

Scotty Nichols barely beats Ted Fehr to win a nine-hundred-dollar pot. With everyone's attention focused on the action, Sid Bennett casually takes the hundred dollars that he was light and slips it into his shirt pocket for a quick two-hundred-dollar profit. John notices Sid's theft, but says nothing. With saliva drooling over his lip, Scotty rakes in the huge pot; his breathing quickens as his fingers sort the money ... he forgets about Sid's lights. Since Sid is a big loser and Scotty is a big winner for the night, the theft has an equalizing effect that benefits John.

Several hands later, Sid pulls the same trick by pocketing his forty-dollar lights for an eighty-dollar profit. John wins the pot and says nothing. As the next hand is dealt, he quietly gives Sid twenty dollars and says, "You owe me another hundred." . . . Sid blushes and then nods in agreement.

4. Robin Hood Cheater (78)

Some players cheat for others without benefiting themselves. The beneficiary is usually a poor player or a big loser. This kind of Robin Hood cheating is relatively common and benefits the good player by—

- distributing losses more evenly among players
- decreasing losses of big losers
- making the hands of both the Robin Hood cheater and his beneficiary more readable.

Sid Bennett often cheats for big losers like Ted Fehr. For example, Sid folds, then looks at Ted Fehr's hand and sees a four-card heart flush. Quickly he grabs Ted's draw card . . . it is a club. Sid then rummages through the discards. Finding a heart, he switches it with Ted's club. . . . Ted smiles and wins the pot with a heart flush.

While Sid's card switch is crude and obvious, no one except John lets himself fully realize what happened. Later in the same game, Sid attempts a partnership with John. This is what happens:

The pot is large. Five players are in for the last bet—including John and Sid, who are sitting next to each other. Sid bets and then his knee nudges John's leg. John promptly folds his three queens. Sid wins with a full house.

"Remember that," Sid whispers to John while pulling in the pot.

A few hands later, Sid Bennett is dealt a pat straight. Again he nudges John, who folds immediately. Sid grins and winks a faded-blue eye at John.

Later that evening, John draws to a lowball hand that he has bet heavily during the first round. But he catches a pair of fives to ruin his lowball hand. Still John bets the maximum in trying to bluff out his two remaining opponents. . . . Ted Fehr folds because Sid is sitting behind him with a pat hand. John's knee nudges Sid's leg. Sid smiles and then shows everyone his eight low as he folds. "Thanks," he whispers to John. Promptly John Finn spreads his hand faceup on the table to win the six-hundred-dollar lowball pot with a pair of fives. . . . Sid looks at the ceiling and sputters dirty words.

Instead of simply saying no to Sid's collusion-cheating offer, John earns a good profit while making his answer clear.

5. Detection (79)

Most cheaters in private games use crude techniques that are easily detectable.* Yet most players ignore even obvious cheating to avoid arousing unpleasant

* See Concepts 128-134 for discussions and details about undetectable, professional cheating.

emotions. When a player detects someone cheating, he often rationalizes it as a rule violation or a mistake rather than cheating. But the good player identifies cheating quickly and can detect even highly skilled cheaters without ever seeing a dishonest move. How does he do this? Cheaters are betrayed by violations of logic and probability. The good player with his sharply focused concentration on his opponents, the game, and the odds has an acute awareness for any improbable playing and betting patterns. This awareness enables him to promptly detect cheating, even without seeing a suspicious move.

Professor Merck suspects Sid of cheating. One night, Sid cheats him out of a $700 pot. After sitting in silence for several hands, Quintin abruptly leaves without a word and slams the front door. Knowing that Quintin detected Sid's cheating and being fearful that he might tell others, John pursues him out of the door. Quintin stops under the street lamp when he sees John approaching. For a moment, neither says a word.

"You saw it too?" Quintin asks, squinting his green eyes.

"I see it every game."

"So why haven't you said something!" the professor half shouts. "He should've been bounced from the game long ago."

"Who's the biggest loser in the game?" John quickly replies. "It's Sid. And you're a big winner. In the past couple years, you've taken Sid for thousands of dollars. Sure he's cheated you, me, and everyone else out of pots. But what if we'd thrown him out two years ago? We'd have done him a forty-thousand-dollar favor."

Quintin's mouth opens. He rubs his chin.

"Sid's a cheater and deserves to be penalized," John continues. "But the best way to penalize him is to let him play. We only hurt ourselves by bouncing him from the game."

"Never thought about it that way," Quintin says scratching his head. "Maybe you're right. . . . Who else knows about his cheating?"

133

"No one who'll admit it. Cheating is a strange thing. Most players have strong feelings against it. . . . Everyone subconsciously knows that Sid cheats. But no one wants an unpleasant emotional experience, so no one sees him cheat."

"Someday, someone will accuse him."

"Perhaps," John continues, "but visible suspicion will occur first. Take yourself . . . he cheated you out of seven-hundred dollars tonight. Yet, you still didn't accuse him. You passed it off till next time. The next time you may have accused Sid or may have passed it off again."

"But what happens when someone does accuse him outright . . . then what?"

"If he's accused outright, we not only lose Sid, but other players might quit. The game might even fold. We must convince any seriously suspecting players that the best action is to let him play. If they won't accept this, then we must either stop the cheating or eliminate Sid from the game."

"So for now, we leave everything as is?"

"Right," John replies with a nod. "And when Sid steals your pot, just remember he'll pay you back many times."

"But why is he a big loser if he cheats?"

"A cheater, like a thief, is unrealistic. He overestimates the value of cheating and plays a poorer game. In fiction, the cheater may be a winner. But in reality, he's a loser and usually a big loser. And this is Sid's case. . . . The good player—the winner—never needs to cheat."

"True, true," Quintin mumbles.

"See you next week," John says as he walks away.

What does John accomplish by this? He keeps the game intact by pacifying Quintin, and Sid continues his cheating and losing.

The good player can lose to cheaters in certain situations. Two or more professional cheaters, for example, can gang up on a good player to reduce his edge odds to a losing level. The good player, however, quickly detects team or gang cheating and either beats it, eliminates it, or quits the game (see Concept 133).

134

For federal tax purposes, net annual poker winnings must be declared as straight *income*.* Poker income can be listed under the heading of "Other" on page two of Federal Income Tax Form 1040. In most states, net poker gains can also be declared as income. Gambling losses can be deducted (on Schedule A) from poker income, but net gambling losses cannot be deducted from taxable income.

Poker players and their winnings are not subject to the federal *excise* taxes on gambling.** . . . Apparently the Federal Government does not classify poker players as gamblers (even though poker income is treated as gambling gains by the IRS).

A 1966 survey by the author (summarized on the following five pages) suggests that poker games are technically illegal in most states. Nevertheless, few if any states apply their anti-gambling laws to private poker games. But house games (where pots are cut or raked for a profit or where players pay collection fees) are vulnerable to legal action in most states.

The table on the following five pages gives information about the legal and tax status of poker in each state.

* *Carmack v. Commissioner of Internal Revenue, 183 F.2d 1 (5th Cir. 1950).*
** *According to the United States Excise Tax Regulation 4401 (paragraphs 4020-4032), poker winnings are not subject to the ten-percent excise wagering tax. And according to Regulation 4411 (paragraphs 4075-4083) poker players, even professional players, are not required to register and purchase the Wagering Occupational Tax Stamp.*

STATE LAWS ABOUT POKER

State Is Poker Legal?*	Source of Information— Legal Reference	State Income Tax 1977
Alabama No	NAACP of Montgomery, Alabama— Alabama State Statutes	Yes
Alaska No	Bar Association Section 11.60.140	Yes
Arizona No	Bar Association— Revised Statutes 13-431	Yes
Arkansas No	Assistant Attorney General— Statutes Annotated 41-2011 and 3809 (Repl. 1964)	Yes
California No	Deputy Attorney General— Penal Code 330: Refers only to stud poker as illegal	Yes
Colorado No	Bar Association— Revised Statutes, Section 40-10-9	Yes
Connecticut No	State Police— Sections 53-272 to 277	No
Delaware Yes	Assistant Attorney General— Title II Code of 1953, Section 665	Yes
Florida No	Attorney General— Section 849.08	No
Georgia No	Assistant Attorney General— Georgia Code, Section 26-6404 and 6401	Yes

*Author's opinion for private games (for guideline use only).

State Is Poker Legal?*	Source of Information— Legal Reference	State Income Tax 1977
Hawaii No	Bar Association— No specific reference given	Yes
Idaho No	Assistant Attorney General— Section 18-3801, Idaho Code	Yes
Illinois No	Legislative Reference Bureau— Criminal Law, Chapter 38, Section 28-1	Yes
Indiana No	Bar Association— Act of 1905, Chapter 169, Statute 10-2307	Yes
Iowa No	Solicitor General— Chapter 726, 1966 Code	Yes
Kansas No	Bar Association— No specific reference given	Yes
Kentucky No	Bar Association— No specific reference given	Yes
Louisiana Yes	Republican Party of Louisiana— No specific reference given	Yes
Maine No	Assistant Attorney General— Revised Statute 1964	Yes
Maryland No	Assistant Attorney General— Maryland Article 27, Section 237-264	Yes
Massa- chusetts No	Bar Association— Section 1, Chapter 37, General Laws	Yes

*Author's opinion for private games (for guideline use only).

State Is Poker Legal?*	Source of Information— Legal Reference	State Income Tax 1977
Michigan No	Democratic State Central Committee of Michigan— Penal Code, 1945, Sections 750.314 and 750-315	Yes
Minnesota Yes	Attorney— Statutes 609, 75	Yes
Mississippi No	Bar Association— Code of 1942, Section 2190	Yes
Missouri No	Governor— State Statute	Yes
Montana No	Attorney General— Section 94-2401, R.C.M., 1947	Yes
Nebraska Yes	Bar Association— No specific reference given	Yes
Nevada Yes	Bar Association— No specific reference given	No
New Hampshire No	Bar Association— 577.7 Gaming	No
New Jersey No	Deputy Attorney General— Statutes 2A:112-a and 218:85-7	Yes
New Mexico No	Assistant Attorney General— Section 40A-19-1 to 3, N.M. Statutes Annotated, 1953 Compilation (P.S.)	Yes
New York No	Assistant Council to Governor— Article 1, Section 9 of N.Y. State Constitution, and Sections 970-998 of N.Y. State Penal Law	Yes

*Author's opinion for private games (for guideline use only).

State Is Poker Legal?*	Source of Information— Legal Reference	State Income Tax 1977
North Carolina No	Bar Association— No specific reference given	Yes
North Dakota No	Bar Association— Chapter 12-23-01	Yes
Ohio No	Bar Association— Section 2915.06, Revised Code	Yes
Oklahoma No	Oklahoma State University— Title 21 of Oklahoma Statutes, 1961, Section 941	Yes
Oregon No	Attorney General— ORS 167.25 and 167.510 Licensed poker clubs only	Yes
Pennsylvania No	Deputy Attorney General— No specific reference given	Yes
Rhode Island No	Attorney General's office No specific reference given	Yes
South Carolina No	Research Clerk— Sections 16-804, 505	Yes
South Dakota No	Bar Association— No specific reference given	No
Tennessee No	Attorney General— Section 39-2001, Tennessee Code Annotated	No
Texas Yes	Governor— Texas Jurisprudence, 2nd volume 26	No

*Author's opinion for private games (for guideline use only).

State Is Poker Legal?*	Source of Information— Legal Reference	State Income Tax 1977
Utah No	Attorney General— Section 76-27-1 to 3, Utah Code Annotated, 1953	Yes
Vermont No	Bar Association— Section 2132 and 13, VSA 2133	Yes
Virginia No	Attorney General— Section 18.1-316	Yes

Washington
No
	Assistant Attorney
	  General—
	Revised Code 9.47.010 to
	  9.47.030: Licensed
	  poker clubs only
		No

West Virginia No	Bar Association— No specific reference given	Yes
Wisconsin No	Bar Association— Chapter 945	Yes
Wyoming No	Attorney— Statute 6-203, 1957	No
District of Columbia ? (not clear)	United States Attorney— Title 22, D.C. Code, Section 1501 to 1515	Yes
Puerto Rico No	Bar Association— No specific reference given	Yes
Virgin Islands No	Attorney— Sections 1221-1226, Chapter 61, Title 14	

United States
Government
Yes
	Deputy Attorney General—
	Legality is up to individual
	  states.
	Winnings are taxable
	  income.	

Author's opinion for private games (for guideline use only).

This section of the Federal Tax form (page two, form 1040) shows how John Finn declares his $54,000 poker income for 1965:

Form 1040

U.S. Individual Income Tax Return 1965

for the year January 1-December 31, 1965 or other taxable year beginning
1965, ending 19 US Treasury Department—Internal Revenue Service

4 Pensions and annuities, rents and royalties, partnerships, & estates or trusts (Schedule B) ▲		
5 Business income (Schedule C) ▲	3,450	00
6 Sale or exchange of property (Schedule D) ▲		
7 Farm income (Schedule F) ▲		
8 Other sources (state nature)		
Monday Poker Games	42,000	00
Other Poker Games	12,000	00
Total other sources ▲ ▶ ▲ ▶	54,000	00
9 Add lines 2 through 8. Enter here and on page 1 line 6 ▲ ▶ ▲ ▶	57,450	00

PART FOUR

OPPONENTS

In poker, all opponents are potential financial assets. The good poker player first gets his opponents involved in the game; he then exploits them to win their money.

XVI
INVOLVEMENT (81)

As players become emotionally and financially involved in a poker game, they become easier to exploit and their chances of quitting the game decrease.

1. Emotional (82)
Emotional involvement can result from gambling im-

pulses . . . and most poker players are gamblers. To them, poker is gambling*. When a gambler loses, he keeps on playing in an attempt to recover his losses. When a gambler wins, he forgets his losses while believing he has finally learned how to win. The gambler's subconscious desire to punish or destroy himself emerges in his consciousness as irrational optimism.

Some players use poker as a narcotic-like diversion to escape reality. Other players develop soul-mate friendships with other players. Such involvements with poker can be emotionally soothing and pleasant and can compensate losers for many large losses.

---

* *Gambling is defined in this book as—"The wagering of money at unfavorable odds." . . . In poker, the good player with favorable edge odds is not gambling, but players with unfavorable edge odds are gambling. Horse players, casino patrons, and losing poker players are gamblers. This definition is consistent with: (1) Webster's definition (Third New International Dictionary, 1961)—"To wager money or stakes on an uncertain outcome." . . . The good player's outcome is certain; therefore, he is not gambling; (2) Funk and Wagnalls definition (The Standard Dictionary, 1962)—"To lose, squander or dispose of by gaming." . . . By this definition, the good player is not gambling, but losing players are gambling; and (3) Random House's definition (The Random House Dictionary, 1966)— "Any matter or thing involving risk or hazardous uncertainty." . . . The good player's situation is essentially riskless and, therefore, is not a gambling situation.*

A gambling situation yields a statistically minus return on money wagered, while a non-gambling (investment) situation yields a statistically plus return on money invested. . . The intensity of the situation (rate of loss or rate of return) is determined both by the time span of the wager or investment and by the percent loss or the percent return. The intensity of gambling and non-gambling (investment) situations are illustrated by the two tables on page 144. On these tables, notice the positions of the Monday-night poker players relative to other investment and gambling situations . . . notice that the good poker player is by far the best investment situation. By contrast, notice that the poor poker player is one of the worst gambling situations.

INTENSITY OF INVESTMENT SITUATIONS

	Estimated per Investment		
Investment Situation	Average Return Rate, %	Time Span	Investment Intensity*
Good Poker Player **(John Finn)**	+25	6 minutes	+2,000,000
Sound Poker Player **(Quintin Merck)**	+ 5	6 minutes	+400,000
Business	+10	1 year	+10
Bonds	+ 6	1 year	+6
Banks	+ 5	1 year	+5
Stocks	+ 4	1 year	+4

* Investment-intensity values are average-return values calculated on an annual basis.

INTENSITY OF GAMBLING SITUATIONS

	Estimated per Gamble		
Gambling Situation	Average Loss Rate, %	Time Span	Gambling Intensity*
Lottery	−50	1 month	−600
Numbers	−40	1 day	−15,000
Average Poker Player **(Scotty Nichols)**	− 1	6 minutes	−90,000
Casino Poker	(varies according to casino rake**)		
Crap Shooting	− 1	1 minute	−500,000
Horse Racing	−15	12 minutes	−700,000
Poor Poker Player **(Sid Bennett)**	−10	6 minutes	−900,000
Poor Poker Player **(Ted Fehr)**	−10	6 minutes	−900,000
Roulette	− 3	30 seconds	−3,300,000
Slot Machines	−20	5 seconds	−130,000,000

* Gambling-intensity values are the average-loss values calculated on an annual basis.
** Poker can be a gambling situation even for the good

2. Financial (83)

For a losing player, financial involvement is a form of emotional involvement. When losses force him to use his savings or to borrow money, he keeps playing in a vain attempt to recover his losses. An occasional win gives him enough encouragement to hold him in the game.

A winning player can also get financially involved and entrapped if he becomes too dependent on his poker income. He can even turn into a chronic loser if a series of losses disrupts his income. How does this happen? If his temporary loss of poker income causes a loss of objectivity, then the quality of his play will deteriorate. If this cycle of decreased objectivity and increased deterioration continues, his future losses will be assured. Memories of past winnings will then sustain him through heavy losses.

> **John Finn and Quintin Merck bet only when they judge the odds to be in their favor; they are not gamblers. But the other players in the Monday night game are gamblers. . . . Each player is emotionally and financially involved as shown on page 146:**

---

player if the pots are regularly cut or raked by the house as they are in public casinos. A large, arbitrary cut can reduce or eliminate the profitable edge odds of a good player. And while the good player can retain a great advantage over the other players in a casino poker game, he cannot stop this house cut. Also, he cannot take control of the public game and its players as he can in the private game. Still the good player can earn a guaranteed income from public poker (Nevada-type casino poker or Gardena-type club poker) if he adjusts his game to a public-professional style of poker (see Concepts 121-127).

	Emotional Involvement	Financial Involvement
John Finn	(minimum involvement)	Receives substantial income
Quintin Merck	Supports ego Finds companionship Relieves boredom	Receives moderate income useful for boasting about his poker skill
Scotty Nichols	Avoids drinking problems Escapes business disappointments	Tries to regain his past winning form
Sid Bennett	Hides insecurities Finds companionship Releases tensions	Seeks hot streak to recover past losses
Ted Fehr	Satisfies gambling compulsion to hurt himself Escapes domestic problems	Hopes for big win to parlay on the horses

XVII
EXPLOITATION (84)

Once players are involved in the game, the good player can take greater advantage of them through—

- their personal weaknesses
- their play of cards
- their betting and raising
- hypnosis
- distractions
- agreements.

146

1. Personal Weaknesses, Favors, and Bribes (85)

Most poor poker players are hooked or involved in games through their personal weaknesses. The good player exploits those weaknesses. He knows that one or more of the following weaknesses exist in almost all players:

altruism	ignorance	nervousness
capriciousness	impulsiveness	parasitism
carelessness	inattentiveness	preoccupation
compulsiveness	inconsistency	self-pity
dishonesty	inexperience	stubbornness
exhibitionism	instability	subjectiveness
faith	irrationality	superstitiousness
fear	laziness	timidness
greed*	mysticism	worry

* Greed can also be a personal strength.

Each personal weakness grows from a player's resistance to objective thinking and rational behavior.

The good player identifies and records the personal weaknesses of each opponent in his notebook. He then uses these weaknesses to influence their playing decisions, to read their hands, and to manipulate them into faster betting paces, higher stakes, and poorer quality poker. He regularly reviews and revises his notes on their weaknesses in order to—

- refresh his memory
- devise new and better ways to manipulate his opponents
- better understand each opponent
- detact changes in opponents.

John Finn identifies and lists the weaknesses of poker players as shown on the next page.

Personal Weaknesses

John Finn	Quintin Merck	Sid Bennett	Scotty Nichols	Ted Fehr
greed*	greed*	capriciousness	carelessness	capriciousness
	laziness	carelessness	faith	compulsiveness
	stubbornness	dishonesty	fear	faith
	superstitiousness	exhibitionism	greed (unhealthy)	fear
		impulsiveness	inattentiveness	impulsiveness
		inattentiveness	laziness	instability
		irrationality	mysticism	irrationality
		laziness	preoccupation	laziness
		stubbornness	self-pity	preoccupation
			subjectiveness	self-pity
			timidness	subjectiveness
			worry	superstitiousness
				worry

* A personal strength

The following incident shows how John uses an opponent's personal weaknesses to win money:

Missing his flush in draw poker, John finds himself in a good position to bluff, so he bets $50. Scotty and Sid fold immediately. Ted Fehr holds two pair and thinks he should drop, but is desperate and considers calling. John must prevent him from calling.

Everyone knows that Ted is superstitious about pennies and that he never keeps any . . . especially when gambling. So when Ted leans over and shows Sid his hand, John takes a penny from his pocket and slips the coin under the edge of Ted's money.

"Call!" Sid bellows as he gazes blankly at Ted's two pair. "He's got nothing."

"Yeah," Ted says and then grins as he picks up his pile of money to call. "What!' his grin fades as the penny tumbles from his money. "No wonder I'm losing!" he yells while picking up the coin and throwing it across the room. As the penny bounces off the wall and rolls around the floor, Ted folds his hand and says, "At least that penny made me fold. I saved fifty bucks . . ." His voice fades when John shows his winning hand . . . a four flush. Ted's eyes water . . . his superstition costs him a two-hundred-dollar pot.

Consider another example of John exploiting an opponent's weakness:

Sid Bennett injures his foot and cannot leave the house. At the last moment, John switches the game to Sid's house so the injured man can play. Knowing there will not be a good supply of food at Sid's house, John stops at a delicatessen and invests a dollar in a gigantic Italian submarine sandwich nicely wrapped in cellophane.

At three in the morning, Scotty Nichols grips his stomach. He rummages through Sid's skimpily stocked kitchen and devours handfuls of dry cereal; he even gulps down a quarter-filled bottle of ketchup.

The next hand is seven-card stud, high-low with two twists. John's hole cards are the ace and the joker*; he has another ace faceup . . . the best possible start for high-low poker. He wants the maximum number of callers. Now is the time to use his dollar investment . . . he reaches under his chair and pulls the huge sandwich from a brown paper bag. All eyes turn toward the juicy submarine. Scotty moans as his tongue laps around his puffy lips.

John lays the elongated sandwich across the pot. "The winners split it," he declares. . . . Scotty's face is sweating, and his stomach is growling.

With eyes fixed on the sandwich, everyone calls the first bet. John aggressively bets his strong hand . . . many players keep calling. The final bets are large . . . Scotty keeps calling with a poor hand. "Should fold," he says catching his breath. "But that sub . . . yum." . . . The red-faced man spends over a hundred dollars on calls. Three other players also call as their eyes remain fixed on the sandwich. The pot is the largest of the night . . . over seven-hundred dollars. John wins both high and low with an ace-high full house and a six-five low. He also wins back the sandwich, which he later uses to build another pot.

With a dollar investment, John Finn exploits his opponents' lack of discipline to win many extra dollars.

The good player continually profits from man's most pervasive weakness—laziness. Laziness foments desires to garner values without effort. This, in turn, leads to seeking unearned approval, respect, and money. The good player uses these wishful desires to manipulate his opponents with "favors" that symbolize (and falsely promise) approval, respect, and money. His victims bend to his will in seeking these pseudo favors.

"Favors" and bribes that the good player extends and withdraws for his personal profit include—

- loans

---

* *The joker (also called the bug) is a wild card for low . . . and an ace for high, also good for filling straights and flushes. In high-low games, the joker can be used as both a high card and a low card in the same hand.*

- advice
- compliments
- sympathy
- showing of cards.

Out of the loser's desire for "favors" and approval from a respected winner, the good player can often get, for example, a loser's support for changes in house rules that further benefit the good player at the loser's expense.

2. Play of Cards and Betting (86)

The good player constantly exploits his opponents as they play their cards. He repeatedly lures them into playing poorer and poorer poker. With the proper strategy, he causes them to—

- make mistakes
- improperly estimate the value of their hands
- play a looser game
- play hands that should be dropped
- drop hands that should be called.

An exploitation ploy that John Finn uses (especially in split-pot games) involves the following maneuver to make a hesitant player call a bet:

The game is high-low, five-card stud with two twists. John has a winner . . . a lock on low. Quintin and Ted are playing for high. Quintin bets $20. Ted has a four flush and wants to call, but is afraid that John will raise and Quintin will reraise . . . thus costing him $40 more. He starts to fold. John picks up a twenty dollar bill and holds it over the pot. Now knowing that John will only call and not raise, Ted calls. He then catches a flush on the twist. After more betting and raising, Ted ends up beating Quintin for high. John wins low and makes an extra fifty dollars by not letting Ted fold.

John seldom fakes this maneuver. So when players

151

see him holding the call money, they know with
confidence that he will not raise. But he will often
fake the reverse maneuver of not holding the call
money and then not raising.

The good player also exploits his opponents through
betting. When holding a strong hand, he can build
much larger pots by getting other players to do his
betting and raising. Successful *indirect* betting requires
accurate reading of opponents' hands and knowledge
of their betting habits. Miscalculation of indirect betting
can result in smaller, not larger, pots. Thus when uncertain about his opponents' intentions, the good player
will bet rather than check his strong hand.

Disproportionate betting can throw opponents into
more vulnerable and exploitable betting positions. For
example, by making a bet or a raise completely out of
proportion with the normal or expected bet, the good
player can confuse opponents into making the desired
bet, raise, call, or drop. Disproportionate betting is useful as both an offensive and defensive tool.

Scotty deals draw poker with one twist. John Finn
gets a four-card straight flush. For his best investment
odds, John wants the maximum players calling a bet
big enough to keep them in for the large, last-round
bets. He also wants to avoid raises that would make
players fold. So John opens for $14 instead of the
normal $25. Noses wrinkle. Players with poor hands
smile and call at this bargain price. Potential raisers,
suspicious of the weird bet and fearing a sandbag,
only call. The results are perfect for John . . . everyone calls and no one raises. John's estimated investment odds soar to a highly favorable—

$$\frac{(\$600)\,(.4)}{\$80} = 3.0.$$

But if John had bet the normal $25 and only two
players called, his estimated investment odds would
have tumbled to—

$$\frac{(\$250)\,(.5)}{\$75}=1.7.$$

Now suppose John had bet $25, someone raised to $50 and everyone else folded. If John had called the raise (which he probably would not have), his estimated investment odds would have fallen to an unfavorable—

$$\frac{(\$222)\,(.4)}{\$100}=0.8.$$

By making the disproportionate $14 bet, John sets up the hand for maximum profits while gaining control of the betting. Moreover, if he checks his bet on the next round, usually one or more players will feel deprived of a full opening-round bet and thus bet aggressively. John can then passively let them do the betting and raising for him. On the other hand, if John bets on the next round, the others players will probably remain defensive and avoid betting or raising.

So with this disproportionate $14 bet, John increases his investment odds and leaves himself in a flexible betting position. By John's checking, his opponents will bet aggressively; by John's betting, his opponents will remain defensive. Thus he can conveniently turn the betting into either an offensive tempo (by checking) or a defensive tempo (by betting) . . . whichever is most advantageous to him.

3. Hypnosis (87)

Because the good player can intensely study and closely scrutinize each poker opponent, he quickly gets to know their minds and psyches. With planned experiments, he can discover hypnotic or subconsciousness responses in many players and then actually hypnotize certain players—particularly the dull, emotional, or mystical players. Typical hypnotic stimuli are—

- staring into the subject's eyes (psychological)

- moving a finger through the pot (visual and motion)

153

- breathing audibly during a tense silence (sound)

- tapping fingers on the table (sound and motion).

While the good player can get certain opponents to bet, call, or fold by hypnosis, he uses this technique cautiously because hypnotizing actions can give away his own hands and intentions.

> After the draw, John Finn takes the final raise for $100. He has Scotty Nichols beat and wants him to call. Scotty groans. Looking at the huge pot, he sees John's finger slowly stirring the pile of money . . . stirring slowly and smoothly. Ten and twenty dollar bills are moving in circles. Scotty's floating brown eyes start rotating with the money. His chubby hand slowly picks up a hundred-dollar bill. He calls the bet.
> Scotty tries to smile as John pulls in the pot. Eventually he may become aware of this hypnotic trick. But then John will simply use another trick. . . . John estimates his earnings per life of hypnotic trick range from several hundred to several thousand dollars. He also estimates that in 1965, hypnotic tricks netted him an extra two thousand dollars.

4. Distractions (88)

The good player can exploit his opponents more easily when they are distracted. A radio or television for sporting events has excellent distraction value. A late newspaper is usually good for several hands of distracted play from opponents checking horse-race results, the stock market, and the news. Pornographic literature offers an absorbing distraction. Good spreads of food and assorted drinks provide steady and effective distractions.

Availability of beer and liquor usually benefits the good player. One drink takes the sharpness off a player's ability to think and concentrate. Even a single beer will reduce the effectiveness of a superior player. This is why the good player never drinks before or during the game. And this is why the good player is glad to see superior-playing opponents take a drink.

Moderate amounts of alcohol have less effect on poor players because their concentrations are already at reduced levels. The poor player must drink enough to become intoxicated before his edge odds are reduced to even lower levels. But the advantages of having intoxicated opponents are sometimes cancelled by disadvantages such as slowing up the game and causing drinking problems that may drive desirable players from the game.

Each week, John Finn is a good fellow and brings beer to the game along with the late evening paper containing the complete stock market closings and horse-race results. Ted and Sid read this paper while playing their hands. Every now and then they lose a pot to John because of this distraction.

These newspapers cost John $5.20 per year, but are worth about a thousand dollars a year in distractions ... a 200:1 return on his investment, or about twenty dollars per newspaper.

By encouraging and creating distractions, John Finn increases everyone's confusion. At the same time, he keeps the actions moving. But in the Monday night game, he discovers, that his opponents will play for significantly higher stakes when using cash rather than faster-moving poker chips. (In most games, the reverse is true, and thus the good player normally prefers using poker chips—see page 114.) ... But to offset the slower-moving cash, John speeds up the game by alternating two decks of cards between each shuffle and deal.

Using an array of distractions, John increases his edge odds by about twenty percent. This means eight-thousand-dollars additional income per year (at his current winning rate). He estimates that while playing their hands, his opponents are distracted 35% of the time. And they are distracted a much higher percentage of the time when not involved in the action. The following table estimates the in-action distractions of each player:

155

	Eating	Gossiping	Daydreaming	Radio, TV, Newspaper	Miscellaneous	Total
			Time Distracted, % (when in action)			
Quintin Merck	2	5	10	5	2	24
Scotty Nichols	10	2	15	2	5	34
Sid Bennett	2	25	5	10	5	47
Ted Fehr	slight	slight	25	15	2	43
John Finn	0	1	slight	slight	2	4

5. Agreements (89)

The good player sometimes makes profitable agreements with other players. Occasionally, he can make an agreement with a loose player whereby each time either one wins a pot he will pay the other, for example, five dollars. Such an agreement will give the good player a guaranteed, side income. Even when the loose player is a big loser, he will usually win more pots than the good player. Many poor players will gladly make such an agreement because they erroneously believe that a winner must win more pots than a loser. Also, most losers desire an association with a winner (the good player); such an association boosts the loser's self-esteem by helping him feel on the same level with the winner. Often a loose player happily maintains such an agreement indefinitely without ever admitting or even realizing that he is providing the good player with a steady, side income.

Compared to John Finn, Sid Bennett plays more than twice as many hands, wins about fifty percent more pots, but loses nearly three times as often. He eagerly accepts John's suggestion to pay each other five dollars every time one of them wins a pot. Two years later, Sid is still pleased with this arrangement as indicated by his comments:

"At least I keep collecting these side bets," he says with a broad smile as John wins a huge pot and gives him five dollars. "Don't understand why you made such a stupid bet."

"Ha!" Quintin Merck snorts. He knows John makes money from that agreement. John knows it too, and his notebook data prove it:

The Sid Bennett Agreement

	#+Weeks, Avg.	#−Weeks, Avg.	Net Income
1964	40, +$30	10, −$10	+1100
1965	40, +$35	8, −$10	+1320

So far, Sid has lost $2,420 on John's stupid bet and is very happy about it . . . sort of an ideal arrangement for John.

157

XVIII
MONEY EXTRACTION (90)

The good poker player is involved in a long-term process of extracting maximum money from the game as well as from each individual player.

1. Winning Too Fast (91)
Money extraction at the maximum rate is not always in the best, long-term financial interest of the good player. Uncontrolled, maximum money extraction can cause the following problems:

—Players who would be long-term sources of important income may quit the game.

—Stakes or rules may be disadvantageously changed.

—Unfavorable attitudes may develop.

—Game may break up.

These problems suggest that the good player can win too fast. To extract maximum money, he often decreases his winning *rate* in order to control the flow of money. In other words, maximum-money extraction may require a slower winning rate.

2. Uncontrolled Money Flow (92)
Over a period of many games, money uncontrolled flows in a pattern similar to that illustrated by the *top* diagram on page 160. As the good player accumulates performance data on each player, these money-movement patterns become increasingly obvious.

Data for uncontrolled money flow are tabulated on page 159. Notice the heavy losses absorbed by poor players A and B compared to players C and D. In this game, the good player E is extracting winnings through a natural, uncontrolled money flow. But poor player A may quit, for example, because continuous losses hurt his pride. And poor player B may insist on

Uncontrolled Money Flow for Ten Games

Dollars Won (+) or Lost (−), $

Player— Rating—	A Poor	B Poor	C Weak	D Sound	E Good	Irregular Players***
12/4/61	+200	−200	+100	+200	−220	−100
12/11	−200	+300	−100	+50	−80	+50
12/18	−100	−200	−150	+50	+440	+50
1/8/62	−150	−400	−200	−250	+860	+100
1/15	−350	Absent	Absent	+200	+260	−100
1/22	−400	−100	+550	0	−100	+50
1/29	Absent	−300	+250	+150	+240	−350
2/5	−200	+100	−250	−150	+680	−200
2/12	+400	+50	−200	+100	+20	−350
2/19	−100	Absent	−100	+100	+520	−400
Totals	−900	−750	−100	+450	+2620	−1350
Average*	−100	−95	−10	+45	+262	−135
Edge Odds, %**	−22	−21	−2	+10	+59	−30

* Averages are calculated by dividing the number of games attended into the net winnings or losses of each player.

** The biggest winner for each of these ten games averages plus $445 per game. Edge odds of the good player, for example, are then calculated as $262/$445 x 100=59%.

*** These are the average winnings or losses for all of the irregular players combined.

159

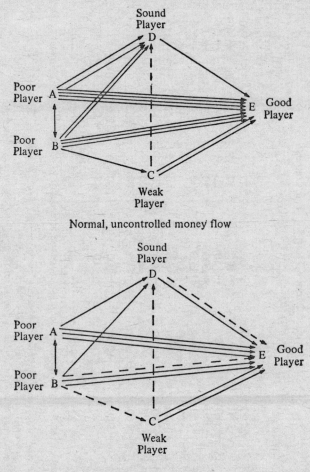

Normal, uncontrolled money flow

Controlled money flow

Broken arrow represents half the money flow of a solid arrow.

160

lower stakes because his sharp losses are causing him acute financial problems. The good player may be risking his future earnings unless he alters the money flow to a controlled pattern similar to that illustrated by the *bottom* diagram on page 160.

The ideal money-flow pattern for the good player occurs when he wins at the maximum rate that each player can tolerate. . . . This usually means winning less from the poorest players and more from the better players.

3. Controlled Money Flow (93)

The good player evaluates the money-extraction patterns on both a short-term and a long-term basis. If a controlled pattern seems desirable, he then determines how the money flow should be altered (extent and direction). In a controlled pattern, he usually extracts money more evenly from his opponents . . . he extracts less from the poorer players and more from the better players. Controlled money flow shifts everyone's performance as shown in the table on page 162.

This controlled pattern costs the good player an average of $22 per game. But if the money flow were not controlled, the continued heavy losses of poor players A and B could have destroyed the game, which would have cost the good player his winnings over these one-hundred sessions. This $22 per session is his insurance premium for keeping the game going at favorable conditions. The good player keeps performance records to determine the cost, value, and effectiveness of his control over the money flow. This control normally costs him 10-15% of his net winnings.

The good player usually takes control of the money flow during the early rounds when his betting influence can be the greatest at the lowest cost. He alters the money-flow patterns by the following methods:

— Helps and favors the poorest players at the expense of the better players whenever practical.

— Drives the poor player out with first-round bets when a better player holds a strong hand. And

Performance Data

(Averages for 100 games—data extrapolated from the 1961-1962 Monday night games)

Player— Rating—	A Poor	B Poor	C Weak	D Sound	E Good	Irregular Players*
Uncontrolled money flow, $/game	−102	− 85	− 22	+ 54	+196	− 41
Controlled money flow, $/game	− 58	− 52	− 35	+ 6	+174	− 35

Average values for the irregular players.

conversely, he uses first-round bets to keep the better players in when a poor player holds a strong hand.

—Avoids, when practical, playing against a poor player after everyone else has folded in order to decrease his advantage over the poor player at a minimum cost. He also tries to make his least favorable plays (e.g., his experimental, image-building, and long-term strategy plays) against the poorest players.

John Finn spends some of his winnings to hold big losers like Sid Bennett and Ted Fehr in the game. The following data from John's records for 1965 indicate that this is a profitable expenditure.

Breakdown of 1965 Poker Income and Insurance Costs

Source of Income	Estimated Net Income, $	Estimated Insurance Costs, $ (calculated losses)
Quintin Merck	2,500	100
Scotty Nichols	5,500	500
Sid Bennett	13,000	2,000
Ted Fehr	9,000	700
Others	12,000	1,200
Total	42,000	4,500

Without paying this insurance, John theoretically could have won $4500 more in 1965. Yet without paying this insurance, the greater psychological and financial pressures on the big losers might have forced them to quit . . . and each big loser is worth much more than this $4500 insurance cost. Also, if several big losers had quit, the poker game could have been destroyed. John, therefore, considers this insurance cost as an important and profitable investment.

How does he spend this $4500? This money buys him the valve that controls the money flow. He watches the losers closely. When they are in psychological or financial trouble and on the verge of quitting, he opens the valve and feeds them morale-boosting money until they are steady again.

Winning players are of little value to John. There is no need to help them or boost their morale; he keeps the valve closed tight on them. He may even spend money to drive them out of the game if they hurt his financial best interests.

John Finn never spends money on any player except to gain eventual profits.

PART FIVE

GAMES

More players and more games mean more income for the good player. He increases his poker activity by—

- finding other games
- organizing games
- expanding current games
- maintaining or reviving games
- starting new games.

Other poker games offer new sources of income. Even if the stakes are not worthwhile, the good player enters new games in order to—

- take control of them and then increase their betting paces and betting stakes to worthwhile levels

- evaluate the losers . . . some may be good candidates for higher-stake games

- make contacts with new players that may lead to still other poker games and other new players.

John Finn first enters the Monday night game on June 6, 1960; the stakes are not worth the effort required to play winning poker. But he takes control of the game, reorganizes it and then steadily increases the pace and stakes. The table on page 84 tabulates his progress during the next five years as his profits in this game climb from $200 in 1960 to $42,000 in 1965.

1. Finding Game (95)

Practically every regular poker game needs, at times, additional players. Likewise, most games need more permanent players. When a "desirable" player spreads word of his poker interest, he usually gets invitations to other games. Most poker players consider a player desirable if he—

- plays a clean game
- arrives on time
- is cooperative and congenial
- acts respectful toward other players

- plays to the end regardless of his winnings or losses

- keeps the game organized.

The good player by design has these "desirable" traits, but considers such traits in his opponents as neither important nor desirable. Since he is interested only in extracting maximum money from the game, desirable opponents are—

- poor players

- steady players

- players with plenty of money

- players that will not harm the game.

Ironically, most players will invite the costly, good poker player to their game in preference to a profitable, poor player.

The players in the Monday night game consider John Finn a desirable player and an asset to the game. They refuse to realize that he is their biggest liability . . . a staggering liability of $42,000 per year. They are glad John is in the game because he is cooperative, congenial, and respectful. He plays a clean game, always arrives on time, and plays until the end. They are grateful that he keeps the game organized. He is a pleasant, soothing, comfortable player. Everyone appreciates him.

John knows this; he works hard to keep his opponents satisfied and happy. His fee for the effort— $42,000 per year.

2. Becoming a Permanent Player (96)

Once in a game, the good player gets a repeat invitation by making the other players feel favorable and obligated toward him. He does this with "thoughtful" but Machiavellian gestures such as—

- lending money at the first opportunity

- offering his own cigars, candy, and gum to the players (even if he does not smoke, eat candy, or chew gum)

- helping to pick up the cards between deals

- sympathizing with losers

- praising winners

- complimenting good plays of his opponents

- helping to clean up after the game

- offering to bring refreshments (especially beer) to the next game.

If the new game is financially worthwhile, the good player plans his behavior to get a permanent invitation by—

- avoiding the image of being a tight or a tough player

- keeping quiet about his activities in other poker games.

The good player generally will not press for maximum edge odds until he becomes a permanent player. Once a permanent player, he concentrates on taking control of the game. He builds the ego of a key player (one with important influence over the game) in order to win his friendship and confidence. With the support of a key player, he is in a strong position to take control of the game.

The first time John Finn plays in the Monday night game, he is a swell fellow—humble, quiet, even timid . . . and very considerate in passing out his cigars and admiring everyone's poker skill. Best of all, he loses money and plays loose. And he never slows down the game or irritates anyone.

A fish, an ideal player, a nice guy . . . so everyone thinks. How about those nutty plays he makes? Raising, then drawing four or five cards. Loosest player I've ever seen. Did you see how he lent Sid fifty dollars? Sid never even asked him for a loan. He even offered to pick up the refreshments for the next game. Sure hope he becomes a regular player. At least he'll come back next week to collect Sid's loan.

Over the next few sessions, John puts zest into the game. He plays wild, exciting poker. Everyone knows he is bound to be a big loser. His popularity grows; his friendships deepen. He establishes his supporters, and no one has an excuse to get rid of him. Soon John becomes a permanent player . . . he then takes control of the game.

Five years later, he has taken $90,000 from the game, but he is just as popular. . . . John Finn never gives anyone a reason to dislike him.

In public games (casino or club poker) or in other one-shot games, especially those with strangers, the good player will press for immediate and maximum advantages over his opponents. Many of his tactics are opposite to those he would use in regular games. . . . His behavior may be almost unbearably tough, un-friendly, and aggressive. He concentrates on extracting money at a maximum rate from the weakest players. He is not concerned about being a nice fellow if his opponents have no future value to him.

3. Quitting Game (97)

The good player quits a game that is not financially worthwhile or that conflicts with a more profitable game. He normally quits under the best possible cir-cumstances and retains good relationships with every-one. Even after quitting, he may occasionally play in this game to renew his contacts and to recruit players for bigger games.

John Finn quits the Thursday night game because it is not profitable enough for him to consume another weekday night on poker. He quits under congenial circumstances and occasionally returns to play and recruit new players for the bigger games. In the past two years, he has recruited four players from this game for the higher-stake Monday and Friday night

169

games. He wins an estimated $10,000 from these four players in 1965.

4. *Breaking up Game* (98)

The good player sometimes breaks up a game to free its players for more profitable games. If he controls the game by keeping it organized, he can destroy this game simply by not organizing it. He can then feed these players to other games.

Besides the Monday night game, John Finn regularly plays in a Friday night game and occasionally in Tuesday and Thursday night games. The low-stake Tuesday game has the least profit potential, but one of its players would be a good addition to the high-stake Monday game. John estimates his entire income from the Tuesday game is less than the money he could win from this one player if he were shifted to the Monday night game. So John breaks up the Tuesday game by focusing his aggression on the two worst players, causing them to suffer consecutive, morale-damaging losses. After three weeks, these two losers quit. The game collapses when John makes no effort to reorganize the players.

By destroying this game, John gains a free night along with a new player for the high-stake, Monday night game. Also, he can now feed the other players from this defunct Tuesday game into the Friday and Thursday games.

XX
ORGANIZATION (99)

The financial potential of a game depends on how well it is organized. The good player organizes a game by—

- scheduling it on a regular basis at a time and place best for maximum attendance
- establishing a firm starting time

- contacting players before each game to get commitments to play.

1. Regular Game (100)

Compared to the occasional game, the regular weekly game is easier to organize because players can plan for it in advance. A regular weekly game also provides more frequent opportunities for money extraction. But most importantly, poker players get more emotionally and financially involved in games that are regular and frequent.

If a game is about to collapse because certain players are losing at rates beyond their financial limits, the good player may temporarily reduce the betting pace or stakes. Or occasionally, he may temporarily reschedule the game on a less-frequent, bi-weekly or monthly basis instead of reducing the betting pace or the stakes.

In keeping the Monday night game going on a weekly basis, John Finn increases the stakes until some players are losing at rates beyond their financial limits; he then lowers the stakes. He may raise and lower the stakes several times before permanently establishing them at a higher level.

In going to higher stakes, the losing tolerances of players increase as they adjust and get accustomed to their greater losses. When John lowers the stakes, the big losers are usually the first to insist on returning to higher stakes.

Sometimes John stabilizes a shaky game by bringing in new players. These new players not only contribute to his income, but they help hold the game at higher stakes. By controlling the betting pace and stakes and by adding new players, John has kept the highly profitable Monday game going on a regular weekly basis for the past six years.

2. Starting Time (101)

An indefinite starting time can eventually destroy a game. If players must wait for others to arrive before starting the game, then these early-arriving players may come later the next week to avoid waiting . . .

thus causing progressively later starting times and a subsequent loss of disgruntled players. The following methods encourage players to arrive on time:

—Make a firm starting time clear to all players.

—Emphasize the reason and importance of being on time.

—Admonish late-arriving players.

—Establish fines or penalties for late arrivals.

—Fill the game early so late-arriving players will not get a seat.

The Monday night game is supposed to start at eight o'clock. As more and more players arrive late, the game starts later and later. Eventually players start arriving at ten and eleven o'clock. Attendance begins to drop, so John Finn takes action. He suggests a five-dollar fine for anyone arriving after the game starts. The players, disgusted with the late starting times, all agree.

The following week, six players arrive by eight o'clock and the game starts at eight-fifteen . . . the earliest start in months. At nine o'clock, Quintin Merck wanders in.

"Get it up!" Sid roars.

"Uh, what ya mean?" Quintin grumbles as he seats himself at the table.

"You're late," Sid says grinning. "Five-buck fine, buddy."

"Ah, don't give me that kid stuff. Deal the cards," Quintin says. He then puffs hard on his cigarette.

Sid deals Quintin out.

"Hey!" Quintin slaps his hand on the table. "What about my hand?"

"You ain't playing till you pay your fine," Sid says. The other players nod in agreement.

"We play for thousands of dollars and you boy scouts hound me for five bucks," Quintin growls while throwing a five-dollar bill at Sid.

The following week, all the players are at Scotty's house by eight o'clock. Since the fine was put into effect, the game never starts later than eight-fifteen.

It's amazing, John thinks to himself. They'll casually lose thousands through lack of effort, but they'll make a big effort to avoid a five-dollar fine.

3. Quitting Time (102)

As a game continues through the night and into the morning, most players tire and their abilities to concentrate on poker decrease. This increases the good player's edge odds. He, therefore, encourages an indefinite or late quitting time. But if players start avoiding the game because the late hours are interfering with their jobs or harming their health, the good player may enforce an early quitting time (at least temporarily) to keep the losers playing and to preserve the game. He will also quit early in lower-stake games that are not worth staying up all night for. The good player often breaks up a game when he leaves in order to keep the poorer players from losing their money to the better players after he is gone. He breaks up the game so he can win this money for himself in future games.

Making players quit early is easier when the last round is played at higher stakes. Higher stakes not only benefit the good player, but serve as a psychological climax to the game. If the good player wants to enforce an agreed-upon quitting time, he plans the final round so the last deal ends with him. He then gathers the cards after he deals the last hand, cashes in his chips, and leaves before anyone can start a new deal.

But the need for a definite or an early quitting time decreases if any player, winner or loser, feels free to leave whenever he wishes. Furthermore, the game becomes more relaxed under these conditions and more profitable for the good player.

John Finn plays all night on Mondays because the additional profits he garners after midnight are worth his time. In 1965, he plays about four-hundred hours of Monday night poker and wins $42,000. Of this amount, $23,000 is won after midnight at the rate of $115 per hour, while $19,000 is made before midnight at the rate of $95 per hour. The following data show another important reason why John plays all night in this high-stake game.

Estimated Edge Odds, %

	PM 8:00–12:00	AM 12:00–4:00	Change
John Finn	+56	+62	+ 6
Quintin Merck	+15	+ 5	−10
Scotty Nichols	− 2	− 8	− 6
Sid Bennett	−24	−16	+ 8
Ted Fehr	−24	−18	+ 6
Others	−27	−31	− 4

These data show that John's edge odds increase by 6% after midnight. Also, the losing rates of poorer players (Sid and Ted) decrease at the expense of better players (Quintin and Scotty); this advantageous shift in money flow is accomplished without costing John money. In other words, John controls the money flow at lower costs during the late hours.

In determining the value of playing all night, John considers the effects on his job, health, and personal life. He evaluates each game, and then enforces an earlier quitting time in games of lesser value.

The data on page 175 indicate that personal considerations outweigh the additional $28,000 that John could have earned by playing as late and as often in the lower-stake games as he does in the high-stake, **Monday night game.**

Game	Quitting Time	1965 Income (# games)	Estimated Income for 50 Games Played until 4:00 AM
Monday	None (4–5 AM)	$42,000 (50)	$42,000 (d=0)
Tuesday and Thursday	12:30 AM	$ 2,500 (17)	$17,600 (d=$15,100)
Friday	1:00 AM	$ 9,500 (48)	$22,400 (d=$12,900)
Totals		$54,000	$82,000 (d=$28,000)

d = The difference between columns 3 and 4.

4. Contacting Players (103)

A list of players and a telephone are two important tools for organizing a game. The good player usually asks other players to help him organize the game. (Eager players and recent winners will normally help.) To conceal his anxiousness for losers to play, the good player asks other players to call the big losers. If negative feelings develop about his organizing efforts, he simply stops telephoning anyone for a few games. His "strike" quickly makes the other players appreciate and support his organizing efforts.

The best time for telephoning players is late in the afternoon before the game. This is early enough so everyone can plan for the game and late enough so those available will seldom have a subsequent excuse for not playing. The good player then knows who his opponents will be for that evening.

Mimeographed or offset forms (as shown on page 177), which list the players' names and telephone numbers along with a column for their responses, are convenient. By filling out these forms and periodically reviewing them, the good player obtains valuable information about the—

- health of the game

- attendance patterns

- character of his opponents and their motives for playing

- losers with declining attendance records who may need special treatment to bring them back as regular players

- ways to keep the game organized and players interested.

DATE _____

Player	Phone # (*)	Called by (Time)	Response	Comments
MONDAY GAME				
Quintin	LM 8-7295 (O)			
Merck	LM 4-1467 (H)			
Scotty	YO 6-3460 (O)			
Nichols	TF 7-0446 (H)			
Sid	YO 4-8391 (O)			
Bennett	KI 8-7382 (H)			
Ted	EV 9-5267 (O)			
Fehr	732-8793 (H)			

177

Charlie		
Holland	YO 4-9006	(O)
	KI 8-3388	(H)
Aaron	YO 4-1147	(O)
Smith	732-5493	(H)
Others		
Mike	?	
Bell		

* *(O)=office phone, (H)=home phone*

MONDAY GAME

Player	Phone # (*)		Called by (Time)	Response	Comments
Quintin Merck	LM 8-7295 (O) LM 4-1467 (H)		John (3:30)	Yes	Quintin will call Sid and Charlie.
Scotty Nichols	YO 6-3460 (O) TF 7-0446 (H)		John (3:40)	Yes	Seems shaky and upset, but eager to play. Must be a personal problem.
Sid Bennett	YO 4-8391 (O) KI 8-7382 (H)		Quintin (5:30) (6:30)	– Yes	Check—not contacted. Check—OK
Ted Fehr	EV 9-5267 (O) 732-8793 (H)		John (3:45) (5:30) (7:00)	– – Yes	Not contacted. Must be at the races. Not contacted. OK, 30 minute discussion about the game, finances and credit. Sounds like he's in bad shape.

179

Charlie Holland	YO 4-9006 (O) KI 8-3388 (H)	Quintin (5:30)	No	Stunned and disgusted by heavy loss last week . . . probably will play next week.
Aaron Smith	YO 4-1147 (O) 732-5493 (H)	John (3:35)	Yes	Check—OK, excited about winning last week.
Others Mike Bell	?	Scotty (5:40)	Yes	Check—OK, concerned about recent losses.

* (O) = office phone, (H) = home phone

In some games, players do not expect telephone calls. The game is played on a regular basis, and everyone just shows up. While such a game is convenient, the good player generally prefers to organize each game because his telephone calls provide opportunities to—

- get or provide "confidential" information

- increase his control over the game

- propagandize players and talk to them about their problems

- obtain definite commitments, which make the game less vulnerable to collapse from a lack of players.

John Finn telephones the players each Monday afternoon and fills out the mimeographed form as shown on page 179.

5. A Place to Play (104)

A game kept in one location makes the game easier to organize, which generally benefits the good player. Usually, at least one player is willing to establish the game at his house permanently. The good player seldom plays in his own house in order to avoid the impression that it is "his game." If necessary, a player is induced to keep the game permanently at his house by, for example, cutting the pot for weekly cleaning expenses. . . . A game played at one location offers the following advantages:

—Game is more stable.

—Burden of locating suitable places to play is eliminated.

—Players not contacted always know where the game is.

Still a game played at different locations each week offers advantages such as—

- closer control over who is invited (e.g., Undesirable players, such as other good players, cannot drop in and play if they do not know where the game is located.)

- more flexibility because the game can easily be changed to locations offering the greatest advantage

- decreased possibility of a robbery (particularly in a high-stake game).

Every Monday night the game is played at Scotty Nichols' house. This stable and dependable location helps John keep the game organized. When Scotty leaves town on a vacation for six weeks, the game shifts to Sid Bennett's house where the danger for any high-stake game is revealed . . . the danger of an armed robbery:

Sid loves to brag about the game to everyone. Now that the game is at his house, he makes his wife watch him play. Then after the third week at Sid's house and to the shocked disapproval of the players, Sid invites his street-paving crew to watch the action. When the players arrive, they find the poker table ringed with a gallery of seats occupied by a dozen beer-drinking laborers wearing bib overalls. The tar-covered men laugh and joke while waiting for the show to begin.

John frowns as he notices the spectators' eyes bulge when the big money comes on the table; the laborers are fascinated by the game. Two of the men remain until the game ends at four in the morning.

"You playing here next Monday?" one of them asks.

"Yeah," Sid chuckles, "Same time, same place . . . you can count on that." Now John frowns even more. And after the game, the players severely criticize Sid for bringing the spectators.

The following week there are no spectators. But at three in the morning, Sid's kitchen door opens. A man in a nylon stocking stretched over his head rushes to the game room. He pulls a revolver from a shopping bag and aims the gun at the players.

"Stand up and empty your pockets," he orders. Obedience is swift and silent. The thief walks around the table, grabs the cash in front of each player, drops the money into his shopping bag, and leaves without a word. John steps to the window and sees two men drive away in a pickup truck.

"I'll call the police," Sid says lifting the telephone.

"No," Quintin Merck replies waving his hand. "That'd get us involved. We'd all get bad publicity."

"Yeah, it'd be in all the papers," Sid says while hanging up. "Think that guy is someone from my paving crew." . . . The players discuss the holdup for an hour and estimate that four-thousand dollars in cash was stolen. They all agree that the big money in their game is a strong incentive for a robbery. A lot of cash can be stolen at low risk, certainly at less risk than a bank holdup. The players make future security plans that include locked doors, well-covered windows, prohibiting spectators, and not discussing the game with non-players.

They decide to keep playing each week at Sid's house until Scotty Nichols returns from vacation. While John realizes the hazard of a robbery is greater when the game is played regularly at the same house, he figures the advantages of a stable game location outweigh the probability of another robbery.

XXI
EXPANSION (105)

The good player gains the following advantages by filling a poker game to capacity:

—The game becomes more stable.

—More sources of income (players) become available.

—Choices for selecting profitable opponents (losers) increase.

—Losses are spread more evenly among losers.

—Confusion increases.

—Greater control over the game is possible.

—Betting pace and stakes are easier to increase.

—If tight play offers better edge odds, any such tight play is less obvious and less resented in a full game.

A poker game is expanded by adding new players and by improving the attendance of current players.

1. New Players (106)

The good player mentions poker to all potential losers. He gauges his comments to bring out their poker interests. The more he mentions poker, the more potential players are revealed. He hunts for losers, and evaluates all potential players with respect to the maximum income that could be extracted from them.

> John Finn tries to fill the Monday night game with at least eight players. He has a nucleus of five players (Sid, Ted, Scotty, Quintin, and himself) who have played regularly over the years. Two or three other players regularly circulate in and out of the game; they usually survive three to twelve months, sometimes longer. Then eight or nine different men play sporadically or when coaxed. These irregular players provide important income and are valuable for filling out and stabilizing the game.
>
> About half of the new players are introduced to the Monday game by John. His major source of new players is other, lower-stake poker games. Mentioning poker to social and business contacts generates a few players, especially for the smaller games. Some of these players later graduate to the big game.

a. Keeping players (107)

If a new player is a financial asset, the good player keeps him in the game by—

- being friendly and helpful to him (especially if the new player is timid or nervous)

- making him feel that the game is relaxed and enjoyable

- countering remarks and actions by other players that may upset him (Probably more players quit poker because of hurt feelings than because of hurt finances.)

- avoiding overpowering or scaring him

- not taking full advantage of his weaknesses

- making him feel that he is a welcome member of the group

- favoring him whenever possible

- flattering him when he wins and offering him sympathy when he loses

- giving him encouragement and advice about the game.

John Finn brings a new player, Aaron Smith, to the big Monday night game. Although Aaron plays in the lower-stake Friday night game, he is timid and nervous. Knowing that Aaron will lose many thousands of dollars if he becomes a permanent player, John sits next to him and helps him whenever possible. He protects Aaron from upsetting losses that could scare him out of the game. He shields him from derogatory remarks that could insult him out of the game. John knows that Aaron will absorb large losses and take insults gracefully once he gets accustomed to the game and its players.

Whenever John folds, he studies Aaron's hand and gives him sound advice; he helps him to a winning night. Aaron is excited . . . his confidence increases and his fear decreases. Whenever Sid throws an insulting remark at Aaron, John counters with an ego-boosting comment. By his third game, Aaron Smith is hooked; he loves the Monday night game and its players. At this point, John withdraws his help and Aaron is on his own.

When Aaron Smith (or any big loser) gets discouraged and contemplates quitting, John Finn extends his protection to hold the loser in the game through his crisis.

b. Rejecting players (108)

If a new player is a financial liability, the good player gets him out of the game. The simplest way to eliminate an undesirable player is not to invite him to the next game. If this is not possible, the good player forces him out by—

- encouraging and instigating unpleasant and unfriendly incidents toward him

- insulting him and hurting his feelings

- refusing him credit

- telling him not to play again.

Scotty Nichols brings a new player, Boris Klien, to the Monday night game. John Finn quickly realizes that Boris is a winning player who will take money out of the game. This will increase the financial strain on the losers, which would force John to reduce his winnings in order to keep these losers in the game. Boris is a financial liability and, therefore, is an undesirable player. John wants him out of the game, quickly and permanently.

"Highball draw with a twist," Quintin Merck announces. John notices how Boris carefully watches the deck for flashed cards during the deal.

John checks. Boris opens for $5.

"Five bucks? . . . we ain't playing penny-ante," Sid says while raising to $30. "You've gotta bet something in this game."

"I'll just call; now you can reraise to fifty," Quintin adds as he winks at Boris.

"I'll raise . . . fifty-five dollars," Boris responds in a clipped voice.

"Hey, he knows what he's doing," Sid whispers. "He sandbagged us."

On the draw, Boris raps his knuckles on the table. "Pat!" he says sharply and then bets $50. Sid folds and Quintin calls.

On the twist, Quintin draws one card. Boris again plays pat and then holds a fifty-dollar bill over the pot.

"Put your money in if you're betting," John Finn snaps and then turns to Quintin and continues, "That's an old bluff trick . . ."

Boris scowls at John.

"Forget it," Quintin says, folding his hand without realizing what John is telling him. "I just had two little pair."

Boris grabs the pot and shouts, "Looky here!" He then spreads his cards faceup across the table to reveal a worthless hand.

"He's got nothing!" Ted Fehr rasps. "He pulls a pat bluff on his first hand and wins a three-hundred-dollar pot!"

"Wise guy," Quintin grunts as his blinking green eyes gaze at Boris' worthless cards. . . . The other players sit in frowning silence.

Over the next hour, Boris Klien plays very tight. He avoids all action until a lowball hand with John Finn. The pot is large; and after the last bet, only Boris and John remain. Boris turns his cards faceup and declares his hand. John says nothing, so Boris starts pulling in the pot.

"Get your hands off my money," John snarls.

"Uh? What do ya mean?" Boris asks. "I won, didn't I?"

"Can't you read?" John says while turning his winning hand faceup on the table. He then snatches the pot from under Boris' stiffened fingers.

"Why didn't you declare your hand?" Boris complains.

"Why don't you look at my cards?" John growls out of the twisted corner of his mouth. "This is a poker game buddy boy. Cards speak for themselves, remember?"

"Wish I hadn't come to this game," Boris mumbles to Scotty Nichols. "I'm not only losing, but I'm getting a bad time."

"Wish I hadn't come myself," Scotty whines. "Lost all the money I won last week."

"Yeah, but I . . ."

"Listen," John says shaking his finger close to Boris' face, "No one made you play. If you don't like our game . . . get out!"

Three hours later Boris Klien is winning over four-hundred dollars.

"He's taking all our money," Sid Bennett remarks.

"I started out losing four hundred," Boris says trying not to smile. "I'm still stuck a hundred."

"Liar!" John snaps. "You're up four-hundred bucks. . . . Scotty, where'd you dig up this clod?"

"At this point, I don't know or care," Scotty mutters. "I'm losing plenty, and Boris won most of it."

"This is my last round," Boris says. "I've . . ."

"The bore is even a hit-and-run artist!" John cries while slapping his hand on the table. "Plan on this being your last round . . . permanently."

Boris frowns. Then looking at his pile of money, his frown disappears.

"Seven-card stud, high-low with qualifiers and one twist," John announces as he deals. "Trips-eight*," he adds in a whispering voice.

After the sixth card, John raises on his low hand and drives out the other low hands. By the last card, only Boris remains; he calls John's final $30 bet. . . . John wins low.

"Don't know why you were wasting our time by betting," Boris says, showing his two pair. "We just split the pot. Obviously you're low and I'm high."

"Look at that hand!" John hoots as he points to Boris' cards. "The sucker calls all my big bets and doesn't even qualify for high. I get the whole pot!"

"What do ya mean I don't qualify?" Boris sputters. "I got two pair."

"Three of a kind qualifies for high, you creep," John says as he shoves Boris' cards into the deck.

"Trips for qualifiers!" Boris shouts. "They've been two pair all night."

"I announced trips-eight," John says with a laugh. "You'd better clean your ears, clod."

---

* *Trips-eight means that three of a kind are needed to qualify for high, and an eight low is needed to qualify for low.*

"I heard him announce it," Ted Fehr mutters weakly.

"Yeah? . . . Well, then it'd be impossible for me to call," Boris says reaching for the pot. "I'm taking back my last bet."

"It stays in the pot," John growls slapping his hand over the money. "When you make a stupid play, buster, you pay for it."

"I've had enough," Boris says while getting up to leave.

"You're winning," Scotty whines. "Sit down and play awhile."

"Let the rock go. We'll play longer without him bothering us," John says. Then turning to Boris, he makes a sharp hitchhiking motion toward the door. "So long, sucker, hope we never see you again."

"I won't be back," Boris huffs.

"Good!" John yells. Boris grabs his coat and leaves, slamming the front door.

"He'll never come back," Scotty Nichols says while scratching his head. "Why so rough on him? He's an honest player."

"He's a milker," John explains gently. "He hangs back and waits for a big hand to kill you with. Look how he hurt you tonight. . . . Why should a stranger come to our game and leech money from the regular players? Not only that, he cries when he wins, tries to take back bets, lies about his winnings, and leaves early when he's ahead."

"Don't understand it," Scotty says. "Seemed like a nice guy outside of the game. Maybe we should give him another chance."

"Don't ask him back," John replies. "He'd ruin our game."

"You're probably right," Scotty says nodding his head. "I'll tell him to stay away."

"Besides, he's a good player," Sid Bennett adds. "We need more fish with lots of money."

"More players like Sid," Quintin titters as his leathery face breaks into a smile.

c. Women players (109)

Since ability, competence, and character are human or neuter traits rather than sexual traits, women players can function identically to men players . . . a woman can be as good a poker player as a man. Still, the good female player will probably encounter more difficulty in controlling men players and in getting invitations to high-stake poker games.

The good poker player considers opponents only from a financial viewpoint. If a woman player is an overall financial asset, she is a welcome player. A woman player can cause men to be less objective, thereby increasing the good player's edge odds. But, on the other hand, control over men players and attempts to increase the betting stakes can be more difficult when a woman is present.* For this reason, the good player usually keeps women out of the game.

As the game starts, Scotty informs the players that Sid is bringing his wife, Stephanie Bennett, to play poker. All object to having a woman, particularly the wife of a player, in the game. Quintin even threatens to quit if she plays.

"I don't want her playing either," John says. "But she's already expecting to play. . . . Let her play tonight; we'll keep her from playing again."

. . . Just as the players finish their first hand, Sid and Stephanie arrive. She is wearing a tight dress with a hemline well above the knees. All the players stand up to greet her.

"Just treat me like one of the boys," says the woman while touching her hair that sweeps up in a French twist with curls on top; she sits down and crosses her long, curving legs.

"Impossible," Quintin rasps. His nose sniffs the air.

The game becomes erratic; eyes keep focusing on the woman. When Stephanie is in a hand, the betting becomes subdued; the players are reluctant to bet into her. When she is not in a hand, the betting and raising become heavier than usual as the men show off in front of the perfumed woman. John Finn takes full advantage of their distorted betting to increase his edge odds.

* *Women players often bring out and amplify the dominant characteristics in men players, making them more difficult to manipulate and control.*

After two hours of playing, Stephanie is winning about fifty dollars and her husband, Sid, is losing three-hundred dollars. Some players begin to fidget and grumble under the strain of her presence. John gets involved with Stephanie in a game of five-card stud with two twists. On the third up card, she has a pair of aces showing and bets $15. Sid raises to $30 with his pair of kings showing; Stephanie raises back. Quintin folds while mumbling that Sid is raising to build the pot for his wife.

"Aye," Sid snorts, "Greed is a many-splendored thing." . . . Abruptly John raises to $60. Sid emits a gagging cough.

After the next card, John has a king, queen, jack and the ten of diamonds showing—a four card straight flush. On the twist, Stephanie pairs her fives to give her two pair showing—aces and fives. . . . John stays pat.

"Pat!" Sid exclaims. "He's got to have the flush or straight."

John bets $25, and Sid folds. Stephanie calls and then twists her hole card. John plays pat again and bets $30. . . . Sid advises his wife to drop.

"He might be bluffing," she says while starting to call.

"Naw!" Sid shouts. "Not after staying pat with all that betting and raising."

"I can't take your money," John says, waving his hand. "I've got the diamond flush."

"Thanks for saving me money," Stephanie replies as she throws away her cards.

John Finn peeks at his hole card—the jack of clubs. He then quickly mixes his worthless cards into the deck. Handing Stephanie twenty-five dollars, he says, "Here's your last bet. Guess I'm not a good gambler. Can't take money from a woman. So I'll quit while you're playing."

"Oh, no," Stephanie says handing the money back and standing up. "I lost it fairly. And you already lost money by not letting me call that last bet. . . . You keep on playing. I'm tired and going home now. . . . I've had my fling at poker."

191

Sid Bennett drives his wife home and then hurries back to the game.

"Stephanie should play instead of you," Quintin says when Sid returns. "She'd win if you'd . . ."

"That lovely woman doesn't belong in this tough game," John interrupts. "Don't let her play again."

"You're right," Sid sighs as he counts his money. "I'll never let her play again."

2. Improving Attendance (110)

Players are attracted to a full game. In fact, they become eager to play in games that are completely filled. So an effective way to expand a game is to fill it. For example, if eight players are the maximum for a game, the good player makes sufficient telephone calls to invite nine or ten players . . . or more. When the game is so crowded that some players cannot be seated, an interesting phenomenon occurs . . . irregular players become regular players, and the scheduled starting time becomes rigidly adhered to. Good attendance is also encouraged by keeping the game well organized and by maintaining the proper atmosphere. Excess attendance means excess players who can be shifted to other games.

John tries to keep the Monday night game filled. The full game helps draw the big losers back each week. The crowded table and fast action excite the players, especially poor players like Sid and Ted who feel they are missing something if left out of the action.

A packed game increases John's flexibility. With excess players, he can increase the stakes and pace more quickly since the loss of one or two players would not seriously hurt the game. Excess players also lessen the need for him to reduce his earnings to keep losers from quitting.

XXII
MAINTENANCE (111)

Maintenance of a poker game determines its health. The good player keeps losers in the game by protecting them, helping them, lifting their morale, and by making the game attractive.

1. Making Game Attractive (112)

A player often tolerates heavy financial losses if he enjoys the game. Also, an attractive game will draw new players. . . . The good player makes the game more attractive by—

- encouraging a carefree and relaxed atmosphere
- keeping players out of serious arguments or feuds
- preventing or ameliorating complaints about the game
- selecting the more pleasant and weaker players for the game, especially when available players are abundant
- keeping the game well organized
- keeping the action exciting
- providing good refreshments and new cards.

John Finn makes certain that at least a dozen new decks of cards are available for every Monday night game. Although the pots are cut to pay for these cards, the players appreciate this luxury. Losers like Sid feel important when they can call for a new deck of cards at their whim. . . . This makes them feel like big gamblers in a big game. And big gamblers in a big game bet more money.

Other small deeds by John also help make this high-stake game relaxed and carefree. For example, he spends six dollars and buys a dozen green plastic eye-shades. At three in the morning as most players are glumly reflecting their losses, John pulls the eyeshades from a brown bag and hands one to each player. Everyone appreciates this sudden, thoughtful gift. When Scotty suggests they cut the pot for the eyeshades, John refuses with a shaking head and a waving hand. All players smile as they don their green shades and laughingly make remarks about gambling at Vegas and on Mississippi river boats. John Finn smiles too.

2. Helping Losers (113)

Poor players are valuable assets to the good player. He keeps them in the game by shielding them from—

- personal comments that could hurt their feelings

- arguments

- unpleasant players

- personal problems of other players

- bad credit.

Poor players and big losers are usually grateful for the good player's "protection." They avoid identifying that he is the one who sets them up for their heavy losses. Still, if big losers never win, they will lose interest and may quit the game long before they are broke. So occasionally, the good player helps them to a winning night. He helps poor players (relative to better players) by—

- increasing the ante

- increasing the betting pace for early bets

- decreasing the betting pace for late bets

- interpreting the rules to favor the poorest players

- assisting the poorest players whenever possible.

But the good player helps others only to the extent that he can profit himself.

Big losers like Ted Fehr think that John is helping them when indeed he is bankrupting them. Consider the following incident with Ted Fehr.

Ted is losing over a thousand dollars. It is four in the morning; Quintin and Sid get up to leave.

"Hey! Play a little longer," Ted says in a shaky voice. "Don't quit now. I'm stuck a fortune. . . . I never quit when you're hooked."

"You never quit, 'cause you never win," Sid laughs.

"I'm going," Quintin grumbles. "You can win it back next week."

Ted turns his sweaty face toward John and rasps, "We can't quit now."

"Look," John says raising his hand, "Ted is way down. Give him a chance for a comeback. Everyone play another hour at double stakes. We'll all quit at five o'clock sharp."

"Yeah," Ted says now smiling. "Everyone play another hour at double stakes."

Quintin Merck objects to the higher stakes. Sid, who is winning nearly a thousand dollars, objects to playing another hour. But they both sit down to resume playing.

"Thanks," Ted says leaning over and patting John on the shoulder. "You're the one guy who always gives losers a break."

At five o'clock the game ends. In that extra hour, Ted loses another eight-hundred dollars . . . he is pale and staggers around the room with unfocused eyes. In that extra hour, John wins another thousand dollars . . . he leaves quietly.

After a few days, Ted forgets his losses; but he always remembers the favors his friend John does for him . . . such as keeping the game going when he is losing.

3. Raising the Morale of Losers (114)

The good player raises the morale of losers whenever possible. Sympathy and understanding properly offered can keep losers in the game indefinitely . . . or until they are bankrupt. Yet, after suffering sharp losses, some players develop attitudes that could decrease the good player's profits . . . attitudes such as those demanding a slower betting pace or lower stakes. A good player can often change these attitudes by talking to the losers in private about their troubles . . . private "little talks" usually have comforting and therapeutic effects on big losers.

New player, Mike Bell, is a valuable financial asset to John Finn. After losing several weeks in a row, Mike becomes discouraged. Fearful that he may quit, John moves to boost his morale. By leading him into several winning pots, he carries Mike to a winning night. Then with the following dialog, he further boosts Mike's morale:

"The way you're winning, you'll break the game," John says. "How much you ahead?"

"A few big bills," Mike says as he splits a high-low pot with Quintin. Suddenly he looks up at John and grins while adding, "I've been lucky."

"Lucky? The way you caught that full house—I call that skill," John remarks while adjusting his voice to a deeper tone. "Why'd you throw your ace and keep the ten kicker?"

"The other three players drew one and two cards," Mike replies in a gloating tone. "They probably were going for low hands . . . so they'd be holding aces rather than tens. My chances were best for drawing another ten." Mike Bell then glances around. Bored expressions cover all faces except John's; he listens with an opened mouth while slowly nodding his head up and down. Mike leans toward him and says in a low voice, "I drew the ten to catch the full house, didn't I?"

"Right," John replies. "Pretty smart thinking."

"Ban Mike from the game!" Sid cries. "Smart thinking is illegal in this game . . . gives wise guys too much advantage over us blokes."

"Don't listen to him," John says as he puts his hand on Mike's shoulder. "We respect a man that plays good poker."

"Look who's talking about good poker!" Sid cries again. "You win lowball games with full houses. You hear about that one, Mike?"

"Sure did. Scotty told me all about it," Mike answers. He then shakes his finger at John. "Don't ever pull that on me. I'd call you out of my grave."

"At least John plays more than two hands a night," Sid says. "If we all played tight like Quintin, the game would fold from boredom."

Mike Bell counts his winnings, smiles, and then says to John, "Guess I'll be playing permanently in this game."

4. Off-Days (115)

When a good player has an off-day or is not feeling well, he may skip the game to avoid a breakdown in his concentration or discipline. Or he may play on an off-day (knowing he may not be playing at his best) in order to—

- alter the consistency of his play

- make money with decreased but still favorable edge odds

- maintain the continuity of the game (Even when he misses a game, he helps organize it whenever possible.).

John Finn seldom misses the Monday night game. Even when feeling below par, he still makes an effort to play. Consider the following Monday night game:

"Where's John?" Mike Bell asks.

"Recovering from the flu," Scotty replies.

"But he called me this afternoon about playing," Mike says with a wrinkling forehead.

"He'll organize the game even if he's sick."

"Mighty thoughtful guy."

"He's also mighty thoughtful about taking all your money," Quintin grumbles. "He's won a fortune in this game."

"Still he takes your money pleasantly . . . hardly mind losing to him," Mike says. "He's always fair."

197

"But he's tough on anyone who's wrong," Sid adds. "Remember how he tore apart Boris Klien?"

. . . About midnight, John walks in and says with a weak smile, "I'm never too sick for a poker game."

"Good!" Sid cheers. "We need your money."

"I took a nap after dinner," John replies as he sits next to Sid. "Woke up about eleven feeling pretty good. I'm ready for action."

After two hours, John Finn is losing over six hundred dollars.

"You're playing a lousy game," Sid remarks. "You're losing almost as much as me."

"When my luck turns bad, I lose big," John says while forcing a sigh. "Losing over a thousand. . . . I'm going for the all-time record loss."

"Great act," Quintin Merck mumbles, "Great act."

5. Leaving Game Early (116)

When a good player must leave early and wants the game to continue, he minimizes any disturbance and resentment over his leaving by—

- announcing before the game starts that he must leave early

- announcing his last round before going, then quietly leaving without breaking up the game.

The Monday night game usually breaks up about four or five in the morning. Occasionally it continues into the next day. John Finn seldom leaves before the end. . . . The longest Monday night game on record is twenty-seven hours (from eight-thirty Monday night until eleven-thirty Tuesday night). This is how John leaves after twenty-two hours:

At seven in the morning, Scotty's wife chases the players from the house. Heavy loser Ted Fehr is playing with money from the second mortgage on his restaurant. He has a thousand dollars left and begs everyone to continue playing at his place. The five players eat breakfast at a diner and then go to Ted's barren apartment.

Ted continues to lose . . . slowly at first, then at

an increasing rate. By eleven in the morning, most of his cash is gone. He plays carelessly and is involved in nearly every hand. He no longer seems to care . . . he even smiles when he loses a pot.

John Finn is a big winner, but avoids getting in hands with Ted. Yet, Sid and Scotty continue to beat Ted and win most of his money. By now, all of Ted's cash is gone; he asks John for a loan.

"They've won all your money," John says nodding toward Sid and Scotty. "They'll lend it back."

By two in the afternoon, Ted's bloodshot eyes gaze into space . . . he has lost all his cash and has borrowed over two-thousand dollars. Now Sid and Scotty are running out of cash, even though they are winning.

"We broke the record—over twenty hours of poker," John announces. "You guys keep playing, I'm leaving at six."

After another round and in the middle of a big hand, John Finn silently leaves. He has most of the cash in the game and escapes without lending money to Ted.

. . . At six-thirty, Ted asks for another loan. Sid and Scotty are out of money. The only person with cash is Quintin, and he refuses to lend Ted any money. Then with trembling fingers, Ted writes another check. When Quintin refuses to cash it, the freckle-faced man sits in a stupor and stares blankly at him with his mouth open. After a moment of eerie silence, Quintin stands up and says, "I'm going home." After another moment of silence, Sid and Scotty stand up to leave.

"No, you can't leave!" Ted suddenly screams rising from his chair; the players start rushing toward the door. "You took all my money! Please don't quit! I'm due for a comeback! I gotta win my mortgage money back! . . . I gotta!" Ted sinks back into his chair with his arms falling to his side as everyone runs out the door. Continuing down the hallway, the players hear him calling out, "Please, give me a break . . . give me a break like John always does . . . like my friend John!"

. . . No one ever saw Ted Fehr again.

XXIII
MAJOR-LEAGUE AND
MINOR-LEAGUE GAMES (117)

For continuous and expanding income, the good player organizes several regular games at different stakes. He runs these games as major-league and minor-league games with a sort of baseball farm-system relationship among them.

1. Major League (118)

A major-league game is the highest-stake game; it is the most valuable game to the good player. He tries to structure this game with players having the most money to lose, compulsive gamblers, and players "trying their luck" in the big game. In this game, the good player continually pushes the pace and stakes to the maximum. The size and health of the big game depend on the availability of poor players and their financial resources. . . . The minor-league or smaller-stake games are a major source of poor players for major-league games.

2. Minor League (119)

The good player can garner worthwhile income from lower-stake games. But more importantly, he uses the lower-stake or minor-league game as—

- a pool for selecting new players for higher-stake games

- a place to break in new players (Many players who never intended to play in higher-stake games will gradually accept higher-stake games after becoming accustomed to or bored with lower-stake games.)

- a proving ground to test and develop new plays, concepts, and modifications before deploying them in higher-stake games

200

- a game where poor players who will never play in the higher-stake games can conveniently lose their money to the good player

- a resting place for players dropping out of higher-stake games (Lower-stake games provide a place to hold valuable losers who are driven out of the big game. Without a lower-stake game to fall back on, these losers might quit poker altogether and never return. But with a lower-stake game, they can continue to play poker. In time, they usually recover their confidence, nerve, or finances and return to the big game.).

When playing in several different games, the good player must carefully plan his schedule in order to budget and invest his limited time into the most profitable poker *and* nonpoker situations.

3. Farm System (120)

The good player controls both the major-league and minor-league games. He directs advantageous transitions of players from one game to another. This system allows him to make the best use of his resources (poker players). He promotes players to higher-stake games when they appear ready to move up. Conditions that indicate when a player is ready for higher-stake games are—

- an increase in his financial resources

- a winning streak to provide him with capital and courage

- development of experience and confidence

- personal situations or problems that make him want to play in higher-stake games.

An obvious sign that a player is ready to drop back to a lower-stake game occurs when he quits playing poker. Approaching him about a smaller game must be tactful to avoid injuring his pride. The proper approach depends on his reason for quitting. Reasons that a player quits a high-stake game include—

- going broke or bankrupt
- discouragement from a losing streak
- loss of too much money
- hurt feelings or pride
- personality conflicts
- personal problems
- time conflict
- health reasons

If the reason for his quitting is identified and if the approach is proper, this player will usually welcome the opportunity to continue playing in a lower-stake game (or even to return to the higher-stake game) rather than to quit poker altogether.

The chart on page 203 summarizes John Finn's system of poker games in 1965 and his annual earnings from each game.

John Finn guarantees himself a substantial income by applying the "Advanced Concepts of Poker". By maintaining the above system of games, he will earn over $1,000,000 from poker in the next twenty years.

Weekly Poker Games

Game League, Purpose	Games Played in a Year Annual Earnings (average $ per game)	Regular Players, #	Irregular Players, #	Major-League Candidates, #
Monday Major, Income	50 $42,000 (840)	5	12	–
Tuesday Minor, New contacts	7 $ 1,100 (160)	4	7	1
Thursday Minor, New contacts	10 $ 1,400 (140)	6	8	2
Friday Intermediate, Farm team, Income	48 $ 9,500 (200)	6	8	4
Totals	115 $54,000 (470)	21	35	7

PART SIX

PROFESSIONALS

XXIV
A GUARANTEED INCOME FROM
PUBLIC POKER (121)

Any man or woman using the "Advanced Concepts
of Poker" can earn a guaranteed income by playing
public poker (i.e., poker in casinos and in commercial
card clubs). But first this person must understand the
difference between *private* poker as discussed in Parts
One through Five of this book and *public* poker as
discussed in Part Six.

The two major differences (or problems) of public
poker are (1) the house cut that permanently extracts

204

large amounts of money from every player in every game, and (2) the widespread professional cheating that pervades high-stake, public poker.

With the information in Part Six, the good player not only can win in most club and casino poker games, but he can also identify those games in which he cannot win. Part Six provides the information needed to accept or reject public poker as a source of income.

XXV
PRIVATE POKER VS.
PUBLIC POKER (122)

Over 95% of all poker played in the United States and throughout the world is private poker. Generally, the good poker player can make much more money from private games than from public (club or casino) games. That is why over three-quarters of this book addresses itself to money extraction from private poker games.

Nevertheless, many private-game players will try public poker sometime during their lives. And almost all private-game players will wonder at times about the following:

—What is it like to play poker in public clubs and casinos? How do these games compare with the games I play in?

—How well would I do in public poker? Could I win consistently? Could I make a living by playing poker in clubs and casinos?

—The constant availability of games, players, and money in clubs and casinos seems attractive, but how much would the house cut and professional competition decrease my odds? Could I beat the professional players? Would I encounter cheaters? Could I beat the cheaters?

This Part Six answers these questions.

To win consistently in public club and casino poker (such as played in the California card clubs and in the Nevada casinos), the good player must use the principles identified in this book . . . he must use those "Advanced Concepts of Poker" that are relevant to public poker.

To compete in public poker, a new player must first understand the differences between private and public poker. The Table on the following four pages summarizes the major differences. By understanding these differences, the good player will know which of the "Advanced Concepts of Poker" are applicable to public poker.

In addition to the differences listed in the Table (pages 207 to 210), public poker differs from private poker in other minor and subtle ways that influence the good player's strategy. Part Six identifies many of these subtle differences; the good player will discover other differences as he plays public poker.

XXVI
THE HOUSE CUT (123)

For the good player, the most negative feature of public poker is the damage that the house cut (time collection or casino rake) does to his profit potential. Card clubs and casinos, through their continuous collections and raking, gradually but permanently remove most of the available cash from all public games. In private games, the bulk of this house-removed cash would have ended up in the good player's pocket. The tables on pages 211 and 213 illustrate the draining effect that the house cut has on the earnings of the good player. If this house cut is sufficiently high (e.g., 20% or more), the good player may be unable to win over the long term, no matter how great his advantage is over the other players.

The far-right-hand columns of the tables on pages 211 and 213 show that the house cut diminishes the good player's earnings much more than the amount

DIFFERENCES BETWEEN PRIVATE POKER AND PUBLIC (CLUB AND CASINO) POKER

	Private Poker (Worldwide)	Casino Poker (Las Vegas, Nevada)	Commercial Club Poker (Gardena, California)
Availability	Whenever and wherever game can be organized.	24 hours, 365 days.	9:00 a.m.-7:00 a.m., 365 days. (On separate days, each club is closed one day a week.)
Game stakes	Any agreed-upon stakes. Usually controlled by the good player. Most flexible.	$1-2 up to no limit. Established by each casino according to market demands. Flexible.	$1-2 up to $20 maximum bet. Established by law. Not flexible.
Speed of play	Very slow to fast.	Fast.	Very fast.
Betting pace	Controlled by good player. Betting pace increased by introducing game modifications such as twists, wild cards, bizarre games.	Controlled by dealer and all players collectively. Generally fast paced within limits of games permitted.	Controlled by all players collectively. Some influence by strongest players. Generally fast paced within limits of games permitted.

Poker games played	All types of poker. Generally controlled by good player.	Mostly seven-card stud and hold 'em. Also highball or lowball draw and stud. A few split-pot games. No wild cards, except jokers in lowball.	Only draw poker, high and low. No oddball games, twists, or wild cards, except jokers in lowball. Stud or open-hand poker prohibited by law.
Profitability for good players	Most profitable.	Varies, depending on house cut or rake. High % rakes (e.g., 20%) eliminates profits for good players. Highest-stake games have lowest % cut.	Better than casino poker because of smaller % house cut ... an advantage partly offset by the higher percentage of better players in Gardena.
Skill of average player	Least.	Intermediate.	Most.
Quality of average professional	Best—the most independent, secretive, honest, and successful of the professionals.	Most dependent on cheating and collusion with dealers, shills, and fellow professionals.	Better than casino professionals, but many are dependent on professional establishment and cheating.
Professionals in high-stake games, %	2-5	10-40	5-30

DIFFERENCES BETWEEN PRIVATE POKER AND PUBLIC (CLUB AND CASINO) POKER

(All data are estimates based on author's direct experience.)

	Private Poker (Worldwide)	Casino Poker (Las Vegas, Nevada)	Commercial Club Poker (Gardena, California)
Extent of cheating	Least.	Most.	Intermediate.
Professionals who cheat, %	10	60	40
Average winnings of top professional players*			
• Without cheating	Unlimited.	$20,000-50,000.	$20,000-25,000.
• With cheating	Winning potential decreases with cheating.	$20,000-$100,000 with cheating in high, table-stake games.	$20,000-35,000 with cheating in highest-stake lowball games.
Cheating techniques (most commonly used)	Crude culling, stacking and peeking by amateurs and losers. Collusion or cheating by professionals or good players is rare.	Undetectable collusion between professionals and house dealers who know hole cards in high-stake stud and hold-'em poker.	Signaling and card flashing between professional partners in highest-stake lowball games. Occasional opportunities for card manipulation.

209

EARNINGS OF PROFESSIONAL CHEATERS VS. GOOD PLAYERS IN PUBLIC POKER: EFFECT OF HOUSE CUTS

GARDENA CLUB POKER

(For 3000 hours of poker per year. All data are estimates based on author's direct experience.)

	Professional Cheating (estimates)	Earnings of Best Professionals* (with cheating)	Earnings of Good players (non-cheating)	House Cut** Per Player	Earnings of Good Players in Equivalent Private Games
High Draw					
$ 5-10	Little	$10,000	$20,000	$12,000	$30,000+
$10-20	Some	$15,000	$25,000	$18,000	$55,000+
$20-20	Considerable	$20,000	$25,000	$24,000	$70,000+
Low Draw					
$ 5 blind	Some	$10,000	$15,000	$12,000	$35,000+
$10 blind	Considerable	$20,000	Uncertain	$18,000	$65,000+
$20 blind raise	Extensive	$25,000	Possible Loss	$30,000	$90,000+

*Earnings are estimated for the best professional players observed in Gardena. The average professional in Gardena (including house shills and proposition players who are paid by the club for starting and maintaining poker games) probably net less than $10,000 per year. The net average earnings of all the professional poker players in Gardena are estimated at $10,000 per year per professional player.

**The average Gardena table extracts an estimated $109,000 per year from its players (see table on page 217).

actually collected from him. That is because the house cut relentlessly drains cash away from every opponent, steadily shrinking the amount of money available for extraction from poor players by the good player. Because of the constantly draining house cut, the poorest players (the good player's most valuable assets) are driven from the game more quickly than are the tougher players. This phenomenon results in higher concentrations of tough or superior players than would occur in comparable games without a house cut. Also, the house cut produces more losers who, in turn, will play tighter poker, thus further diminishing the good player's advantage and edge odds.

Adding to the cash drain in casino poker is the toking (tipping) of the house dealer by the winner of each pot. Because of the arbitrary raking power of most casino dealers, toking is necessary to avoid extra-heavy rakes from future pots that the player may win. Toking increases by as much as 20% the money removed from the game by casinos. Since public card clubs have no house dealers, their customers are spared this additional drain (although toking of floormen does occur in some high-stake club games).

The house cut (rake) in poker is actually higher than the house cut in most major gambling games such as blackjack, craps, and roulette. The primary difference between gambling and playing public poker is that in gambling, individuals play directly against the house (the casino) and have no way to overcome the house cut or house percentage.* But in poker, indi-

---

* *The single exception to the unbeatability of casino games occurs when a Thorpe-type counting system is properly used in blackjack. The validity of blackjack counting systems is limited and provides at best a theoretical advantage of less than 1% (or investment odds of less than 1.01). Furthermore, these systems are entirely mechanical—they are inflexible, difficult and boring to apply, and basically impractical for accumulating any significant or reliable income. Casinos can eliminate any player advantage in blackjack whenever they want to or need to (which is seldom) simply by increasing the number of decks used or by increasing the frequency of shuffles. Moreover, by publicizing their feigned dislike and fear of counting systems, casino management surreptitiously promotes*

EARNINGS OF PROFESSIONAL CHEATERS vs. GOOD PLAYERS IN PUBLIC POKER: EFFECT OF HOUSE CUTS

LAS VEGAS CASINO POKER

(For 3000 hours of poker per year. All data are estimates based on author's direct experience.)

	Professional Cheating (estimates)	Earnings of Best Professionals* (with cheating)	Earnings of Good Players (non-cheating)	House Cut** Per Player	Earnings of Good Players in Equivalent Private Games
High Stud and Draw					
$ 5-10	Little	$ 5,000	$15,000	$15,000	$ 40,000+
$10-20	Some	$10,000	$20,000	$20,000	$ 75,000+
$20-40	Considerable	$15,000	$25,000	$25,000	$100,000+
$40-80	Extensive	$20,000	$30,000	$30,000	$125,000+
$100+	Extensive	$25,000	$30,000	$35,000	$150,000+
Table Stakes	Extensive	$35,000	Possible Loss	$35,000	No Limit
Low Stud and Draw					
$ 5-10	Little	$10,000	$20,000	$15,000	$ 45,000+
$10-20	Considerable	$15,000	Uncertain	$20,000	$ 85,000+
$20-40	Extensive	$20,000	Probable Loss	$30,000	$125,000+
$40-80	Extensive	$30,000	Probable Loss	$35,000	$150,000+
$100+	Extensive	$35,000	Probable Loss	$35,000	$175,000+

*Earnings are estimated for the best professional players observed in Las Vegas. The average professional in Las Vegas (including house shills who are paid by the casino for starting and maintaining poker games) probably nets less than $12,000 per year. The net average earnings of all the professional poker players in Las Vegas are estimated at $12,000 per year per professional player.

**While most Nevada casinos have a harsh percentage rake averaging about 10%, some have a $2-3 maximum rake per hand for higher-stake games. (For high-stake games, a few casinos are switching to a lower-percentage, Gardena-type, time collection.) Even with a $2-3 maximum cut per hand, casinos can remove $1400-2000 per day per table, which is $500,000-700,000 per year per table. Accounting for low-stake games and slack periods, the average casino poker table extracts an estimated $300,000 per year from its players (see footnote on page 267). Additional money lost to house dealers in tokes or tips can exceed 10% of the house-cut total.

viduals play against one another, not against the house or casino. The good poker player can, therefore, consistently extract money from all inferior players. He will win in casino and club poker if his money extraction from the other players is greater than the amount the house extracts from him. Conversely, the loser or the inferior player takes a double loss in public poker . . . the loss to the winners and the loss to the house.

In calculating his edge odds, the good player must include the house as the biggest winner. As indicated in the tables on pages 211 and 213, the house will be the biggest winner in almost every game, with the good player averaging a distant second. In private poker, the good player tries to eliminate any competing big winner as quickly as possible. (Or he quits that game and finds a more profitable game without a competing big winner.) But in public poker, the good player can never escape from or eliminate the biggest winner (the club or casino). By playing only in private games and avoiding the house cut, the good player makes *himself* the biggest winner.**

The time collections of public poker clubs (e.g.,

---

and encourages the use of blackjack counting systems. The burgeoning interest in these systems has caused major increases both in blackjack activity and in profits for the casinos.

** *In private poker, the good player could sponsor a game with pleasant distractions and discipline-breaking amenities (e.g., "free" gourmet buffets, rich desserts, expensive liquors). But the good player acting as the house (with profitable collections or rakes) could cause his opponents to believe that he is sponsoring the games solely for profit (which, of course, would and should be true). Such a belief would make his opponents more defensive and harder to manipulate and, thus, harder to control and extract money from. Besides, the good player can win by finesse all available money without having to compete against himself by mechanically collecting money through a house cut. Also, most states consider running a profitable game with regular house cuts as an illegal gambling operation. Such activity could leave the sponsoring player vulnerable to a criminal complaint filed, for example, by an unhappy loser . . . or by the loser's wife.*

Gardena, California poker clubs*) are generally less expensive and less harmful to the good player's earnings than are the percentage rakes of Nevada casinos**. Still, the Gardena-type time collections relentlessly and permanently remove the major portion of available cash from every game. The table on the following page shows that each year, the six Gardena clubs end up with ten to twenty times more cash than the total amount won by all of the professional poker players in Gardena combined. This table shows that the six Gardena poker clubs extract over $22,000,000 per year from their customers. . . . Poker generates substantial profits for the club owners—even after paying business expenses, high taxes and an annual payroll of over $8,000,000 (according to the Gardena Chamber of Commerce, 1976). Who then are the smartest and most prosperous poker players in Gardena? The quiet and invisible club owners, of course. The club owners truly deserve admiration—what player could ever match their edge odds and consistent winnings from poker?

Still, how do the other poker players fare? If the average professional poker player in Gardena nets about $10,000 per year (estimated in footnote on page 211), then the estimated 100 to 200 professionals in Gardena would extract $1,000,000 to $2,000,000 per year from all the other poker players. After allowing for those seats occupied by the professionals plus the empty seats and vacant tables during slack periods,

---

* *California has four-hundred legal poker clubs. A few other states such as Washington and Oregon also have legal poker clubs. But by far the most important area for public club poker is Gardena, California, where legalized poker began in 1936. Today, Gardena has six of the most prosperous poker clubs in the country and is the mecca for both amateur and professional public club poker players.*
** *Some Nevada casinos are switching from harsh percentage rakes to milder, Gardena-type time collections, especially for their higher-stake games. Increasing competition for poker players is causing this trend toward milder house cuts as more and more Nevada casinos, attracted by the profitability of public poker, are adding poker to their operations or are expanding their existing poker facilities.*

MONEY EXTRACTED BY GARDENA POKER CLUBS VIA TIME COLLECTIONS

	Minimum Collection $1/half hour (for $1-2 game)	Average Collection $2/half hour (Average for all games)	Maximum Collection $5/half hour (for $20 blind-raise game)
Each hour/seat	$2	$4	$10
Each day/seat (22-hour day)	$44	$88	$220
Each year/seat (310-day year)	$13,640	$27,280	$68,200
Each year/filled table (8 seats/table)	$109,120	$218,240	$545,600
Each year/average table (50% filled)	$54,560	$109,120	$272,800
Each year/club (35 tables)	—	$3,819,200	—
Each year/Gardena (6 clubs)	—	$22,915,200	—
Estimated money extracted per year by professional poker players	—	$1,000,000— 2,000,000	—

the nonprofessional players occupy an estimated average of 800 seats in the six Gardena poker clubs. These clubs, therefore, must extract $28,500 per year from each of these 800 seats to account for the $22,000,000 permanently removed each year. This means that the nonprofessional regular customer who plays 40 hours per week must lose an average of $7,000 per year *if* his play is superior to half of the other players in Gardena. (And, as a group, the Gardena players are the best and the toughest poker players in the world.) If he does not play as well as half of the players, he will lose more than $7,000 per year by playing 40 hours per week. If he is a much better player than the average Gardena player, he must extract $7,000 per year from the other players in order to break even. And if he is skilled enough to extract $20,000 per year from the other players by playing *60 hours* every week, he will be in the same class with the average professional poker player by earning $10,000 per year. In other words, except for the few very best and toughest players, all others pay dearly in both time and money for the privilege of playing poker regularly in Gardena. And as shown in the tables on page 211 and 213, players pay even more dearly for the privilege of playing poker regularly in Nevada casinos because of the more costly casino rake.

To earn a steady income from public poker requires an exceptionally tough player with poker skills far superior to the average player. To be a professional poker player in the Gardena clubs or the Nevada casinos requires long, hard hours that yield relatively poor yearly incomes. For the constant high levels of thought and effort required to earn a living from public poker, most professional casino or club players seem to be wasting their abilities in unrewarding careers. And most other public poker players (the losers) are throwing away their time and money with methodical certainty.

XXVII
LEARNING PUBLIC POKER (124)

The good player can extract a steady income from the unlimited supply of players and money offered by public club and casino poker. Still, private poker is basically more profitable than public poker. The house cut, the stiffer competition (resulting from higher percentages of superior and professional players in public poker), and the rigid rules and betting limitations of public poker all serve to reduce the good player's edge odds, flexibility, and income.

1. Club Poker (125)

Public poker in the Gardena card clubs is tough, fast, and different. And as a group, the Gardena poker players are the best in the world. Most newcomers to public club poker lose money not only because of the house collection and the superior competition, but also because of their own confusion, errors, and lack of knowledge. Even the experienced private-game player will be confused, even shaken, the first time he plays public club poker . . . especially if the first time is in Gardena, California.

Unlike casino poker, no house dealers are available in club poker to protect, help, or guide new players. Also, club poker moves faster and is higher pressured than casino poker. The newcomer to Gardena poker often encounters harassment, intimidation, and pressure from other players. The nonprofessional, regular players in the lower-stake games especially try to press for advantages by intimidating newcomers into losing money through confusion and errors. Superior players and professionals in higher-stake games, on the other hand, usually do not harass new players because they want to hold them in the game for longer-term money extraction. Thus, the newcomer can learn public poker more comfortably in the higher-stake games, but he will pay more for his lessons at the higher stakes against the superior competition.

After twenty to forty hours of Gardena poker, the good player begins integrating the unique characteristics of club poker into his own poker experience and skills. The good player will then start detecting patterns among different games and players. As he continues to play club poker, these patterns become increasingly familiar. After a dozen or so games, the good player starts recognizing a stereotype sameness for each kind of club game (e.g., low-stake, high-stake, highball, lowball) and for each class of player (e.g., losers, winners, sporadic players, regular amateurs, regular professionals). Because of the rigid customs and rules in club poker, the playing and betting actions of club players fall into more predictable patterns than do similar actions of private-game players. Once familiar with club poker and its patrons, the good player can enter any club and after a few hands be able to read and predict most actions of both amateur and professional players with good accuracy.

The good player can reduce or even eliminate the cost of learning Gardena poker by rattling his opponents—by switching the pressures and intimidations from him to them. The good player's normal technique for rattling and intimidating opponents requires a confidently bold and aggressive style. But for the newcomer, such a style would be unconvincing and ineffective because of his weak and defensive position during his first few ventures into public poker.

Ironically, that temporary weakness places the good player in an ideal position to use unorthodox behavior and bizarre actions in order to confuse and frighten his opponents. By such actions, he can often nullify the disadvantage of his own initial confusion by throwing his opponents into even greater confusion. Being a stranger, he can effectively induce bewilderment and fear in others through the unknown. For example, feigning insanity induces fear in others. Who would not fear the unknown of a deranged stranger? Few players would dare to pressure or intimidate a psychotic at their table . . . indeed, most players would be rattled into making errors. Feigning a physical disorder such as a severe tic or bizarre guttural sounds also rattles opponents into errors. Feigning muteness eliminates harassments and provides peace.

John Finn first experienced public poker in the Gardena, California, card clubs. He promptly cancelled the disadvantages of being a newcomer by rattling his opponents into errors. He learned public poker at their expense.

Arriving in Gardena for the first time, John Finn parked his rented car in the self-park area behind the Eldorado Card Club. He entered the club through the automatic glass doors. Walking past the darkened lobby partly illuminated by a large, gas-fed fireplace, he abruptly stopped and stared into the brightly-lighted, pit-like playing area filled with rising layers of white smoke. A low, almost quiet rumble of voices rolled from the cloudy pit. For an instant, John felt that he was witnessing several hundred vagabonds huddling around tables in a cavernous Salvation Army hall. He moved to the observation rail that partly circled the poker pit and studied the scene. Some people were poorly dressed, causing the entire crowd to project a tacky appearance. Everyone seemed to homogenize into a blend of middle-aged and elderly men and women. A few looked younger, but most looked pallid and wan . . . some looked cadaverous. About 25% were women—some seemed slack and bored, others seemed tense and desperate. John observed more closely. Contradictory to his first impression, many faces reflected an intelligence and a strength . . . or at least a faded intelligence and perhaps a surrendered strength, especially in the older people. He estimated that 70% of the players were addicted smokers . . . John Finn knew he could extract money from this crowd.

After watching from the rail for thirty minutes and reading through a house-rule booklet obtained in the lobby, John Finn went to the large chalkboard that listed the poker games in progress and the waiting list for each game. The lowest-stake game was $1-2 high draw, jacks or better to open. John gave the boardman the false initials "J.R." to be wait-listed for this low-stake game. In ten minutes, "J.R." was announced over the speaker system. Moments later, John was sitting in his first public poker game.

After an hour, John was still winless and had forfeited two pots because of technical errors: On his first forfeited pot, he had turned up his pair of queens to show openers after no one called his final bet. When he tossed his other three cards facedown on the discards, a collective shout from the other players informed John that his hand was dead. (According to Gardena house rules, all five cards—not just openers —of the opening hand must be spread faceup before any of these cards touch the discards.) John forfeited the pot. Several hands later, he held three kings. His only opponent held two pair and stayed pat. John was the dealer. He drew one card, but forgot to burn a card (deal a card into the discards) before drawing. Again a collective shout informed John that his hand was dead. The player with two pair promptly spread his cards faceup, grinned, and yanked the pot into his pile of chips.

John decided he had learned enough from that game and wanted to establish a stronger psychological position in a higher-stake game. Looking at the gameboard, he noticed that a $3-6 draw game had no waiting list. John played one more hand. He opened with three tens. Everyone folded. He promptly spread his hand faceup and pulled in the forty-cent ante—his first pot in public poker. As he stood up to leave, a wizened old woman sitting across from him looked up, stretched her skinny neck and cackled, "Hey buster, don't tell 'em where ya won all that money."

Moving to the $3-6 game, John already knew his strategy. He would nullify the disadvantages of his inexperience by rattling his opponents into yielding advantages to him.

Silently sitting in the empty seat, he put his chips on the table, anted for the next pot, touched his fingertips together in a praying position, bowed his head, and waited for the cards to be dealt. Someone asked him a question. John did not look up or even acknowledge the question. He looked at no one, said nothing, and moved with squared, mechanical-like motions. Between movements he sat with fingertips joined and stared silently at the "action spot" on the table or at his stack of chips. The conversation at the table diminished as the players began casting glances at him. John knew they were worried about his behavior.

His total withdrawal gave John Finn a two-way advantage: First, he could shut out all interference and distractions from the other players, allowing him to concentrate, learn, think, and plan strategy. Second, the other players were reluctant to pressure or intimidate him because they were nervous about his strange behavior. Everyone left him alone. John had the solitude and time to think and act deliberately, thereby decreasing his confusion and errors.

But this technique, being a short-range tool, needed constant reinforcement as new players entered the game and as other players became tired of John's behavior and began challenging it with intimidations. For example, after a profitable hour of this silent playing, John bowed his head as a portly player entered the game and sat beside him. The stout man began chatting with other players. After two hands, he noticed John's silent, mechanical-man behavior and jabbed John's shoulder several times while blurting, "Hey man, you alive? You some kind of a robot? Say something so I know I'm not playing against a computer."

Without moving or looking at the man, John kept staring at his chips while answering in a low monotone, "Doctors at state hospital make me like this ... to control myself. They keep accusing me of being paranoid ... they keep lying about me. They keep accusing me of being violent. This way I stay controlled and peaceful."

Several players shuddered. But the portly neighbor pressed on, "Hey man, what hospital? Who's your shrink? I need someone to make me stay controlled and peaceful. I need someone to make me quit gambling and eating. Man, how do I get committed to that hospital?" ... He punched John's shoulder again.

John Finn jumped up, pointed a stiff finger at the man's face and shouted, "You a cop or something! You from the C.I.A.? You writing a book? Don't bug me! Don't bug me or I'll lose control!"

The stout man picked up his chips. "No ... no

223

offense, sir," he said. "I'm leaving. See, I'm leaving."
He stood up and left.

Everyone became silent. Another player abruptly stood up and left. John played two more hours in peace while winning a hundred dollars. As other players left, new players entered the game. Gradually players became hostile toward John's mechanical behavior. So he decided to reinforce his act again at their expense.

The opportunity came several hands later. Before the draw, John had the last bet and raised the maximum on his two pair of jacks and fours. He drew one card and caught the third jack for a full house. He knew his three opponents held weak hands; they would check and probably fold on any betting strength from him. After catching his full house, John had to change his strategy in order to build a larger pot for himself. So he used his abnormal behavior to elicit bluffing and betting action from his opponents: With a jerk, John rose from his seat and faced the player on his left. Lifting his upper lip to expose his teeth, he bowed and whispered, "Thank you, sir, for my straight flush." Turning clockwise, John bowed and uttered his thanks to every player. With each bow, he flashed the jack of hearts and the four of clubs in his carefully arranged hand that concealed his other three cards. He then slumped into his seat, closed his eyes, lowered his head to the table, and continued muttering words of thanks.

The first player snorted and bet the maximum. The second player raised. And the third player called. Without lifting his face from the table, John shoved all of his chips toward the pot and said in a muffled voice, "Reraise the maximum." After long pauses, each player called. Still pressing his forehead against the table, John spread his full house faceup across the pot. All three players threw down their cards and promptly left the table. Another player stood up and left. The game had been broken. John grabbed the $110 pot, picked up his chips, and left.

Perhaps John Finn overacted in that last hand, causing the players to flee. But so what? Unlike private games, each public game is a one-shot combination of opponents. What they think, feel, or experience

has little bearing on future games. So by acting ab-
normally, John rattled his opponents and won an
extra-large pot plus an additional hundred dollars
earlier . . . all while learning to play club poker in
Gardena. If John had not rattled his opponents, he
probably would have lost money in that game . . .
probably a hundred dollars or more. A little planned
acting made at least a $300 difference. With his bi-
zarre aggressiveness, John replaced his initial weaknesses with actions that intimidated and confused his
experienced opponents into making multiple errors.
By unorthodox thinking and careful planning, he beat
his opponents while learning their game.

2. Casino Poker (126)

Casino poker is easier to learn (especially in major
casinos) than club poker because the nonplaying casino dealer controls the game and protects the new
player by guiding him through unfamiliar rules and
customs. This help from the dealer reduces the new
player's technical errors and allows him more thinking
room to analyze the game and to execute strategy. The
good player makes a wise investment by toking (tipping) dealers who provide him with pressure-relieving
protection and helpful information. With the dealer's
protection and help, the new player can win pots that
he might otherwise have lost or forfeited because of his
inexperience. But in the faster-moving higher-stake
games, dealers are more reluctant to help or protect
the newcomer. Yet even here, the inexperienced good
player can beat experienced professionals by rattling
them with unorthodox actions.

In first moving up to higher-stake casino poker,
John Finn twice assumed the role of a mute in order
to play in peace and to gain thinking time necessary
to turn certain high-pressure losing situations into
winning hands. On another occasion, John faked a
severe tic to successfully bluff a superior professional
player out of a $240 lowball pot: John made a $60
bluff bet while knowing his only remaining opponent
had a weak but callable hand. When this opponent
started moving his chips toward the pot to call the

$60 bluff bet, John looked directly at him, groaned, and then yanked the right corner of his lip up with a simultaneous wink of his right eye while jerking his right shoulder to his ear . . . he did this several times in rapid succession. With each yank, his right arm spasmodically twisted toward his opponent, momentarily exposing the two, three, four, and five in his hand—his paired five remained concealed. The startled but observant opponent folded his ten low. John's "physical disorder" cleared up as the dealer pushed the pot toward him. Instead of losing $100, John earned $240 with a five-second act.

Once John Finn had control of casino and club poker, he dropped most of his short-term ploys for the more profitable long-range strategy of tough, sound poker based on the "Advanced Concepts of Poker."

Choosing when to use unorthodox or bizarre acts and choosing which act to use depend on the game and its players. Such acts benefit the good player when he is first adjusting to or learning a new game situation—such as casino or club poker. Once the new game situation and its players are under his control, the good player can then use his straight poker skills more effectively than his unorthodox, bizarre, or sometimes ludicrous acts.

3. Notes on Public Poker (127)

John Finn made the following notes while playing poker in the Gardena card clubs and in the various Nevada casinos:

1. Advantages of private poker over club and casino poker: (1) No house cut to drain away profits. (2) The same players are available week after week for the long-range manipulation necessary for increasing money extraction and a growing poker income.

2. Advantage of club and casino poker over private poker: The constant supply of fresh players allows maximum aggressiveness and ruthlessness without fear of destroying the game. If best strategy

226

dictates, unrestrained effort can be directed toward upsetting opponents. No need to mollify losers. Establish psychological dominance early. Avoid excessively obnoxious tactics that might alienate club or casino management and result in banishment from their establishments.

3. The six card clubs in Gardena, California, provide simultaneous action for up to 1680 poker players. Over 400 licensed card clubs in California and more than 50 Nevada casinos continuously offer thousands of fresh poker players for money extraction, every hour of every day and night, all year around.

4. Major poker clubs and casinos always offer a selection of games and players. Carefully select the most advantageous game with the weakest players. Keep aware of the other games, and promptly abandon any game for a more advantageous game (e.g., more profitable stakes or weaker players).

5. Seek games with careless players, nervous players, women players, drinking players, players with tattoos or unkempt beards, and especially players wearing religious crosses or medals, good-luck charms, astrology symbols, or other mystical amulets. Avoid games with high ratios of calm, controlled, or intelligent-looking people.

6. Because of his initial confusion and inexperience when first learning public poker, the good player's statistical game (the mechanical aspects—the figuring of odds and money management) is weaker than his strategical game (the imaginative and thinking aspects—the strategy and bluffing). Conversely, the statistical game of most public-game professionals is stronger than their strategical game because of their greater dependence on mechanical routines, rotes, and rules designed to yield statistically maximum investment odds on every play. Their more rigid consistency makes

227

them more readable and predictable. The good player, on the other hand, does not strive for maximum investment odds on every play, thus leaving him more flexible and unpredictable.

7. Collection fees or time cuts in public games range from $2 per hour for a $1-2 game to about $12 per hour for games with bets of $20-40 and higher. The casino rake (from every pot) can range from a 5% maximum up to a 25% maximum . . . or even higher. Maximum rakes in casinos are usually posted in the poker area.

8. House cuts are less harmful to the good player's profits in the faster-moving, higher-stake, time-cut games (versus the slower-moving, lower-stake, pot-raked games).

9. In public poker, lowball games are generally less flexible (more mechanical) than equivalent highball games. Therefore, the good player can usually use the "Advanced Concepts of Poker" more advantageously in highball games. But the faster betting pace of lowball can outweigh this advantage. Professional players, however, cheat more frequently and more effectively in highstake lowball.

10. The narrow and fixed betting ratios (e.g., $10-20) in all public club games and in most casino games diminish the effectiveness of the good player's poker skills, especially in executing bluffs and power plays. Casino table-stake games usually offer the best profit opportunities for the good player experienced in public poker.

11. Most casino and club shills (house players) play conservative and predictable poker (especially women shills), making them dependable decoys and unwitting partners for manipulating other players.

12. In public poker, women are generally weaker players than men. Many women lack the aggres-

siveness necessary for good poker. They play more mechanically and more predictably than men. In Gardena, during weekdays, up to 40% of the players are women. (The percentage of women players drops in half by nightfall.) Many are poor players ... some are desperate players gambling with their Social Security checks and grocery money. Still, an estimated ten to twenty good, tough women professionals work the Gardena clubs. Successful women professionals are much rarer in the Nevada casinos.

13. Opponents generally play looser and poorer poker on or immediately after paydays (e.g., on the first of the month and on Friday nights).

14. Best to enter games fresh and rested at 1:00 a.m.- 5:00 a.m. (while faking tiredness, nervousness, or even drunkenness) in order to work over groggy players, drunk players, loose winners, and desperate losers.

15. To conceal poker abilities and to throw good players off guard, wear a religious cross.

16. Rattle opponents through physical invasions of their "territories" (e.g., by using elbows or hands, by pushing poker chips or money around, by knocking over drinks). Foist feelings of outrage, guilt, inferiority, or fear onto opponents through personal, verbal attacks. Temper bad-boy behavior only to avoid physical attacks or banishment from games.

17. Give no player a break. Make opponents sweat. Never grant mercy to an opponent.

18. In highball, elevate height with extra chair cushions. The higher a player sits, the more carelessly exposed hands he can observe. In lowball, diminish height and sit low in order to see more cards flash during the shuffle and on the draw.

19. Observation of well-known and self-publicized

professional poker players, including those who play in and have won the World Series of Poker, reveals a composite character (with individual exceptions) of a prematurely aged, physically unfit, heavy smoker who is prone to boasting, gross exaggeration, and gambling. Yet he is a character who is basically intelligent and shrewd —but vulnerable to manipulation through his flaws. He is a character who through his weaknesses can be exploited and beaten by the good player.

20. The good player is probably the biggest loser in poker . . . especially in public poker. Surrounded by losers, he consumes his intelligence and time in a situation that provides a guaranteed income, but offers neither an interesting nor a productive future.

In six days, John Finn put both public club and casino poker under his profitable control . . . at least for the lower-stake and medium-stake games. For the higher-stake games, John had an additional major problem to deal with . . . the problem of professional cheating.

XXVIII
PROFESSIONAL POKER
PLAYERS (128)

Professional poker players fall into two classes: (1) professionals that extract money from private games, and (2) professionals that extract money from public games.

Successful private-game professionals explicitly or implicitly understand and use many of the "Advanced Concepts of Poker." Private-game professionals are usually quiet, ostensibly self-effacing, independent loners who never need to join an establishment* or

* *Professionals who get involved with establishments or cliques usually limit their potentials and acquire rigid, stereotype characteristics that the good player can identify. On*

cheat to extract maximum money from their opponents. (Cheating would actually decrease both their investment odds and their long-range edge odds.) Private-game professionals generally prosper more and spend fewer hours playing poker than do public-game professionals.

While all public-game professionals explicitly or implicitly must understand and use enough of the "Advanced Concepts of Poker" to generate a regular income, many public-game professionals misunderstand or violate various key concepts. For example, many public-game professionals not only openly boast about their poker abilities, but they compromise their independence by joining a tacit professional establishment. Many of these professionals increasingly depend on cheating (at the expense of playing good poker) to extract money from non-establishment players. Because of their compromised independence and their reliance on cheating for survival, most of these public-game professionals limit their potential winnings . . . and their future.

XXIX
PROFESSIONAL CHEATING (129)

Perhaps the most profound difference between private poker and public poker (club and casino) is the collusion cheating practiced by many professional players in public poker. Few outsiders or victims detect or even suspect professional cheating in public poker because such cheating is visually undetectable. Public-game professionals execute their collusion so naturally and casually that upper management of major casinos

---

identifying the stereotype characteristics of these professionals, the good player can predict their actions and consistently beat them—even when they cheat. The good player or the superior professional, on the other hand, usually remains independent and avoids stereotype characteristics. And often his opponents never even realize that he is a good player who is winning all of their money.

and card clubs remain unaware of their cheating, even when it routinely occurs in their own casinos and clubs. Many public-game professionals accept and practice collusion cheating without qualms. They consider their cheating a natural and legitimate trade tool that enables them to offset the draining effect of the house rake or collection.

All of the important classical and modern professional cheating methods and devices are listed below:

Card Manipulations	Card Treatments	Other Devices
★ blind shuffling	★ daubing (Golden	check copping
★ crimping	Glow, nicotine	cold deck
★ culling	stains, soiling)	★ collusion
dealing	corner flash	partners
seconds,	denting and	★ card
bottoms,	rounders	flashing
middles	luminous readers	★ crossfiring
★ false cutting	marking	★ signals
★ false riffling	nailing	★ spread
foiling the cut	(indexing)	holdouts
palming	punching	shiners
★ peeking	sanding	
★ pull through	slicked-aced deck	
★ stacking	stripping	
★ Las Vegas	waving	
riffle		
★ overhand		
stack		
★ riffle cull		
and stack	[See Glossary in Appendix
★ undercut	C for definitions of these
stack	terms.]

★ *Professional cheating methods most commonly used today in public poker.*

To win consistently at high-stake casino or club poker, the good player has two choices: (1) join the professional establishment and become a part of their collusion-cheating system,* or (2) develop and use techniques to profit from the cheating of others. But in certain games such as high-stake lowball, collusion cheating by professionals can prevent even a good player from winning. As identified in Chapter XXXI, professional collusion cheating in lowball poker can diminish the good player's investment odds so greatly that he cannot win, even with his superior alertness, poker skills, money management, and startegy.

The table on pages 235–236 summarizes some of the important cheating techniques that professional poker players use in public clubs and casinos. This table also includes the classical but crude cheating techniques occasionally used by amateurs.** Contrary to popular belief, almost any player can master effective and undetectable cheating methods with only a few hours of practice. A forthcoming book, "Neocheating" by Frank R. Wallace and Max Cortine identifies, illustrates and describes in clear detail most of the cheating techniques that professional players use today in poker clubs and casinos. In club poker, the alert player detects professional cheating most often in the highest-stake lowball games in which signaling systems and card-flashing col-

---

* *Most public-game professionals admire and respect the good poker player and readily accept him into their establishment (especially in Gardena and Las Vegas). Their ready acceptance of the good player seems contradictory to their best interests since such acceptance increases competition for the losers' money. But these professionals both respect and fear the independent, good player. He is a threat to their system. They eliminate this threat by making him a part of their system. By contrast, the private or non-establishment good player rejects and tries to get rid of any competing player who is good enough to drain money from the game.*
** *Classical cheating (e.g., stacking specific hands, second dealing, holding out cards) seldom occurs in club or casino poker. Occasionally amateurs, strangers, or newcomers attempt classical cheating in public poker. But since their techniques are almost always crude, they are usually caught and banished from the game. Few professional cheaters today approve of or practice that kind of obsolete, mechanical cheating. The modern cheating methods are easier, more effective, and essentially undetectable.*

lusion are devastatingly effective. In casino poker, the alert player detects collusion cheating most often in the highest-stake stud and hold-'em games.

Not all public-game professionals are cheaters or part of the professional establishment.* Not all high-stake public games have cheaters present or even have professionals present. But any high-stake public game free of cheaters and professionals is ripe for exploitation and quickly attracts professionals and cheaters. Still, out of justice and fairness, the good player never considers anyone to be a cheater until he has adequate proof of cheating. While justice is a moral end in itself, the good player also strives to be just and fair in order to know more accurately what is going on and thus avoid costly errors. Being just and fair not only boosts a player's self-esteem, but also boosts his profits. . . . The good player resists the temptation of blaming tough or painful losses on being cheated (rather than on coincidence or on his own errors). Because of the extra-quick folds and the extra-aggressive bets used to beat cheaters, the good player can make an expensive error by misreading an opponent as a cheater.

Since cheating harms the long-range business interests of all public card clubs and casinos, management of the major clubs and casinos seriously oppose any form of cheating. They have always taken firm measures to eliminate and prevent cheating in their operations. For them, cheating means only bad publicity, lost business, lower profits, and potential legal and licensing problems. Without cheating, clubs and casinos can eventually extract all the money gamblers have to offer. With cheating, clubs and casinos could eventually go out of business.

Using tight controls and effective surveillance systems, the management of major casinos keeps all gaming operations (except poker) free of major, organized, or chronic cheating. All casino games, except poker, function between casino and player, allowing management to closely monitor and tightly control the action.

* Likewise, not all private-game professionals are independent loners or above cheating.

CHEATING TECHNIQUES USED IN PUBLIC CLUB, CASINO, AND PRIVATE POKER

	Uses	Methods
Manipulation Techniques—more common in private poker		
Classical and amateur manipulations (solo)	Least effective, most detectable. Shunned by today's professional establishment. Crudely used by amateurs in private games. Effectively used only by the rare, classic cardsharp who is highly skilled, dexterous, and experienced.	Classical deck stacking, holding-out cards, palming, second and bottom dealing, shaved decks, shiners, marked cards, and various mechanical devices used to cheat opponents.
Full flashing of draw and hole cards (dealer to partner)	More effective for stud and hold-'em games.	With smooth, imperceptible motions, the dealer lifts or tilts cards just enough for his partner to see. Done only when others are not looking or are unaware. The dealer may also allow his partner to see cards during the riffle.
Modern and professional manipulations (solo)	Most effective, easiest to learn, usually undetectable, and is used by professional players in both private and public poker. Neocheating.	New methods of culling cards, blind shuffles, false riffles, false cuts, and foiling cuts as described in this book.
Collusion Techniques—more common in club poker		
Partial flashing of draw and hole cards (dealer to partner)	Most effective for high-stake, lowball draw.	Player sits low enough to see shades of darkness, blur intensities, or the actual values of cards being dealt facedown—with or without the dealer's help.*

Collusion betting (partner to partner)	Most common in high-stake lowball and in bluff-dependent games.	Requires system of "strength of hand" and "when to bet, raise, or fold" signals between colluding partners.
Combined Techniques—more common in casino poker		
Collusion and manipulation (house dealer to partner)	Most effective and common in casinos with house dealers who manipulate cards and work in collusion with professional players.	The dealer culls or manipulates memorized cards to top of deck. He then knows everyone's hole cards and signals his partner when to bet, raise, or drop.

* *Good players train themselves to evaluate the shades of darkness or blur intensities of partially flashed cards (e.g., darker shades or more intense blurs indicate higher value cards—valuable information for lowball). If a player sees flashed cards without dealer collusion, he is not cheating since the same advantage is available to all players who choose to be equally alert. Alert players also watch for flashed cards as the dealer rifles, shuffles, and cuts.*

But in poker, the game functions between player and player (not between casino and player), leaving the management unable to monitor and control the action. That uniquely uncontrollable situation combined with the undetectability of professional collusion cheating makes poker the only casino game in which management has no practical way to detect or eliminate professional cheating. Also, casino management and its employees are less motivated to ferret out poker cheating because in poker, the players (not the casino) lose money to cheaters. But in other games, the casino (not the players) loses money to cheaters.

In May, 1976, a major poker-cheating conspiracy was publicly exposed in the Las Vegas MGM Grand Hotel and Casino, the world's largest gambling establishment. The police arrested the cardroom manager, the floorman, two dealers, and five outside partners— all were charged with illegal conspiracy and felony swindling. The authorities caught those "professionals" only because they were amateurish and crude in their techniques of culling, stacking, and peeking—allegedly they even resorted to copping chips from pots. But the MGM cheating scandal did not involve or even touch on the professional cheating that flourishes with casual finesse in higher-stake poker games, unchecked and undetected by casino managements.

Even if professional cheaters were eliminated from a high-stake game, a wave of new professionals and cheaters would fill the vacuum in order to exploit the "easy pickings" inherent in any new or clean public poker game. The financial incentive is too great to prevent professionals and cheaters from quickly moving into high-stake poker games filled with tourists, losers, and other easy amateurs.

What will happen when management and the public become increasingly aware of this uncontrollable professional cheating? Casinos can simply drop poker from their operations (or at least eliminate cheater-prone, high-stake poker) with only a minor effect on their business. But how will commercial poker clubs handle undetectable professional cheating? Their entire business depends on poker, which in turn depends on the trust and confidence of their most important customers—the losers. Unless management can control and eliminate chronic professional cheating, the commercial poker clubs could encounter business difficulties if the majority of their customers (the losers) began discovering and understanding the extent of professional cheating in their games.*

Since many professional poker players depend on collusion for a living and since their cheating is generally undetectable, management currently has no practical way to eliminate their cheating. One long-range solution may be mechanical or electronic shuffling and dealing devices that would not only eliminate undetectable dealer-player collusion, card flashing, and most card manipulations, but could reduce operating costs by eliminating dealers, accelerating the action, and automating house collections. In turn, lower operating costs could result in lower-percentage house cuts. Also, elimination of competition from professional cheaters would further increase the profits of good players and independent professionals who win through their own skills rather than through cheating.

XXX
WHY PROFESSIONALS
CHEAT (130)

The canons of poker, as clearly understood and tacitly accepted by every player, allow unlimited deception to win maximum money from ownerless pots. Therefore, everyone can and should freely use unlimited deception in every poker game. But no one should use deception outside of poker. If a person "plays poker" outside of a poker game, he becomes a dishonest person. But even *in poker* a person becomes dishonest if he violates the understood and accepted

---

* *Also, some chronic or heavy losers might sue those card clubs and casinos in which they had systematically lost money to professional cheaters. But the losers would probably need corroboration from some professional cheaters to support any serious litigation.*

canons of poker by usurping money through cheating. (Cheating is any manipulation of cards or any collusion that gives a player or players advantages not available to other players.)

Many poker players, including most professionals, do not fully distinguish between what is honest and what is dishonest, in and out of a poker game. For example, many professional players who day after day lie and practice deceit in poker ironically do not grasp the *rightness* of their poker deception. To them, lying and deception in poker become little different from cheating in poker. Their ethics become hazy and ill-defined. They feel the only barrier to crossing the line from lying and deception to cheating and stealing is the threat of being caught. By removing this threat (i.e., by undetectable cheating techniques), they cross over the line and begin cheating.

The failure to understand the black and white moral differences between deception in poker and cheating in poker is one reason why many players react so strongly (often violently, sometimes murderously) against a cheater. They fear that without strong anti-cheating reactions everyone would easily cross over the line from deceiving them to cheating them. Sensing their own capacity to cheat, they assume the same capacity to cheat resides in everyone. Thus even if they never cheat others, they fear that others will cheat them. Generally those who would react most violently against cheaters are those who would most readily cheat others —only their fear of being caught and evoking similarly violent reactions from their opponents restrains them from cheating.

Most amateur poker players hold the classical but misleading views about cheating. They perceive nearly all cheating being done either by bumbling amateurs who are easily caught or by highly dexterous and invincible cardsharps who have perfected sleight-of-hand skills through years of laborious practice and dangerous experience. In holding those misleading classical views, most amateur poker players remain unsuspecting of the casual, natural-appearing collusion cheating practiced among the professional establishment.

239

As the stakes of public games increase, the percentage of professional players increases—and their motivation for cheating increases. Every player should increasingly expect and look for cheating as he progresses to higher-stake club or casino games . . . right up to the highest-stake games, including the finals (down to the last three players) of the $250,000 World Series of Poker Hold 'em Tournament held annually in Las Vegas, Nevada. Some of the finalists in the World Series of Poker are public-game professionals who have worked among the professional establishment for years. Few members of the professional cheating establishment would have qualms about making collusion arrangements in the World Series of Poker. For example, two of the three, final players could safely and swiftly squeeze the third player out of the game with collusion betting to assure both of the remaining players a $125,000 return on their original $10,000 stakes (their entry fees). By their collusion, the final two players improve their investment odds—they eliminate any possibility of losing while guaranteeing themselves a large win.*

When, how, and why does a public-game profes-

---

* Since the author has not played in the World Series of Poker, no accusations of collusion or cheating are made about any World Series tournament held to date or against any participant. This chapter and the next chapter provide information on professional cheating in order to warn players of the cheating possibilities that exist in all public poker games, including the World Series of Poker. At some unspecified time, the author will quietly and anonymously enter the World Series of Poker, not only to win everything, but to gather first-hand information for future editions of the "Advanced Concepts of Poker."

If a collusion opportunity in the World Series of Poker were available to a good player such as John Finn, he would reject the offer not only because it would involve cheating (with its unfavorable, long-range consequences), but also because the odds would probably favor his winning all the money anyway . . . especially if he knew his final two opponents would be trying to drive him out by collusion cheating. On the other hand, if a shrewd professional player were in collusion with a skilled house-dealer mechanic, neither John Finn nor anyone else could beat that combination.

sional begin cheating? Imagine a lonely public-game player struggling against the house cut to become a full-time professional and suddenly discovering a friendly professional establishment with an ongoing cheating system readily available to him . . . an undetectable cheating system requiring no special skills and available for his immediate profit. Such a player, especially if he is a mediocre or marginal professional, will often embrace that opportunity by tacitly cooperating with the establishment professionals in perpetuating their system. He accepts their collusion cheating as a trade tool required for playing competitive, professional poker. As he blends in with those professionals and adopts their system, he becomes increasingly dependent not only on their establishment but on collusion cheating to survive. He loses his independence and becomes a stereotype public-game professional. With a sense of professional righteousness, he becomes a cheater.

XXXI
BEATING PROFESSIONAL CHEATERS (131)

The alert player who is familiar with the basic professional cheating techniques can detect any cheating, even the most skilled and invisible cheating, without actually seeing the cheating. An alert player usually can tell who is cheating, what technique is being used, and exactly when the cheating is occurring by detecting patterns and combinations of illogical betting, raising, pace, and playing style by his opponents.*

* To detect invisible cheating, a player must be involved in at least one hand and perhaps several hands in which cheating occurs in order to observe the illogical poker patterns and variables. For that reason, every player must be cautious about high-stake or no-limit games in which he could be lured into a single cheating setup and financially wiped out before detecting any cheating. Furthermore, the good player must not relax his vigilance after identifying a cheating pattern in a high-stake game—he must watch for a double-cheating ploy during which he is distracted with minor cheating that he can easily handle while being set up for a one-shot, big-hand play designed to

241

Once a player has detected and confirmed cheating in public poker, he has five options:

1. Join the cheating.
2. Beat the cheaters through their poorer playing, greater readability, and greater predictability that result from their cheating.
3. Eliminate the cheating.
4. Expose the cheating.
5. Quit the game.

The good player rejects the first option as not only being dishonest and unhealthy, but as being the least profitable option. Several of John Finn's encounters with professional cheating described in this chapter illustrate the other four options.

Although John Finn played mainly in private poker games because of their greater profitability, he did spend the summer of 1976 playing public poker in the Gardena, California, card clubs and in the Las Vegas, Nevada, casinos. In both the clubs and casinos, he discovered professional cheaters operating in the higher-stake games. John's public-game experiences uncovered six common cheating methods used in public poker (see A–F on the following pages). He also learned how the good player routinely can beat

---

wipe him out. Indeed, the wise player views with suspicion and is prepared to throw away without a bet any super-powerful hand (e.g., four of a kind . . . or a straight flush) that he receives in high-stake games with strangers.

The adroit player, nevertheless, can beat the one-shot, big-hand cheating setup by scalping the bait but not swallowing the hook when the set-up hand finally appears. Being aware of a cheating setup, the shrewd player can sometimes extract extra large bait (e.g., $5000) by staging an illusory huge pay-off (e.g., $100,000). After plucking the bait, he must fold without a bet on the first super-powerful hand dealt to him. Or better yet, he should leave the game before the big hand is sprung—in which case, he may even be able to return for more bait. . . . But the good player is also smart—he never tries conning con artists who might rob, assault, or even kill him for his counterintrigue.

professional cheaters in public poker. More importantly, he identified those situations in which he could not beat professional cheating.

1. Gardena, California (132)
A. Collusion Cheating—Reciprocal Card Flashing

During his first two days in Gardena, John Finn played in each of the six poker clubs. After the second day, he became aware of a network of habitual amateur players, professional players, floormen, and cardroom managers woven through these six clubs. The continuous circulation of poker players among the clubs allowed everyone in that network to effectively communicate (and gossip) with each other. While most of the habitual amateur players in Gardena recognized they were a part of a clique, few recognized that the professional establishment was using them as milch cows.

In the lower-stake games, John Finn found mainly amateurs; the few professionals were usually shills. In these games, he detected no cheating. On the fourth day, he graduated to a $20 blind, lowball draw game. In this game, he discovered from their poker styles and conversations that players in seats 2 and 5 were professionals involved in collusion cheating. Even before identifying them as full-time professionals, he knew they were colluding. Their methods were simple, effective, and unnoticeable. Both players sat low in their seats ... each slumping a little lower when the other dealt. On dealing draw cards with smooth quicker-than-the-eye motions, the dealer would expose key cards as fleeting blurs perceptible only to his partner. The partner would return the favor on his deal. The cheaters accomplished their card flashing without suspicion in spite of the great pressure on dealers in the Gardena card clubs not to flash cards. Only once did John observe a collusion cheater being scolded for his "careless" dealing. Ironically, John observed on numerous occasions noncheating dealers being scolded for flashing cards.

By knowing when his own lowball draw card had been flashed, John Finn could outmaneuver the cheating partners by more accurately predicting what they would do as the result of their knowing his draw card. Furthermore, the cheaters were constantly misled by John's counteractions—they repeatedly misjudged what he would do. John Finn exploited and beat both collusion partners by using the cheating counteractions taken from his notes on lowball cheating and listed below:

1. Save money by folding promptly against a cheater's more readable winning hand.

2. Lure the cheater into making an expensive bluff when he draws a picture card or a pair in lowball and knows you have drawn a high card such as a ten or a jack. The cheater's overconfidence often encourages him to bluff excessively.

3. Set up the cheater for an easy bluff. For example, a strong lowball bluff position develops when the cheater knows you have drawn a good low card (e.g., a six or lower), but does not know you paired the low card.

4. When you do draw a powerful low hand, the overconfident cheater can sometimes be misled into believing you did pair, causing him to call a final bet or to try a bold bluff, especially if the pot is large and if other bluffable players (whose draw cards the cheater also knows) are still in the pot.

5. When the readable cheater bluffs, use his aggressive betting to drive out other players who have you beat. When the other players are driven out, simply call the cheater's bluff. Or when necessary, bluff out the bluffing cheater with a final raise.

[Note: In each of these examples, the cheater would have either won more money or lost less money if he had concentrated on playing sound poker to gain broad information about his opponent—rather than on cheating to gain information only about his opponent's draw card.]

Throughout the night, John Finn used the five approaches listed above to exploit and beat both collusion cheaters. And on occasion, when positioned properly, John saw cards flash between the partners. He used what he saw to further improve his advantage. When the game ended at seven in the morning, the two professional players were big losers. They left the table cursing their "bad luck," never realizing that their own cheating had victimized them.

Over the next several days, John Finn noticed five trends while moving from lower-stake to higher-stake games:

1. The ratio of professional players to amateur players increased. But the proportion of out-of-town losers decreased only slightly.

2. The skill of the professional players increased.

3. The incidence of collusion cheating increased.

4. Cheating became more dominant and profitable in lowball poker (compared to highball poker). Also, professional players became more dependent on cheating in lowball draw, but were more dependent on skill in highball draw.

5. The edge odds for outside players generally decreased, especially in lowball draw. (In the highest-stake, lowball games where the best professional cheaters operate, the edge odds for even the good player could drop to unprofitable levels.)

Because the best public-game professionals and cheaters concentrated on the highest-stake, lowball games (where professional cheating was most effective and most profitable), John Finn found that he could often improve both his edge odds and his investment odds by dropping back a level or two from the highest-stake games. When he dropped to lower-stake games, competition lessened—money extraction was easier and often more profitable because of the

decreased ratio of tough professionals and cheaters to easy losers and amateurs.

In public poker, great pressure is on the dealer not to flash cards, especially in high-stake lowball. But these games offer professional collusion cheaters the greatest profit incentive to flash cards . . . so almost all skilled card flashing occurs in the high-stake lowball games. The flashing motions are usually so quick and smooth that very few outsiders ever notice or even suspect card flashing. And most professional collusion cheaters use cautious discretion and avoid flashing cards whenever they sense suspicion by others. If flashing is suspected, the colluding partners will usually switch to a less effective signaling system or move to another game.

Still most professional cheaters in Gardena use only reciprocal signaling systems because they are not knowledgeable or skilled in card flashing. And while collusion *signaling* is more commonly used among cheaters, card *flashing* is more effective and flexible because the colluding partners need no prearrangements, no agreements, no payments, no splitting of loot, no secret signals, no collusion betting, no deck stacking, and not even card flashing on the initial deal . . . they need only to flash draw cards toward their fellow professionals . . . toward any fellow professional who will tacitly return the favor. Their flashing movements are usually so quick, natural, and guiltless that few if any opponents ever see or even suspect their cheating. And even if suspected, neither their victims nor the poker club management can directly accuse them of cheating without some concrete evidence—of which there is none. Furthermore, the cheaters can have different, unplanned collusion partners for every game so no fixed set of partners can ever be pinned down and accused of collusion cheating. . . . In any case, collusion cheating of all varieties among establishment professionals is becoming increasingly common as they silently extend to one another their mutual, professional "courtesies."

But whenever a poker player cheats, the quality of

his play declines as his time, energy, and thought shifts from sound-poker actions to cheating actions. He usually becomes overconfident and careless about playing poker—his objectivity, concentration, and discipline diminish as his thinking efforts become diluted. His betting becomes distorted and usually overly aggressive. And most importantly, his hands become more readable and his actions become more predictable whenever he cheats.

The classical card-manipulation type of cheating is rare among the Gardena professionals. John encountered that kind of cheating only once, and he made a quick profit from the cheater:

In his final lowball game at Gardena, John sat to the left of a collusion cheater who had switched a card with his partner to win a pot. After the hand, John saw the cheater ditch a face card on the floor. No one noticed the missing card. On the next hand, the cheater summoned the floorman for new cards. The cards were exchanged, but the ditched card remained on the floor. Two hands later, when the same cheater was involved in another pot, John leaned under the table to pick up some money he had purposely dropped. While under the table, he quickly tore the corner off the ditched card and slipped the corner into his jacket pocket.

Several hands later, John had a powerful six low. The cheater on his right had a callable low hand. John reached into his pocket, withdrew the torn face-card corner, and positioned it at the top edge of his cards. Then while concealing his other cards, he accidentally-on-purpose flashed his hand to the cheater, who immediately spotted the "picture card" in John's hand. John bet the $20 maximum. Now positive that John was bluffing a busted lowball hand, the cheater raised. John inconspicuously dropped the torn corner beneath the table and reraised. Since they were the only two players remaining in the hand, the number of raises were unlimited. Nine times they reraised each other the maximum $20 bet. Suddenly the cheater stopped betting. He choked, became tense, pushed back his chair and looked on the floor. Dropping his hand facedown on the table, the red-faced man promptly left the game without even calling John's last $20 raise. John pulled in the $460 pot.

John Finn left Gardena knowing that he could consistently beat both the professionals and the cheaters to earn a regular income from any club game, except possibly from the highest-stake lowball games that were dominated by the best professional players and cheaters.

2. Las Vegas, Downtown (133)
B. Collusion Cheating with House Dealer— Natural-Play Technique

John Finn first encountered professional casino cheating in a large poker room of a major hotel-casino in downtown Las Vegas. The cheating involved the dealer, the casino manager, and his friend—and was unusual because management was involved.*

Initially off guard, John Finn was not suspicious of or looking for cheating patterns because (1) the game was at fairly low stakes . . . $5-10 high stud (although that was the highest-stake game in the cardroom at the time), and (2) the casino manager was not only playing, but was sitting next to the dealer. . . . The game seemed safe from cheating.

Moving clockwise from the dealer's left sat (1) the casino manager, (2) a professional poker player, who was also a friend of the manager, (3) a poor-playing tourist, (4) a regular player, (5) [an empty seat], (6) an ex-poker dealer, (7) John Finn, and (8) a woman who was an off-duty blackjack dealer.

Within an hour, newcomer John Finn was the biggest winner. He was playing aggressively, winning heavily, and badly beating the other players—especially the woman player in seat 8, who was playing poorly.

---

* Likewise, the publicized 1976 poker-cheating conspiracy in the MGM Grand Casino was unusual because management was involved (although low-level management). Normally, even the lowest level management in major casinos are unaware and innocent of professional cheating in their cardrooms.

248

The manager and several other players seemed annoyed and confused over John Finn's unorthodox and unpredictable play. After a shift change of dealers, the woman player switched to empty seat 5. Two hands later, another tourist sat in empty seat 8. He found a loose card beside John's elbow. The card apparently had slid under a napkin left by the woman player, and the dealer never noticed the missing card. (Some dealers can feel when one card is missing by the bulk and weight of the deck.) Several players glanced sharply at John as if they had discovered how he was beating them. The manager left the table and returned moments later.

Before the next hand, a floorman brought two fresh decks of cards to the dealer. John Finn became puzzled on noticing the cards were in a brown box bearing an orange-shield label from the Normandie Club in Gardena, California. Two hands later, John maneuvered into a strong position and was betting heavily. The manager beat him in a series of illogical but infallible calls and bets that did not coincide with the manager's poker style or ability. Staring straight at John Finn, he pushed the large pot to the woman player—the heavily-losing, off-duty blackjack dealer in seat 5. She took the money without appearing grateful or surprised by the manager's "generous" action.

Several hands later, John Finn again maneuvered into a strong and favorable position; he bet heavily, but once more was beaten in a similar series of illogical calls and raises by the manager's friend—the professional player. John became alert and suspicious. At first he thought his hole cards were being flashed, especially since the professional player sat low in his seat. Trying to counter that possibility, John was unsuccessful as he lost two more large pots to the manager, who again won through a series of illogical but infallible moves. John then noticed a slight crimp in his cards . . . such as might occur if a dealer had made a false cut and failed to bend out the crimp. In addition, the dealer gripped the cards in a way to facilitate false cutting. But yet John detected no evidence of card culling, discard sorting, or deck stacking. After certain hands, however, the dealer would periodically glance at face-down discards as he gathered cards for the next deal. Still he made no attempt to rearrange any cards.

John Finn lost another large hand to the manager's friend. While assuming that collusion cheating was occurring, John did not know how or when it was occurring. His counteractions not only failed, but they increased his losses. He had lost his winnings and was losing over two-hundred dollars before realizing how the cheating was occurring. The method was simple, essentially undetectable, yet devastatingly effective. After each hand, the dealer simply gathered the face-up stud cards in a natural way, making no attempt to cull, sort, or stack them . . . he merely remembered the value and order of the exposed cards. If too few cards had been exposed, he would simply glance at some face-down cards. By remembering fourteen cards* and by positioning them in an unchanged order on top of the deck through blind shuffles, false riffles, and false cuts, the dealer would know everyone's hole cards—thus, he would know everyone's exact hand right up until the seventh and final card. From this omniscient position, the dealer would then make all of the playing and betting decisions for his partner (or partners) by signaling when to fold, call, bet, or raise. The playing partner would never need to know anyone's hand, including his own; he would only need to follow the signals of the all-knowing dealer.

On losing his third large pot to the low-sitting professional, John Finn realized that he could not beat this kind of collusion cheating. He further realized that unless he could figure out how to beat this kind of cheating, his only choice was to quit the game. In order to gain some benefit . . . in order to analyze player reactions, John decided to openly declare his suspicion of cheating without revealing how much he really knew. He wanted to leave himself in the most knowledgeable and strongest position should he decide to return to the game.

* *Rapid memorization of large groups of cards can be difficult. But with practice, most players can learn to rapidly memorize fourteen or more cards (even the entire deck) by association, mnemonic, and grouping techniques. [Reference: "Perfecting Your Card Memory" by Charles Edwards, Gambler's Book Club, 1974 ($2.00).]*

After losing the pot, John placed one of his crimped hole cards on the flat palm of his hand and lifted the card to eye level. The dealer was waiting for the card as everyone watched John Finn. "Are these cards marked?" he asked knowing that except for the crimping they probably were not marked. At that moment, he yanked his hand from beneath the card. It fell in an irregular motion to the table. Everyone stared at John . . . everyone except the dealer, the manager, and the professional player—they kept glancing in different directions. John Finn picked up his chips and left. He had learned something.

An all-knowing collusion dealer greatly increases the investment odds for his playing partner while leaving the playing partner immune to errors and detection as well as immune to having his hands and intentions read by the good player. Furthermore, the cheater's cards always appear normal and above suspicion. No dramatic or improbable set-up hands occur. The cheater may fold at any time during the hand and sometimes is beaten on the last card . . . all normal in appearance and above suspicion—except for the cheater's illogical playing and betting patterns and his unnaturally improved investment and edge odds.

More importantly to the good player, this cheating system is difficult if not impossible to beat. The good player has only the seventh and final down card with which to outmaneuver and beat the cheater. (This final card is the only unknown to the signaling collusion dealer.) But by the final bet, the good player's investment odds may be so diminished by the previous four bets controlled by an infallible pair of collusion cheaters that he may be unable to win over the long term. If the cheating technique includes the dealer's knowing or peeking at the final down card or if the game is five-card or six-card stud with no final down card,* the

---

* Six-card stud with no final down card has nearly replaced seven-card stud in Reno and is beginning to replace seven-card stud in Las Vegas. Without an unknown final hole card, five-card and six-card stud give an unbeatable advantage to the dealer-player collusion cheaters.

good player then has no way to beat the dealer-player collusion cheaters—unless he can crack their signaling code and use it against the cheaters without their knowledge.

The strength of their collusion system lies in its simplicity and natural-appearing play. By contrast, the classical cheating systems involve dramatic big-hand or certain-win setups. Such setups are not necessary or even desirable. The dealer-player collusion system undramatically extracts money from its victims. This collusion system is ideal for casino poker because the house dealer* deals every hand, thus leaving the collusion partners in the best cheating position for every hand (unlike club or private poker in which each partner deals only once each round.) This constantly favorable cheating position allows and even requires a slower, more casual and natural method for extracting money from its victims. Furthermore, no player touches or cuts the cards except the house dealer, thus greatly facilitating and simplifying the cheater's card manipulations and false cuts. But in club or private poker, a nondealing player usually cuts the cards, making card manipulations and deck stacking more difficult and risky for the dealer.

C. Collusion Cheating with House Dealer— Culling and Stacking

On the following afternoon, John Finn entered a newly remodeled downtown casino that had introduced poker only a few weeks before. The card area was small and offered only $1-3 stud games. Wanting to examine low-stake casino poker, John Finn sat in the open seat on the dealer's left. Again, he did not

* *Not every house dealer cheats. In fact, most casino dealers never cheat and are probably unaware of any professional collusion cheating occurring around them. When a collusion dealer is temporarily relieved by a noncheating dealer, the collusion partner will sometimes leave, but will often continue playing while waiting for the collusion dealer to return. Agreements with and payments to collusion dealers are usually made off shift, away from the casino. Payments are by a flat rate, by a percentage of winnings, or by a combination of both.*

expect cheating in a low-stake game. He soon realized that the other four players were locals—they all knew one another and the dealer. But none of the players appeared to be professionals or good players. The players and the dealer chatted amicably among themselves. John Finn played the role of an inexperienced tourist by asking naive questions about the rules. The game was loose. On the third hand, all four players stayed until the final card. Sixteen up cards were exposed, including an exposed two pair of aces and queens. Another ace and another queen were also among the face-up cards. John Finn watched with narrowing eyes as the dealer picked up the cards— he picked up an ace and a queen and then three other cards. His hand darted back to pick up the second ace and queen and then three more random cards before grabbing the final ace and queen. He then gathered the rest of the cards.

After carefully squaring the deck, the dealer made several false riffles and a false cut before dealing. John knew what was going to happen. He did not even look at his two hole cards. His first up card was a queen. The first up card of the player on his left was an ace. The player with the ace looked twice at his hole cards and then bet a dollar. Everyone folded to John. He paused and looked at each player and then at the dealer. Everyone was watching him and waiting. The dealer seemed to be smiling. John placed the edge of his right hand firmly over the lower half of his hole cards and tore them in half. He could hear inhaling breaths . . . and then some grunts and coughs. He turned over his two torn queens and placed them faceup alongside his third queen. John Finn reached toward the hole cards of the player on his left. Again everyone inhaled. They remained motionless as he ripped the hole cards of his opponent in half and placed the two torn aces faceup alongside his opponent's third ace. Everyone was silent.

"Redeal." John ordered. The dealer quivered, glanced toward the mirrors in the ceiling, and then quickly collected the old cards—including the torn ones. He redealt from a new deck. Over the next dozen hands, John Finn aggressively manipulated his now tense and compunctious opponents. In twenty minutes, he extracted fifty dollars from the low-stake game and left. As he walked down the aisle of blackjack tables, he glanced back toward the poker area. The dealer and the players he left behind were still staring at him.

That was a mistake, John Finn thought to himself. I revealed too much about myself . . . for only fifty dollars.

3. Las Vegas, the Strip (134)
D. Collusion Cheating through Partner Crossfire Betting

That evening, John Finn entered a major casino on the Strip. The casino had a large poker area. The action was heavy. In addition to many low-stake and intermediate-stake games, several high-stake stud games ($30-60 games of high stud, low stud, and high-low stud) were in progress. John began in a $5-10 game, moved up to a $10-20 game and then graduated to a $15-30 stud game before encountering professional cheating.

The cheating was simple collusion between two professionals who signaled the strengths of their hands to each other. The cheater with the strongest hand or position would indicate to his partner when to check, bet, or raise. Their collusion entrapped or drove out players and increased or decreased the betting pace— whatever was most advantageous to the cheaters at the moment. The collusion partners increased their investment odds by either sucking in or driving out players to improve their betting position and their odds for winning. They entrapped players and then generated bets and raises to build larger pots whenever either cheater held a strong hand. They consistently bilked the tourists and transient players . . . at least until John Finn entered their game.

He promptly detected collusion cheating by the illogical patterns of checks, bets, and raises between the partners. Since the dealer was not involved with card manipulations or flashing, John easily turned the cheaters' advantages into his own advantages. He beat the cheaters because their collusion actions markedly improved his accuracy in reading their hands and intentions. When either partner held a strong hand, John read their strength more quickly and folded sooner—thus saving considerable money. Moreover, when the cheating partners revealed a strong hand and John held a stronger hand, he quietly let them suck other players into the pot. He let them build the pot for him with extra bets and raises. On the final bet, John would end his passiveness with a maximum raise.

Also, the colluding partners doubled their losses to John whenever they bet as a team into pots that John won. If they had not colluded, normally only the player holding the strongest hand (rather than both players) would have been betting into John's winning hand.

To further increase his advantage, John Finn manipulated the readable hands and intentions of these cheaters against the other unsuspecting players. But John reaped his most profitable advantages from the cheaters when they bluffed. (Most collusion cheaters are overconfident and bluff too often.) John would keep calling with a mediocre or even a poor hand as the bluffing partners kept betting aggressively to drive out players who held superior hands. John would then simply call the final bluff to win the pot. Or when necessary, he himself would bluff by stepping in with a raise after the final bet to drive out the bluffer and any remaining players to win the pot with a busted or a poor hand.

In three hours, John Finn converted the two professional cheaters from substantial winners into the biggest losers at the table and drove them from the game. With a $600 profit, he left that table to explore other games. He sat down at a table where four professional players were operating as two separate teams of colluding partners, cheating each other as well as the other three players. John assumed the role of a slightly drunk, wild-playing tourist—an ideal fish. He promptly broke the game open by playing all four cheaters against one another and against the other three players. In an hour, John ripped $900 from the game and then abruptly left the table. As he walked away, some of the players mumbled things about his "unbelievable hot streak" and his "dumb luck."

John walked over to the highest-stake game in the house—a fast-paced, $30-60 lowball, seven-stud game (razz). As he studied the action, he wondered about the unusual house rule that allowed five raises instead of the standard three. The five raises greatly increased the flexibility and advantage of collusion cheaters over their victims. John also wondered about the much higher proportion of professional players and collusion cheaters he observed in this casino. Was the management aware of their collusion cheating? Did the management establish the five-raise rule to accommodate the cheaters? Or were the professional collusion cheaters drawn to this casino because of a five-raise rule innocently established by management to increase the betting action? . . . John assumed the latter to be true.

Standing behind the dealer, John Finn continued to watch the high-stake game. For nearly an hour, he studied the two biggest winners. From their conversation and style, he knew they were professionals . . . but neither seemed to be cheating or colluding. Yet he noticed that in spite of the large pots, the dealer was not being toked (tipped) when either professional won a pot. John Finn studied the dealer more closely: Gathering the face-up cards in a routine left-to-right order, the dealer made no attempt to rearrange the cards. But as players folded, the dealer would make a pile with their face-down discards and then gather their face-up cards and flip them on top of the discard pile. He would then flip the later-round face-up cards directly on top of the discard pile while slipping dead hole or face-down cards underneath the discards. If the hand ended with fewer than fourteen up cards being exposed, the dealer would sometimes glance at several face-down discards and toss them on top of the discard pile.

Although John could not actually see any blind shuffles, false riffles, or false cuts (or verify any illogical cheating patterns*), he speculated that the dealer

---

* The alert player detects and verifies illogical cheating patterns by evaluating the actions of cheaters relative to his own

was memorizing everyone's hole card and then signaling the best moves to one or both of the professional players . . . in a similar way that the dealer was colluding with the casino manager and his friend two days earlier in the downtown casino. And, as in the downtown casino, John Finn concluded that with his current knowledge and experience, he could not beat that kind of dealer-collusion cheating. He, therefore, left the casino without playing in the $30-60 game.

E. Amateurish Collusion Cheating with Sanction of House Dealer

Traveling south on the Strip, John Finn entered another major casino with a large cardroom and observed the various poker games for thirty minutes. After considering the higher-stakes games, he sat in a medium-stake ($10-20) seven-card stud game because more of its players looked like losers. All were out-of-town gamblers and tourists, except for two women players sitting together across from John. Although their conversation revealed they were experienced local players, both women played poorly. Nevertheless, they were winning moderately because of their collusion cheating, which was crude and obvious. They blatantly showed their live hole cards to each other and then coordinated their betting to produce a collective advantage. The other players either did not notice their collusion or were too indifferent or timid to object. By quietly taking advantage of their cheating, John converted the two women from winners to losers. Wanting to play in a higher-stake game, he decided to leave as soon as he verified the dealer's knowledge and sanction of this amateurish collusion

---

playing and betting actions. But without actually playing in the game, an outside observer, even an alertly suspicious and knowledgeable observer, cannot easily see or verify the illogical patterns of a competent cheater . . . at least not in a short period of time. (That is one reason why casino management is seldom aware of professional cheating in poker . . . few people can detect competent poker cheating without actually playing against the cheaters and without knowing how to notice and evaluate illogical cheating patterns.)

cheating (although he knew the dealer himself was not involved in any collusion). . . . Such information would be helpful to John for future high-stake games in this casino.

Two hands later, John lost a fairly large pot to the women cheaters. During the hand, they had flashed their hole cards to each other. Then in a crude and visible manner, they actually swapped their final hole cards during the last round of betting, allowing one woman to win with a full house. After she turned her hole cards faceup, John Finn stuck his arm in front of the dealer when he started pushing the pot toward the woman. John then silently removed all the chips he had put into the pot. "Any objections?" he asked looking at the two women and the dealer. No one objected. John had his information. He picked up his chips and left.

F. Unbeatable Collusion Cheating through Dealer-Player Partnerships

Moving further south on the Strip, John Finn entered a casino that normally offered the highest-stake poker games in Las Vegas. For twenty minutes, he watched six players in a $100-200, seven-card stud game. He detected two professional players in the game and studied them (one was apparently losing slightly, the other was winning heavily). They were working over four out-of-town gamblers, all of whom were losing. While the two professionals did not seem to be in direct collusion with each other, when winning a pot neither player toked (tipped) the dealer. And while the dealer never glanced at face-down cards when gathering cards for the next deal, he did riffle and shuffle the cards several extra times whenever the previous hand produced fewer than twelve face-up cards. Without seeing anything else, John Finn speculated that when the dealer was riffling the cards he was also memorizing the hole cards of every player. John knew he could not beat collusion cheating involving a house dealer who knew everyone's hole cards. So he left without playing.

After three days in Las Vegas, John Finn realized

that professional collusion cheating was well en-
sconced in higher-stake casino poker. He also knew
that the alert, good player could subvert and beat
most forms of professional cheating in public poker.
And most importantly, he identified those collusion
situations in which he could not beat the professional
cheaters . . . at least not until he learned how to
crack their collusion signals quickly and without their
knowledge.

In theory, even collusion cheating involving all-
knowing house dealers can be beaten by the good player
with superior strategy and better money management.
Yet to beat such cheaters, the good player needs to
know what the cheaters know . . . he needs to know
the concealed or hole cards of every opponent through
near perfect card reading. But few if any players can
achieve such perfection. Therefore, most players, no
matter how skillful, will lose money in games dominated by well-executed, dealer-collusion cheating—with
the possible exception of a good player capable either
of near-perfect card reading or of cracking and using
the cheaters' signals.

In any case, justice prevails in poker. The honest,
good player will generally win more money from poker
than will the professional cheater. Furthermore, as a
professional player becomes increasingly dependent on
cheating for his support, he will become increasingly
entrapped in an unproductive career and a limited
future. The honest player, on the other hand, retains
his independence and freedom to seek more creative
and profitable opportunities, both inside and outside
of poker.

XXXII
SURVEY OF CLUBS AND
CASINOS (135)

Pages 263–266 survey the six commercial poker
clubs in Gardena, California. These six clubs provide

210 poker and pan tables with 1680 seats. Throughout California, 400 licensed poker clubs have a potential capacity of 14,000 tables and 112,000 seats.

Pages 267–278 survey one-hundred Nevada casinos. As shown in the summary below, about half of these casinos offer poker and provide almost 250 poker and pan tables:

Nevada Casino Survey of August, 1976

	# of Casinos Surveyed	# of Casinos Offering Poker	# of Poker and Pan Tables
Las Vegas—the Strip	39	23	126
Las Vegas—downtown	23	7	51
Reno—downtown	17	5	25
Nevada—small towns	21	11	18
Nevada—other (estimated)	–	15	25
Totals	100	61	245

The growing interest in public poker and the high profit margins possible from a well-run poker operation are causing a sudden increase in the number of poker tables in Nevada casinos. Only six months after the August 1976 survey of casino poker (pages 267–278), at least a dozen Nevada casinos have added poker to their operations, while many other casinos have expanded or improved their poker operations. For example, a sampling of changes that have occurred in Las Vegas between August 1976 and January 1977 are listed below:

- A second Hughes casino added poker to its operations—the Silver Slipper set up Gardena-type, time-collection poker games (low-stake).

- The Thunderbird changed management (now the Silverbird) and began a low-stake poker operation.

- The Aladdin moved and expanded their poker

operation from a dark corner to the prominent center of their casino.

- Johnny Moss (a well-known, public-game professional) closed his poker operation at the Flamingo Hilton and moved across the Strip to the Dunes. He shifted the Dunes poker room area into the main casino and expanded the entire poker operation. He also organized two regular, exceptionally high-stake games—a $400-800 seven-card stud game and a $1000-2000 razz (lowball stud) game—the highest-stake, regular poker games offered by any casino in Nevada. In those games, a player could win or lose $100,000 in a single sitting, especially in the fast-paced razz game.

XXXIII
THE BILLION-DOLLAR
POKER INDUSTRY (136)

Public poker is a billion-dollar-a-year industry involving 400 California card clubs and more than 60 Nevada casinos.

The public poker industry could collapse if a majority of its customers—the losers—ever fully realized the amount of money that they will lose with automatic certainty to the winners (good players, professionals, and professional cheaters) and to the casinos or card clubs (through automatic rakes or time collections). Once they clearly understand their inevitable and inescapable loser's role, some public players might quit poker to save their time and money—and to raise their self-esteem and standard of living. Others might switch to private poker to eliminate their automatic losses to the house, the professionals, and the cheaters. Still others might switch to other gambling or casino games to eliminate their losses to the good players, the professionals, and the cheaters. Or would they quit or switch? Would the losers abandon public poker in spite of knowing the inescapable multiple tributes they must pay to the house, the good players, the professionals, and the cheaters?

All other legalized games have a sound and honest operating base that mechanically extracts fixed percentages from all players. Professional players and widespread cheating do not exist for any casino game (except poker) because players cannot extract money from other players (except in poker)—and no player can extract money from the house or casino over the long term. Therefore, no true professional player can exist for any casino game (except poker) because no player can support himself by gambling against immutable odds that favor the house or casino.

The public poker industry, on the other hand, is built on a unique establishment of true professional players who make a living by applying superior poker skills, collusion cheating, or a combination of both to consistently extract money from the other public players—the losers.

Could the billion-dollar public poker industry survive if the losers clearly understood their role of being permanent milch cows to the house, to the professionals, and to the cheaters? Perhaps . . . perhaps not . . . depending on how many public players would continue to accept their role as suckers, boobs, and losers.

If the losers ever began rejecting their sucker's role by quitting public poker, the public poker industry would collapse.* Indeed, the entire gambling industry would collapse if their customers ever became imbued with rationality and self-interest and began rejecting their loser's role.

---

* *The demise of public poker could benefit good players in private games by causing an influx of losers into their private games, especially in Nevada, California, and other areas in which public poker now exists. But a disadvantageous influx of public-game professionals and cheaters into their private games could also occur.*

SURVEY OF CLUB POKER IN GARDENA, CALIFORNIA
(August, 1976)

Poker Club (Hours: 9:00 a.m. to 7:00 a.m.)	# of Tables	Draw Games*	Stakes, $	Comments
		(Games on 8/26/76, subject to change)		
Eldorado Club 15411 South Vermont Avenue Gardena, California (213) 323-2800 (Closed Thursdays)	35	High Jacks	1-2 to 10-20	More emphasis on high-stake lowball.
		Low Blind Blind raise	1-2 to 20-20	Attracts toughest lowball professionals.
		Pan 1 table going	1, 2, 3	Rough on beginners and amateurs. Good buffet.
Horseshoe Club 14305 South Vermont Avenue Gardena, California (213) 323-7520 (Closed Wednesdays)	35	High Jacks California High low	1-2 to 20-20	Most crowded. Greatest variety of poker. More higher-stake games. Highest percentage of tough professionals.
		Low Straight Blind open Blind raise Razz	2-4 to 20-20	Roughest on beginners and amateurs. Best restaurant.

263

SURVEY OF CLUB POKER IN GARDENA, CALIFORNIA
(page 2)

Poker Club (Hours: 9:00 a.m. to 7:00 a.m.)	# of Tables	Draw Games*	Stakes, $	Comments
		(Games on 8/26/76, subject to change)		
Monterey Club 13927 South Vermont Avenue Gardena, California (213) 329-7524 (Closed Tuesdays)	35	High Jacks Low Straight Blind	1-2 to 10-20 2-4 to 20-20	Same management as next-door Rainbow Club. Some of the best professionals work these two clubs.
	35	Pan 0 tables going	1, 2, 3, 4, 5	
Rainbow Club 13915 South Vermont Avenue Gardena, California (213) 323-8150 (Closed Tuesdays)		High Jacks Blind Low Straight Blind	1-2 to 15-20 2-4 to 20-20	Same comments as Monterey Club. More emphasis on pan.
		Pan 7 tables going	1, 2, 3, 4, 5	

264

SURVEY OF CLUB POKER IN GARDENA, CALIFORNIA

(page 3)

Poker Club (Hours: 9:00 a.m. to 7:00 a.m.)	# of Tables	Draw Games*	Stakes, $	Comments
		(Games on 8/26/76, subject to change)		
Normandie Club 14808 South Western Avenue Gardena, California (213) 323-2424 (Closed Thursdays)	35	High	1-2 to 10-20	Tendency toward lower stakes.
		Jacks		Fewer professionals.
		High low		Generally less crowded than other clubs.
		Low	1-2 to 10-20	
		Straight		
		Blind		Good club to learn in.
	35	Razz		
		Pan	50¢, 1, 2, 3, 5	
		5 tables going		
Gardena Club 15446 South Western Avenue Gardena, California (213) 323-7301 (Closed Wednesdays)		High	1-2 to 20-20	Same management as Horseshoe Club.
		Jacks		More relaxed atmosphere.
		Low	1-2 to 20-20	More regular players, but fewer professional players.
		Straight		
		Blind		Tendency toward lower stakes.
		Pan	50¢, 1, 2, 3, 4, 5	
		4 tables going		Best club to learn in.

- High draw is played with 52 cards. Low draw is played with 53 cards using the Joker as a wild card.
- Jacks is draw poker that requires a pair of Jacks or better to open. California is draw poker that can be opened on anything.
- High low is not a split-pot game, but is high draw with Aces to open. If the pot is not opened, the game switches to low draw.
- Blind open means the player on the dealer's left must bet. Blind raise means the player to the left of the blind opener must raise.
- Razz played in Gardena poker clubs is not lowball stud, but is a blind, lowball draw game in which the winner of the previous pot must bet double the blind bet.
- Pan (Panguingue) is not poker, but a form of rummy that requires less skill than poker. Little interest to the good players.

266

SURVEY OF CASINO POKER IN NEVADA
(August, 1976)

Casino Las Vegas—Strip (23 casinos with poker, 126 tables)	Maximum House Cut or Rake*	# of Tables	Games Played	Stakes, $**	Comments
Hacienda (702) 739-8911	15% or $3 maximum	3	7 Stud	1-3	Moderate action.
Tropicana	—	0	—	—	Dropped poker in 1975.
Paradise (702) 739-1000	25%	3	7 Stud	1-3	Gambling temporarily suspended.
King 8	—	0	—	—	No poker.
Marina (702) 739-1500	25%	6	7 Stud	1-3	Light action.
Aladdin (702) 736-0111	10% (lowest stake) 5%	4	7 Stud	1-3, 3-6 5-10	Moderate action.
Little Caesars	—	0	—	—	No poker.

* Maximum rake at some casinos is as low as $1.50-2.00 per pot (ask the cardroom manager or floorman for information on game rules and house cut). With 30-40 hands played per hour, this low rake permanently removes $45-80 per hour or about $1000-2000 per table per day. Allowing for lower cuts and slack periods, the amounts removed from a low-rake table with four or five players averages $500-1000 per 24-hour day. The average casino poker table extracts from its players an estimated $850 per day or about $300,000 per year (also see second footnote on page 214).
** The buy-in (the minimum cash value of chips a player must buy to enter the game) is usually ten times the original bet.

SURVEY OF CASINO POKER IN NEVADA
(Page 2)

Casino Las Vegas—Strip	Maximum House Cut or Rake	# of Tables	Games Played	Stakes, $	Comments
Dunes (702) 734-4110	10%, time cut for high-stake poker (e.g., $15/table/20 min.)	5	7 Stud (high, low, and split pot)	1-3, 5-10, 30-60, 50-100, 100-200	Heavy action. Be extra cautious of cheating. High percentage of professionals.
MGM Grand (702) 739-4111	10%	16	7 Stud Pan*	1-3, 3-6, 5-10 50¢, $1	Moderate action. Massive arrests for poker cheating in May 1967.
Caesars Palace (702) 734-7110	10%	11	7 Stud Pan	1-3, 3-6, 5-10 50¢, $1, $2	Moderate action.
Barbary Coast	—	—			Not yet open.
Flamingo Hilton (702) 735-8111	50%	5	7 Stud (high and low) Hold 'em	1-3, 30-60, 50-100, no limit 3-6	Light action.
Flamingo Capri	—	0	—	—	No poker.
Holiday Inn (702) 732-2411	10%	6	7 Stud	1-2, 1-3, 3-6	Moderate action.
Sands	—	0	—	—	No poker.
Castaways (702) 735-5252	10%	2	7 Stud	1-3	Light action. The only Howard Hughes casino that has poker.

*Pan (Panguingue) is a form of rummy that requires less skill than poker and offers little profit potential to the good player.

SURVEY OF CASINO POKER IN NEVADA
(Page 3)

Casino Las Vegas—Strip	Maximum House Cut or Rake	# of Tables	Games Played	Stakes, $	Comments
Desert Inn	—	0	—	—	No poker.
Frontier	—	0	—	—	No poker.
Silver Slipper	—	0	—	—	No poker.
Mr. Sy's Casino	—	0	—	—	No poker.
Stardust (702) 732-6111	20%	15	7 Stud (high and low) Hold 'em	1-3, 3-6, 15-30, 30-60, 50-100 3-12	Heavy action. High percentage of professionals. Be extra cautious of cheating. A faro game starts at 3 a.m.
Royal Las Vegas	—	0	—	—	No poker.
Royal Inn	—	0	—	—	No poker.
Landmark	—	0	—	—	No. Poker.
Hilton (800) 528-0313	10%	16	Draw (high and low) 5, 6, 7 Stud Hold 'em 7 Stud (low) Pan	3-6, 5-10 1-3, 5-10 2-4, 5-10 10-20 50¢, $2	New card room opened in August, 1976.
Silver City (702) 732-4152	10% $2 maximum	6	7 Stud (high and low) Hold 'em	1-3, 3-6 3-6, 5-10	Moderate action. High percentage of regular players.
El Morocco	—	0	—	—	No poker.

269

SURVEY OF CASINO POKER IN NEVADA
(Page 4)

Casino Las Vegas—Strip	Maximum House Cut or Rake	# of Tables	Games Played	Stakes, $	Comments
Riviera	—	0	—	—	No poker.
Westward Ho	—	0	—	—	No poker.
Slots A Fun	—	0	—	—	No poker.
Circus Circus (702) 734-0410	8%	8	6 Stud Hold 'em	2-4, 4-8 1-5	Moderate action.
Mini Price	—	0	—	—	No poker.
Thunderbird	—	0	—	—	No poker.
Sahara (702) 735-2111	10% Time cut for higher-stake poker at $1, 2, 3 /player/30 minutes	15 15	7 Stud (high, low and split) Pan	1-4, 3-6, 5-10 10-20, 20-40, 30-60 50¢, $1, 2, 5	Heavy action. Allows 5 raises. High percentage of professional players. Be extra cautious of collusion betting.
Foxy's	—	0	—	—	No poker.
Moneytree (702) 382-1188	10%	1	7 Stud	50¢-$2	Light action.
Honest John's	—	0	—	—	No poker.
Centerfold (702) 385-3168	10%	2	7 Stud Hold 'em	1-3 1-3	Light action.
Jackpot (702) 382-7472	5%	2	7 Stud Hold 'em	1-3 2-4	Moderate action.

SURVEY OF CASINO POKER IN NEVADA
(Page 5)

Casino Las Vegas—Downtown (7 casinos with poker, 51 tables)	Maximum House Cut or Rake	# of Tables	Games Played	Stakes, $	Comments
Union Plaza (702) 386-2110	25% $3 maximum	14	7 Stud (high and low) Hold 'em Pan	1-3, 3-6, 5-10 1-2, 2-6 50¢, $1, 2, 5, 10, 20	Moderate to heavy action. Casino employees and casino management often play. Be extra cautious of cheating.
Nevada Hotel	—	0	—		No poker.
Golden Gate	—	0	—		No poker.
Las Vegas Club	—	0	—		No poker.
California Hotel	—	0	—		No poker.
Coin Castle	—	0	—		No poker.
Golden Goose	—	0	—		No poker.
Club Bingo	—	0	—		No poker.
Pioneer Club	—	0	—		No poker.
Sundance West	—	0	—		No poker.
Mint (702) 385-7440	25%	9	5, 6, 7 Stud Draw (low) Hold 'em	1-2 3-5 1-2	Moderate action.

271

SURVEY OF CASINO POKER IN NEVADA

(Page 6)

Casino Las Vegas—Downtown	Maximum House Cut or Rake	# of Tables	Games Played	Stakes, $	Comments
Golden Nugget (702) 385-7111	25% $2-3 maximum	12	Hold 'em Draw (low) 7 Stud	1-2, 2-4, 3-6, 5-10, 10-20 No limit, $40 buy-in No limit, $200 buy-in 1-5 50¢-$2	Heavy action. High percentage of regular players in low-stake games. High percentage of professionals in no-limit games. House cut for no-limit games: $1 on $20, $1 on $80, $1 on $1000.
Horseshoe (702) 382-1600	—	—	—	—	No poker, except the annual World Series of Poker in May.
Fremont (702) 385-3232	10% $1.50-2.00 maximum	10	Draw (high and low) 7 Stud Pan	2-5 1-3 1	Moderate action.
Four Queens (702) 385-4011	$2-3 maximum	5	6, 7 Stud	1-2, 1-3	Moderate action.
Lady Luck	—	0	—	—	No poker.
Rendezvous	—	—	—	—	Not yet opened.
Holiday Inn	—	—	—	—	Not yet opened.

El Cortez	—	0	—	—	No poker.
Orbit	—	0	—	—	No poker.
Western	—	0	—	—	No poker.
Silver Dollar (702) 382-6921	10%	1	Draw	1-3	Light action. Straddle bets allowed (pay $1 for right to last bet).
Showboat	—	0	—	—	No poker.

273

SURVEY OF CASINO POKER IN NEVADA
(Page 7)

Casino Reno—Downtown (5 casinos with poker, 25 tables)	Maximum House Cut or Rake	# of Tables	Games Played	Stakes, $	Comments
Sundowner	—	0	—	—	No poker.
El Dorado	—	0	—	—	No poker.
Fitzgerald's	—	0	—	—	No poker.
Harold's	—	0	—	—	No poker.
Primadonna (702) 329-2251	5%	5	6 Stud Hold 'em Draw (low)	3-6 1-5, 5-10 2-10, 2-20	Moderate action.
Harrah's (702) 329-4422	5%	4	6 Stud Hold 'em Draw (low)	3-6 3-6 2-10	Moderate action.
Overland	—	0	—	—	No poker.
Palace Club (702) 329-2993	5%	5	6 Stud Hold 'em Draw (low)	3-6 1-5, 5-10 2-10, 2-20	Moderate action.
Cal Neva (702) 323-1046	5%	7	6 Stud Hold 'em Draw (low)	3-6 3-6 2-10	Moderate action.
Gold Dust	—	0	—	—	No poker.

SURVEY OF CASINO POKER IN NEVADA
(Page 8)

Casino Reno—Downtown	Maximum House Cut or Rake	# of Tables	Games Played	Stakes, $	Comments
Horseshoe (702) 329-0076	10%	4	7 Stud	2-4	Light action.
Nugget	—	0	—	—	No poker.
Silver Spur	—	0	—	—	No poker.
Moneytree	—	0	—	—	No poker.
Mapes	—	0	—	—	No poker.
Jessie Beck's	—	0	—	—	No poker.
Holiday	—	0	—	—	No poker.

Lake Tahoe

Poker is currently offered only at the Sahara-Tahoe, (702) 588-6211; the North Shore Club, (702) 831-3100; and the Hyatt (Incline Village), (702) 831-1111. Harrah's, (702) 329-4422, scheduled to start poker on the South Shore in the winter of 1977.

Carson City

Poker is offered at the Ormsby House, (702) 882-1890.

SURVEY OF CASINO POKER IN NEVADA
(Page 9)

Small-Town Nevada Casinos (11 casinos with poker, 18 tables)	Maximum House Cut or Rake	# of Tables	Games Played	Stakes, $	Comments
Beatty					
Exchange Club	—	0	—	—	No poker.
Boulder City					
The only locality in Nevada where gambling is prohibited by law.					
Goodsprings					
Town is too small and isolated to support poker or any gambling, even a slot machine.					
Hawthorne					
El Captain (702) 945-3322	10%	2	7 Stud Hold'em Draw (low)	50¢-$2, 1-5 2-5 No limit	Light action.
Joe's Tavern (702) 945-2302	5% and 10%	2	7 Stud Hold'em	50¢-$2 2-5, 5-10, no limit	Light action.
Henderson					
Eldorado (702) 564-1811	10%	1	Dealer's Choice	2-4	No action.
Rainbow Club	—	0	—	—	No poker.
Indian Springs					
The Oasis (702) 879-3356	?	1	—	—	Poker every Thursday night.

276

SURVEY OF CASINO POKER IN NEVADA
(Page 10)

Small-Town Nevada Casinos	Maximum House Cut or Rake	# of Tables	Games Played	Stakes, $	Comments
Jean					
Pop's Oasis (702) 874-1381	25%	1	7 Stud	1-3	No action.
Laughlin					
Nevada Club					Lack information.
Mesquite					
Valley Inn Club					Lack information.
North Las Vegas					
Jerry's Nugget	—	0	—	—	No poker.
Silver Nugget (702) 642-9494	8%	2	7 Stud	1-3	Light action.
Pahrump					
Calvada Inn	—	0	—	—	No poker.
Pittman					
Skyline (702) 565-9116	5%	1	Dealer's Choice $100 buy-in	No limit	No action.
Railroad Pass					
Railroad Pass (702) 293-3297	5%	1	7 Stud	1-3	Friday and Saturday, 7 p.m.

277

SURVEY OF CASINO POKER IN NEVADA
(Page 11)

Small-Town Nevada Casinos	Maximum House Cut or Rake	# of Tables	Games Played	Stakes, $	Comments
Searchlight					
El Rey	—	—	—	—	Closed.
Sandy's (702) 297-1201	25%	1	5 or 7 Stud, or Hold 'em	Determined by dealer	No action.
South Point					
Monte Carlo (702) 298-2355	?	1	Dealer's Choice		No action.
Sparks					
John Ascuaga's Nugget (702) 358-2233	5% $2 maximum	5	6 Stud Draw (low)	2-4, 3-6 2-10, 4-20	Moderate action.
Stateline					
Tower Club	—	0	—	—	No poker.
Tonopah					
Mizpah	—	—	—	—	No. poker.

Other areas of Nevada
Estimate that 15 additional casinos throughout the state regularly offer poker and provide an additional 25 poker tables.

PART SEVEN

POKER NOTES

XXXIV
POKER NOTES—1968
to 1977 (137)

This chapter compiles and summarizes some additional poker ideas and concepts accumulated during the decade since the "Advanced Concepts of Poker" were first published.

1. Who is Buying the Poker Manual? (138)
More winners than losers are buying the Manual. The most profitable advertising for the Poker Manual comes from success-oriented publications such as

Forbes, Fortune, and *The Wall Street Journal*. A scanning of letterheads from orders confirms that the majority of Poker Manual buyers are successful individuals. In other words, winners are more interested than losers in improving their performance. . . . That is logical.

The Poker Manual threatens the rationalizations of all chronic losers by exposing their self-deceptions. The Manual strips away their excuses and facades. The Manual exposes their fooleries for all to see. Many losers resentfully reject the identifications made throughout the Manual. As long as they reject the identifications, they will remain losers. . . . Yet any loser who owns the Manual can become a winner if he chooses to understand and heed the "Advanced Concepts of Poker"—which may mean quitting poker.

2. What Will Happen when All Players Own the Poker Manual? (139)

As sales of the Poker Manual expand, more and more players ask "What will happen when all poker players own the Manual?" Will the advantage gap between good players and poor players narrow? Will the potential earnings for those players applying the "Advanced Concepts of Poker" diminish?

The answer to each of the last two questions is no. The potential earnings of good players should increase as the circulation of the Poker Manual increases. This paradox is explained by examining the nature of the game, the good player, and the poor player in the following four paragraphs:

Thousands of players around the world already own the Poker Manual. By clearly identifying the total nature of poker, the Manual is gradually but permanently changing the game and its players. The "Advanced Concepts of Poker" are dispelling the myths that have always worked against the good player in his efforts to create faster-paced, higher-profit games. The Manual eliminates most objections to profitable poker innovations such as split pots, twist cards, and lowball variations by disproving the myth that such pace-increasing variations change poker from a game of skill to a game of luck. As the distribution of the Poker Manual continues, the more profitable, fast-paced games will become increasingly acceptable and easier to introduce—thus allowing the good player to increase his profits at faster rates and to higher levels.

But will the dispelling of other poker myths (e.g., the validity of luck) improve the performances of poor players and chronic losers, thus decreasing the edge odds for the good player? On the whole, the answer would be no. A few poor players (those who would work to steadily improve their game regardless of the Manual) will benefit from the Manual. But most poor players are static players who will not use the "Advanced Concepts of Poker" or do anything to improve their game. Why? Consider the nature of chronic losers: Most chronic losers have deeply entrenched habits that militate against the ingredients of good poker—*discipline, thought*, and then *control*. The "Advanced Concepts of Poker" demand intensive discipline and continuous thought—the very efforts that chronic losers seek to avoid. In fact, they build elaborate rationalizations or excuses to avoid any such discipline and thought. They play poker to "relax" their minds. Applying the "Advanced Concepts of Poker" would contradict and threaten their rationalized excuses for losing.

Exposing chronic losers to the "Advanced Concepts of Poker" is similar to exposing chronic alcoholics to the logical advantages of being sober, or to demonstrating the unbeatable casino odds to inveterate gamblers. Few chronic losers will change their self-destructive habits when confronted with their problems and errors.* Those who have read "Man's Choice" or

* *On reading the "Advanced Concepts of Poker," some chronic losers temporarily become wary of the good player and alert to some of his techniques. But in most cases, their alertness soon fades and their awareness sinks even lower because of a tranquil confidence that develops from now "knowing" the good player's techniques and from now "being savvy" to his tricks. They quickly let themselves forget that his techniques and tricks continue to extract money from them.*

"Psychuous Sex" can understand the unwillingness of most chronic losers (such as Ted O'Breen and Rocco Torri) to help themselves. . . . Most losers simply reject the identifications made by the "Advanced Concepts of Poker" and continue to be losers. And that is why the circulation of the Poker Manual will not diminish the good player's profits.

Yet any loser at any time can choose to use his mind* to make himself a winner. The mind is the instrument required to use the "Advanced Concepts of Poker". . . . Winners make themselves winners by choosing to effectively use their minds. And losers make themselves losers by choosing to default on the effective use of their minds. . . . Responsibility for the results of poker rests squarely and solely on the individual.

3. Why Does the Author Reveal the "Advanced Concepts of Poker"? (140)

In addition to the answer above (that revealing the "Advanced Concepts of Poker" will not diminish the good player's profits), the author gives two additional answers:

1. Compared to playing poker and extracting money from a limited number of players, the potential profit is much greater for selling the "Advanced Concepts of Poker" to 47,000,000 poker players domestically and to an estimated 75,000,000 poker players worldwide.

2. After writing the Manual and identifying the full nature of poker, the author stopped playing poker. Why? The author, Dr. Frank R. Wallace, provides the following answer:

   "If an income of $1,000,000 per year could be

---

* *The effective use of the mind is not related to intelligence. A genius can (and often does) default on the effective use of his mind to make himself a loser. Conversely, a man with mediocre intelligence can elect to use his mind effectively—to beat competitors of superior intelligence.*

guaranteed for the rest of my life by playing poker, but poker could be my only profession, I would decline the proposition. The third footnote in the Introduction to the Poker Manual explains why. The footnote reads: 'This Manual identifies the true nature of winning poker as a highly profitable but a time-consuming, nonproductive activity that requires bringing out the worst in one's opponents. In certain cases, therefore, poker can work against the good player's self-esteem and happiness no matter how much money he wins.' . . . The footnote is based on the premise that the source of a person's self-esteem and happiness lies in his or her own productivity.* That premise is not an opinion—it is a fact based on human nature. A person must be productive to be happy. Too few people understand the nature and source of happiness. As a result, too few people attain much happiness from their lives.

"By consuming large segments of time in nonproductive activities such as poker, an individual shrinks his or her potential for productive achievements. No amount of money generated through nonproductive activities can produce the abiding happiness and satisfaction possible through productive accomplishments. Besides in the long run, a person will almost always earn more money by pursuing productive routes rather than nonproductive or destructive routes.

"Furthermore, in poker, the good player must strive to surround himself with losers . . . with people who are constantly defaulting on the use of their minds—the opposite kind of people whom the good player could respect and enjoy. This cannot be a satisfying or rewarding way for him to consume large, irreplaceable portions of his life.

"Indeed the good player may be the biggest loser

* *Productivity is defined as adding to the sum total of mankind's material, intellectual, physiological, psychological, or aesthetic well-being. Humans earn genuine self-esteem, happiness, and satisfaction through the pursuit of productive goals.*

in the game. He may be sacrificing valuable segments of his life to the neurotic and self-destructive needs of chronic losers."

4. John Finn's Notes on Private Poker—1968 to 1977 (141)

(See pages 226–230 for John Finn's notes on *public* poker.)

1. Beat opponents through their personal weaknesses . . . through their irrationalities. Smoking, for example, is a self-destructive irrationality that represents vulnerability—a lack of
discipline and control. If an opponent constantly hurts himself through irrationalities such
as smoking (or drinking excessively, chronic
gambling, mysticism, dishonesty, or physical
unfitness), he can certainly be manipulated into
hurting himself through a much more subtle
irrationality such as poker.

2. Probe all opponents for weaknesses and irrationalities that can be manipulated in order to
extract maximum money from them.* . . . Also
identify and eliminate one's own weaknesses
and vulnerabilities (or at least guard against
losing money through one's own weaknesses).
And constantly strive to identify and correct
one's own errors—and then capitalize on cor-

---

* *An extreme example of manipulating the personal weakness of an opponent for profit occurred in the Monday night
game when a wealthy loser (Sid Bennett) quit the game because
of a succession of heavy losses. Under the facade of a joke,
John Finn persuaded the other players to cut the pots in order
to hire a prostitute to service Sid—compliments of the Monday
night game. When the deed was done, Sid laughingly returned
to the game to play with his "good old buddies" again. With
his self-esteem decreased and his "obligation" to his buddies
increased, Sid Bennett played and lost heavily for three more
years in the Monday night game. John estimated that he directly won $40,000 of the $60,000 that Sid Bennett lost over
those three years.*

rected errors (i.e., by springing trap plays on those alert opponents who had been aware of and capitalizing on one's past errors).

3. Be alert to changes. Opponents can undergo drastic changes during a poker session. In a few minutes, an opponent can change from a tight, careful player to a loose, reckless player—or vice versa. To maintain best investment odds, constantly monitor and adjust to all changes in all opponents.

4. To evaluate more accurately the quality of poker played by any individual, analyze his game in two separate segments—his statistical game and his strategical game. The statistical game is the shorter-range, card-playing and money-management aspects (the mechanical aspects) that depend on an understanding of the odds or probabilities and on discipline and control. The strategical game is the longer-range, imaginative aspect that depends on alertness and on independent and objective thinking effort. . . . The good player usually beats professional players and cheaters with a superior strategical game.

5. Concentrate on areas that provide maximum advantages. For example, in a game with weak players, concentrate more on opponents' play and do more manipulating. In a game with strong players, concentrate more on one's own play and do less manipulating (which can give away one's own hand and intentions). Better yet, avoid playing with strong players. _

6. Breathe deeply to release tensions, especially in the neck, shoulders, and buttocks. Tension-free relaxation makes a player more effective for extracting money from opponents. Also, being physically fit (especially being aerobically fit via regular roadwork) can make a significant contribution not only to one's stamina,

but to one's ability to concentrate and implement the "Advanced Concepts of Poker."

7. Use hypnotic motions to condition and train players to react favorably—to "obey commands" (e.g., to fold, bet, or raise).

8. With strong hands, open as seldom as possible (i.e., only when no one else is going to open). Usually a mistake or a disadvantage to open with a strong hand if a subsequent player would have opened. Often can profitably check strong hands from deeper positions than most players realize (e.g., can profitably check four sevens from a deeper position than two high pair). Not too serious if no one opens after checking a strong hand, since opening against all non-bettors would normally result in a small pot with few, if any, callers . . . and then they would be weak callers. The rewards of winning larger pots by check raising are greater than the risks of losing smaller, passed-out pots. But generally avoid underbetting hands—especially strong hands.

9. Opponents holding openers or good hands tend to be more alert. Players who suddenly start policing the game usually have at least openers. Players glumly staring at their cards will seldom open. Players who are tense and not looking at their cards (but are alertly looking at the pot or other players) will usually open.

10. By learning to read opponents' hands accurately, the card odds become less important as the manipulation of opponents to increase the size of pots and the number of successful bluffs becomes much more important.

11. Since neither total inconsistency nor total consistency are possible, all hands of all opponents potentially can be read by the observant good player.

12. Usually the more an opponent tries to hide the strength of his hand, the easier and more accurately can his hand be read. The player who never looks at his cards until his turn to bet is often the hardest player to read, but he leaves himself with less time to plan strategy relative to his cards.

13. Evoke give-away reactions from opponents by hesitating before betting. Pretend the pot is light and then count the chips to induce give-away reactions. Also evoke card-reading or give-away reactions with surprise moves, unusual acts, or point-blank questions. To extract useful information or reactions, ask opponents point-blank questions about their hand, their bet, or what they plan to do. . . . Be careful not to give away one's own hands or intentions by these tactics.

14. When holding winning hands, provide excuses and reasons for losers to call or bluff. Losers often look for excuses and reasons to call or bluff.

15. Reading bluffs of opponents offers major money-making opportunities. Players often reveal pat-hand bluffs by not looking at their cards long enough to assure themselves of pat hands. When bluffing, many players try to project confidence and strength with fast bets or by feigning relaxation or cheerfulness. Also, players who back out of bluffs early in a hand will often try to bluff again within the next few hands.

16. The purpose of every bluff should be to win the pot. The advertising value of a bluff is only a secondary benefit.

17. In early developed bluffs, make players believe that they must improve their hands to win. In general, cancel bluff plans if opponents do improve their hands.

18. To reinforce a loose-player image, never admit to folding good hands and generally show weak hands that win. Never reveal poker skills or the ability to read opponents' hands by betting too confidently, by folding too quickly, by giving "lessons," or by explaining strategy.

19. Fiction and movies like "The Cincinnati Kid" offer clichéd and misleading views of poker, cheating, and good players. In reality, prosperous good players are not flamboyant "big-man" types. Instead they strive to appear mundane. They are non-famous. They are Clark Kents. They are stealthy and clandestine. Moreover, they play wide-open, fast-paced games—not five-card stud. And they never need to look under tables or examine overhead lamps to protect themselves from cheating. But the stereotyped, fictionalized, and romanticized views of poker and good players provide helpful and deceptive covers for the real-life good players as they surreptitiously extract all available money from all opponents.

5. Supplements to the Poker Manual (142)

Owners of the Poker Manual can increase their understanding of their opponents by reading Frank R. Wallace's novel, "Man's Choice." In a plot free of stereotypes, a dozen poker players dramatize the nature and development of winners and losers in poker and in life.

"Psychuous Sex Guaranteed for Life" is a newer and more valuable book by Dr. Wallace that unravels the philosophical, psychological, and emotional minds of all poker players—of all human beings from impotent losers to confident winners. The half-million-word book shows how a person can switch from a loser's mind to a winner's mind.

Owners of the Poker Manual will recognize the main characters in both "Man's Choice" and "Psychuous Sex." Here is the key:

Poker Manual (nonfiction, 1968)		_Man's Choice_ (fiction, 1970)		_Psychuous Sex_ (nonfiction, 1976)
John Finn	=	John Flagg	=	John Finn, John Flagg, and Eric Flame
Sid Bennett	=	Sid Glickman	=	Sid Glickman
Ted Fehr	=	Ted O'Breen	=	Ted O'Breen
Quintin Merck	=	Quintin Marini	=	Quintin Marini
Scotty Nichols	=	Scotty Drummond	=	Scotty Drummond
Aaron Smith	=	Aaron Silver	=	Aaron Silver
Mike Bell	=	Mike Morgan	=	Mike Morgan
Charlie Holland	=	Max Pursyman	=	None
Boris Klien	=	Boris Krupp	=	Boris Krupp
None	=	Rocco Torri	=	Rocco Torri

CONCLUSION

Poker is merciless.

Poker is a game of money and deception. The consequences are always deserved. The penalties go to the weak—the rewards go to the strong. The loser dissipates his time and money. The winner earns satisfaction and money. . . . But what is the net result of poker? Is it merely time consumed and money exchanged with nothing positive produced? Is the net result a negative activity?

Poker exposes character . . . poker is a character catalyst that forces players to reality. Those who evade thinking and act on whims cannot escape the penalties. Those who use their minds and act on logic are rewarded. The results are clear and true: The lazy evader fails—he can never fake success. The thinking performer wins—he is always rewarded.

The good poker player functions rationally. He views all situations realistically. With objective thinking, he directs his actions toward winning maximum money. He pits the full use of his mind against the unwillingness of his opponents to think. . . . The good player cannot lose.

In poker, man is on his own. He must act as an individual. No one will help him. Success depends on the rational use of his mind. Success depends on exercising his positive qualities and overcoming his negative qualities. Success depends on him alone. In poker, man can function entirely for his own sake. The results are his own. The loser has made himself a loser. The winner has made himself a winner.

Poker is sheer justice.

APPENDIX A

HISTORY

The memoirs of an English actor (Joseph Crowell) touring America in 1829 described a game being played in New Orleans in which each player received five cards and made bets—then whoever held the highest combination of cards won all bets. Mr. Crowell was probably describing the earliest form of poker or its immediate predecessor, the Persian game of Âs.

The first direct reference to poker was found in Jonathan H. Green's book, "An Exposure of the Arts and Miseries of Gambling" (G. B. Zieber, Philadelphia, 1843). Green described poker games on a steamer running between New Orleans and Louisville. His book indicated that poker began in New Orleans about 1830.

Research on the evolution of poker (outlined on page 295) revealed that poker descended directly from the Persian game of Âs Nâs and not, as commonly believed, from the French game of Poque, the German game of Pochen, or the English game of Bragg. But these and other European games soon exerted their influence on the original game of poker, as shown on pages 295 and 296.

Sailors from Persia taught the French settlers in New Orleans the gambling card game, Âs, which was derived from the ancient Persian game of Âs Nâs. The Frenchmen would bet by saying, for example, "I poque for a dollar," . . . and would call by saying, "I poque against you for two dollars." Those were the betting expressions used in their game of Poque, a three-card game first played by commoners in France and then by Frenchmen in America as early as 1803. Poque was similar to Bouillotte, a card game popular with the aristocrats in France just prior to the French Revolution in 1789.

Combining the words "Âs" and "Poque," the game

became known as "Poqas." Then influenced by the German bluff game of Pochen and the southern accent, the pronunciation of "Poqas" became "Pokah." Under Yankee influence, the pronunciation finally became "Poker."

Poker moved from New Orleans by steamboat up the Mississippi and Ohio rivers. From the river towns, the game spread East by the new railroad and West by covered wagons. Between 1834 and 1837, the full fifty-two-card deck replaced the original twenty-card deck. Soon after that, the flush was introduced. During the Civil War, modifications such as open cards (stud poker), the draw, and the straight became popular. When the joker was introduced as a wild card in 1875, the European influence on poker ended. Further development of the game was essentially American.

Jackpot poker (draw poker requiring both an ante and a pair of jacks or better to open) began about 1875. Split-pot and lowball poker started around 1903. Two Missouri assemblymen (Coran and Lyles) introduced a bill to the state legislature in 1909 to control and license poker players in order to prevent "millions of dollars lost annually by incompetent and foolish persons who do not know the value of a poker hand." In 1911, California's Attorney General (Harold Sigel Webb) ruled that closed poker (draw poker) was skill and beyond anti-gambling laws . . . but open poker (stud poker) was luck and, therefore, illegal. That stimulated the development of new draw games and the use of wild cards. The variety of poker games grew steadily, particularly during the first and second world wars. In the 1960s poker variations further developed with innovations such as twists (extra draws) and qualifiers (minimum hands to win).

In 1968, Wallace's "Advanced Concepts of Poker" was first published. By 1972, the publication had become the largest-selling poker book in the world. The "Advanced Concepts of Poker" fully identified for the first time the potentially ruthless, manipulative, but highly profitable nature of poker. In addition, the characteristics of consistent winners and chronic losers were identified. Also defined and identified for the first time were the effects of the betting *pace* versus the betting *stakes* and the advantages gained by the good player when complex and fast-paced games were played. The "Advanced Concepts of Poker" clearly distinguished the financially profitable nature of poker from the financially destructive nature of gambling.

EVOLUTION OF POKER

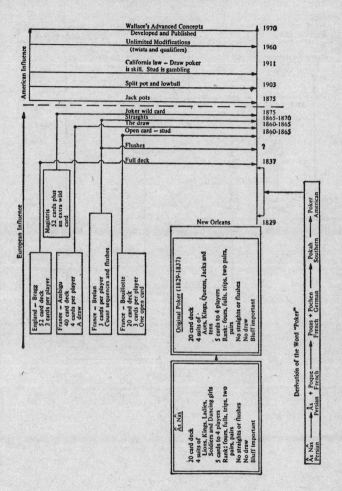

	1970
Wallace's Advanced Concepts Developed and Published	1970
Unlimited Modifications (twists and qualifiers)	1960
California law — Draw poker is skill. Stud is gambling	1911
Split pot and lowball	1903
Jack pots	1875

American Influence

Joker wild card	1875
Straights	1865-1870
The draw	1860-1865
Open card — stud	1860-1865
Flushes	?
Full deck	1837

European Influence

Magistris — 52 cards plus an extra wild card

New Orleans — 1829

England — Bragg
52 card deck
3 cards per player

France — Ambigu
40 card deck
4 cards per player
A draw

France — Brelan
3 cards per player
Count sequences and flushes

France — Bouillotte
20 card deck
3 cards per player
One open card

Original Poker (1829-1837)
20 card deck
4 suits of
Aces, Kings, Queens, Jacks and tens
5 cards to 4 players
Rank: fours, fulls, trips, two pairs, pairs
No draw
Bluff important

Âs Nâs
20 card deck
4 suits of
Lions, Kings, Ladies, Soldiers and Dancing girls
5 cards to 4 players
Rank: fours, fulls, trips, two pairs, pairs
No straights or flushes
No draw
Bluff important

Derivation of the Word "Poker"

| Âs Nâs | → | Âs | + | Poque | → | Poqas + Pochen | → | Pokah | → | Poker |
| Persian | | Persian | | French | | French German | | Southern | | American |

295

DERIVATION OF POKER

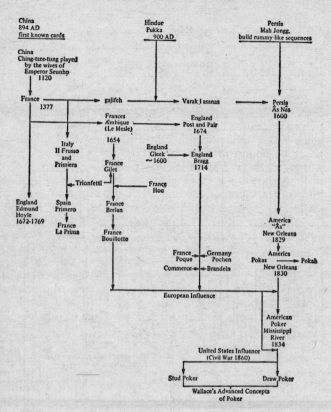

China
894 AD
first known cards

Hindue
Pukka
900 AD

Persia
Mah Jongg,
build rummy like sequences

China
Ching-tsze-tung played
by the wives of
Emperor Seunho
1120

France ────────────→ gajifeh ──────→ Varak Jasanas ──────→ Persia
1377   As Nas
                                                            1600

         Frances   England
         A'mbique ──────────→   Post and Pair
         (Le Mesle)   1674

Italy   1654   England
Il Frusso   Gleck ──→ England
and   France   ~1600   Bragg
Primiera   Gilet   1714

    └─Trionfetti─┐   France
                 France Hoc
England Spain   Brelan
Edmund   Primero
Hoyle   ↓   America
1672-1769 France France   "As"
          La Prima Bouillotte   New Orleans
                                          1829
                                                            America
                          France ←─ Germany   Pokas ──→ New Orleans ──→ Pokah
                          Poque   Pochen   1830

                       Commerce ←─ Brandeln

                       European Influence ────────────────────────────┐

                                          American
                                          Poker
                                          Mississippi
                                          River
                                          1834

                    United States Influence
                    (Civil War 1860)

              Stud Poker   Draw Poker

                    Wallace's Advanced Concepts
                    of Poker

296

APPENDIX B

BIBLIOGRAPHY

Early poker literature tried to establish firm rules for the game. Unlike other card games and being a uniquely dynamic game (a competitive money-management game rather than a routine card game), poker could never be bound in rigid rules. Continuously changing within a loose framework of traditions, poker remained a versatile, living game always subject to infinite modifications and variations—with over 150 varieties of poker described in the literature.

As early as 1674, "Cotton's Complete Gamester's" (published in England) described a card game called "Post and Pair," a predecessor to "Bragg," which in turn was a predecessor to poker with a full deck. Bragg and the art of bluffing were first described in Cotton's 1721 edition. "Poque," a French card game that influenced the development of poker, was described in the eighteenth century editions of "Acadence Universelle des Jeux."

Until 1850, there were no printed rules for poker.* Neither of the two American Hoyles then in print (George Long, New York, 1825, and G. Cowperthwait, Philadelphia, 1838) mentioned poker. The English Hoyle ("Bohn's Handbook of Games") made no reference to poker in either its 1850 or 1887 edition. But the 1850 American reprint of Bohn's book men-

* *The common reference, "Poker according to Hoyle," is curious because the English writer and lawyer, Edmund Hoyle (1672–1769), never heard of poker; he died sixty years before the game originated. Hoyle was a famous Whist player, and his original book described three card games—Whist, Piquet, and Quadrille. But his authority for card game rules grew until all card and board game rules became known as "Hoyles." Since many different "Hoyles" now exist, "Poker according to Hoyle" depends on the editor and publisher of that particular Hoyle.*

tioned poker in a tacked-on addendum. Also in 1850, "Hoyles' Games" (H. F. Anners, Philadelphia) had a brief note about poker that described a full deck, ten players (therefore, no draw) and a bonus paid for any hand of trips or better. In 1857, Thomas Frere's "Hoyle" (T. W. Story, New York) described poker without referring to a draw.

The first mention of draw poker appeared in the 1867 edition of "Hoyles" (Dick and Fitzgerald, New York). Also, that edition was the first book to mention an ante, a straight (which beat two pair, but not trips), and the straight flush (which beat four of a kind). The 1875 edition of "Hoyles" (Dick and Fitzgerald, New York) mentioned jackpot poker and the joker used as a wild card.

The first printed poker rules in England were written by General Robert E. Schenck, the United States minister to England. He introduced poker to the guests at a country house in Somersetshire. The hostess, a prominent duchess, persuaded him to write down the rules. In 1872, the duchess privately printed these rules for her court. The game caught Queen Victoria's fancy, and the popularity of poker spread through Great Britain. Poker in England soon became known as "Schenck poker."

In 1875, a description of poker appeared in Cavendish's "Round Games of Cards" (De La Rue & Co.).

After 1875, books about poker appeared regularly in America, England, and Europe. Data on all poker books (whose locations and dates of publication are known) published in the one-hundred years between 1875 and 1975 have been tabulated on the opposite page.

Number of Books	%	Country Where Published
93	72.6	United States
22	17.2	England
8	6.2	France
2	1.6	Italy
1	0.8	Germany
1	0.8	Holland
1	0.8	India
———	———	(for 1875–1965)
128	100.0	

Years (in 10-year intervals)	Number of Poker Books Published
Up to 1875	2
1876–1885	13
1886–1895	18
1896–1905	13
1906–1915	11
1916–1925	9
1926–1935	9
1936–1945	4
1946–1955	11
1956–1965	17
1966–1975	20
	———
	127

[Note: From 1976 to March 1977 an additional 5 poker books were published.]

Since the original publication of Frank R. Wallace's "Advanced Concepts of Poker" in 1968, the Manual has dominated the poker-book market with ten printings and three revised editions. About twenty other poker books were published from 1968 to 1977, but none have yet sold beyond their first printing. Brief reviews of all poker books published since 1968 are given in the Addendum Bibliography on pages 312–315.

For the 1977 edition of Wallace's "Advanced Con-

cepts of Poker," each of the 120 original concepts were
revised and 22 new concepts covering professional
poker, cheating, casino poker and public club poker
were added.

A bibliography of over 150 poker books is tabulated below:

Books on Poker in The Library of Congress

Catalog Number	Subject Heading "Poker" Library of Congress Card Information (verbatim)
1. GV1251 A15	Abbott, Jack. A treatise on Jack pot poker, with the game of sancho pedro, when played for stakes. New Orleans, Clark & Hofeline, printers, 1881. 64 pages
2. GV1258 A43	Allen, George W. Poker rules in rhyme, with chances to improve the hand by drawing. St. Louis, Mo., 1895. 74 pages
3. GV1251 B6 (other editions)	Blackbridge, John. The complete poker player. A practical guidebook to the American national game: containing mathematical and experimental analysis of the probabilities at draw poker. New York, Dick & Fitzgerald, 1880. 142 pages
4. GV1253 B8 1916 (other editions)	Brown, Garrett. The autocrat of the poker table, or, How to play the game to win. 3rd ed., Boston, R.G. Badger, 1916. 105 pages
5. GV1251 C15	Cady, Alice Howard. Poker: the modern game. With passing description of its origin. New York, American sports publishing company, 1895. 37 pages
6. GV1251 C65	Coffin, George Sturgis. Fortune poker; a world-wide roundup of the

traditional American game. Complete with new laws according to Hoyle. With a forward by Ely Culbertson, Philadelphia, D. McKay Co., 1949. 198 pages

7. GV1251
C67

Coffin, George Sturgis. The official laws of poker. Baltimore, Ottenheimer, 1956. 64 pages

8. GV1251
C68

Coffin, George Sturgis. Pocket guide to the play of poker. Baltimore, Ottenheimer, 1956. 64 pages

9. GV1251
C95

Curtis, David A. The science of draw poker; a treatise comprising the analysis of principles, calculation of chances, codification of rules, study of situations, glossary of poker terms necessary to a complete understanding of the great American game. New York, D. A. Curtis, 1901. 216 pages

10. GV1253
D62

Dowling, Allen Nicholas. Confessions of a poker player by Jack King (pseud.) New York, I. Washburn, Inc., 1940. 209 pages

11. GV1253
D62

Dowling, Allen Nicholas. Under the round table by Jack King (pseud.) Philadelphia, Dorrance, 1960. 219 pages

12. ?

Edel, Edmund. Poker ein spieler— roman. Charlottenburg, E. Beyer, 1912. 176 pages

13. GV1253
E26

Edwards, Eugene. Jack pots; stories of the great American game. With over fifty original pen and ink illustra-

Catalog Number	
	tions. Chicago, Jamieson-Higgins Co., 1900. 342 pages
14. GV1251 F5	Fisher, George Henry. How to win at stud poker . . . instruction for the novice, principles of strategy, problem hands, hand valuation, card probabilities, complete set of rules, history of the game, etc. Los Angeles, The Stud Poker Press, 1933. 111 pages
15. GV1251 F63	Florence, William Jermyn. The gentleman's handbook on poker. New York, London, G. Routledge Sons, Ltd., 1892. 195 pages
16. GV1251	Foster, Robert Frederick. Practical poker. New York, Brentano's 1905. 253 pages
17. GV1251 G47	Gilkie, Robert J. Experimental drawing at poker from five thousand hands. Dorchester, Mass., 1886. 13 pages
18. GV1251 G5	Girardet, Philippe. Philosophie et mathematique du poker. Paris, M. Senac, 1929. 160 pages
19. GV1251 G77 (other editions)	Gray, E. Archer. Hints on poker. Washington, D.C., 1886. 16 pages
20. GV1251 H2	Hardison, Theodore. Poker; a work exposing the various methods of shuffling up hands, as well as other ways of cheating that are resorted to by professional gamblers, also embracing the cardinal principles by which every sleight-of-hand trick known with

cards may be played. St. Louis, Hardison Publishing Co., 1914. 120 pages

21. GV1251
H4

Heineman, Walter Raleigh. Draw poker; a compilation of rules governing the game of "Jack pots," by Jack Pot (pseud.). New York, Chrisholm Printing Co., 1923. 48 pages

22. GV1251
H52
(other editions)

Henry, R. J. Poker boiled down . . . the latest authentic rules . . . on the great national game . . . 1st edition. Boston, Massachusetts, Tourist Publishing Company, 1890. 13 pages

23. GV1233
H6
(temporary
entry)

History and anecdotes of card games (especially poker). 43 cuttings from newspapers, etc. . . . bibliographical notes in ms . . . Gift of Prof. Brander Matthews

24. GV1251
J2
1947
(other editions)

Jacoby, Oswald. Oswald Jacoby on poker, with a forward by Grantland Rice, and an introduction by William E. McKenney. Rev. ed. Garden City, New York, Doubleday & Company, Inc., 1947. 175 pages

25. GV1251
J22

Jacoby, Oswald. Winning poker. New York, Permabooks, 1949. 189 pages

26. GV1251
K59

Keller, John William. The game of draw poker. Including the treatise by R. C. Schenck and rules for the new game of progressive poker . . . New York, White, Stokes & Allen, 1887. 84 pages

27. GV1251
M15

MacKenzie, Collins. Jack pots. A collection of poker stories. By A. Pair (pseud.). Chicago, the Illustrated Publishing Co., 1887. 160 pages.

28. GV1251
    P32

Patton, F. Jarvis. How to win at draw poker. Showing all the chances of the game. New York, Dick & Fitzgerald, 1896. 45 pages.

29. GV1253
    P6
    (Office)

Unknown. Poker as it was played in Deadwood in the fifties. Palo Alto, California, Wheatstalk Press, 1928. 5 pages (A reprint from an article in Hutching's California magazine in August, 1858-Vol. III, pg. 85)

30. GV1253
    P77
    (Houdini
    Collection)
    (other editions)

Poker; how to play it. A sketch of the great American game with its laws and rules, and some of its amusing incidents. By one of its victims. London, Griffith & Farran, 1882. 109 pages

31. QA/273
    P96

Proctor, Richard Anthony. Chance and luck: a discussion of the laws of luck, coincidences, wagers, lotteries, and fallacies of gambling; with notes on poker and martingales. London, Longmans, Green & Co., 1887. 263 pages

32. GV1251
    R3
    (other editions)

Radner, Sidney H. The key to playing poker and winning. Owing Mills, Maryland, Ottenheimer Publishers, 1964. 189 pages

33. GV1251
    R37

Reese, Terence. Secrets of modern poker. New York, Sterling Publishing Co., 1964. 148 pages

Catalog Number	Library of Congress Card Information (verbatim)
34. GV1251 R4	Renaudet, G. Le poker; regles completes et commentaires, L'art de gagner au poker; poker a 52 cartes; a 48, 44, 40, 36 et 32 cartes; freeze out; la partie a la cave; calud des probabilities; le blugg, physiologie du jeu. Paris, S. Bornemann, 1922. 31 pages
35. GV1253 R47	Rhoades, William Morston. Poker, smoke, and other things; fun and pictures. Rules of poker, recipes, toasts, mixed drinks. Chicago, the Reilly & Britton Co., 1907. 69 pages
36. BF21 A7 (other editions)	Riddle, Ethel Maris. Aggressive behavior in a small social group; bluffing, risking and the desire to beat . . . studied by the use of a poker game as an experimental technique. New York, 1925. 196 pages (Also published as a Ph.D. thesis in psychology, Columbia University)
37. GV1251 R65	Rottenberg, Irving. Friday night poker, or, Penny poker to millions, by Irv Roddy (pseud.). New York, Simon & Schuster, 1961. 222 pages.
38. GV1251 S32	Schenick, Robert Cummings. Rules for playing poker. Brooklyn, New York, Private printing, 1880. 17 pages (1st edition, 1872)
39. GV1251 S32 1881 (Toner Collection, Office)	Schenick, Robert Cummings. Draw poker. Published for the trade, 1880. 8 pages

40. GV1251
   S5

Smith, Russell A. Poker to win. El Paso, Texas, 1925. 110 pages

41. GV1251
   S68

Steig, Irwin. Common sense in poker. New York, Cornerstone Library, 1963. 188 pages

42. GV1251
   7

Steig, Irwin. Poker for fun and profit. New York, McDowell, Obolensky, 1959. 181 pages

43. GV1251
   T2

Talk of Uncle George (pseud.) to his nephew about draw poker. Containing valuable suggestions in connection with this great American game. New York, Dick & Fitzgerald, 1883. 50 pages

44. GV1251
   U55

United States Playing Card Co. Poker; official rules and suggestions, endorsed by Association of American playing card manufacturers. Cincinnati, Ohio, The United States Playing Card Company, 1941. 64 pages

45. GV1251
   W3

Walter & Philip (pseud.) Il poker familiare, come si giuoca in Italia. 2nd edition, Milano, U. Hoepli, 1945. 81 pages

46. GV1253
   W4

Webster, Harold Tucker. Webster's poker book glorifying America's favorite game; a handy volume for the hearthside consisting of fifty portraits; informative and diverting text on the joys, rules, love and pitfalls of poker; sideline suggestions and interpolations; authoritative data on the history and technique of poker; including hints from Hoyle and a forward by George

Ade; together with a compartment containing a set of poker chips and a pad of I.O.U. forms ready for instant use. New York, Simon & Schuster, 1925. 126 pages

47. GV1251
W5
1944
(other editions)

Wickstead, James M. How to win at stud poker. Louisville, Kentucky, Stud Poker Publishing Co., 1944. 115 pages

48. GV1251
W55

Winterblossom, Henry T. The game of draw poker, mathematically illustrated; being a complete treatise of the game, giving the prospective value of each hand before and after the draw, and the true method of discarding and drawing with a thorough analysis and insight of the game as played at the present day by gentlemen. New York, W. H. Murphy, 1875. 72 pages

49. GV1251
X3

Xavier, Francois. Le poker, sa technique, sa psychologie, suivi d'une etude sur le stud poker. Paris, B. Grasset, 1955. 222 pages

50. GV1251
Y3

Yardley, Herbert Osborn. The education of a poker player, including where and how one learns to win. New York, Simon & Schuster, 1957. 129 pages

51. GV1243
C8

Culbertson, Ely. Morehead, Albert H. and Goeffrey, Matt Smith. Culbertson's Hoyle: the new encyclopedia of games, with official rules. New York, Graystone Press, 1950. 656 pages

52 Reference

Encyclopaedia Britannica. Poker. Volume 10, pg. 128, Chicago, William Benton, 1965. 4 pages

53. GV1251
F79

Fox, Richard K. Poker, how to win, together with the official rules. New York 1905. 90 pages

54. GV1243
F85

Frey, Richard L., ed. The new complete Hoyle: an encyclopedia of rules, procedures, manners, and strategy of games played with cards, dice, counters, boards, words, and numbers. Philadelphia, D. McKay Co., 1947. 740 pages

55. GV1239
J3

Jacoby, O., et al. The fireside book of cards. New York, Simon & Schuster, 1957. 364 pages

56. PZ3
L628P

Lillard, John F. B., ed. Poker stories, as told by statesmen, soldiers, lawyers, commercial travelers, bankers, actors, editors, millionaires, members of the Ananias club and the talent, embracing the most remarkable games, 1845-95. New York, F. P. Harper, 1896. 251 pages

57. GV1243
D8

Ostrow, A. A. The complete card player. New York, McGraw-Hill Book Company, Inc., 1945. 771 pages

58. GV1291
P6

Poker-bridge; een nieuw kaartspel. Amsterdam, A. J. G. Strengholt, 1954. 32 pages

59. AP2
W64

Poker chips, a monthly magazine devoted to stories of the great American game. New York, F. Tousey, June-

Nov. 1896. 243 pages (continued as the White Elephant magazine)

60. GV1247   Scarne, John. Scarne on cards. Includ-
    S37   ing a photographic section on cheat-
                 ing at cards. Revised, New York,
                 Crown Publishers, 1965. 435 pages

[Note: The Library of Congress does not catalog books about poker under the subject of "Gambling." The 375 books listed under "Gambling" include books on blackjack, boule, cards (nonpoker), cardsharping, craps, fero, horse-race betting, parimutuel betting, probabilities, raffles, roulette, speculation, trent-et-quarante, and wagers . . . but none on poker. Apparently, the Library of Congress does not consider (classify) poker as gambling.]

Seventy-two other poker books not found in the Library of Congress are listed below:

61. Allan, L., The Laws of Poker, Mudie, 1929, 41 pages.
62. Ankeny, Nesmith, Scientific Poker, Harper, 1967.
63. Ante—I Raise You Ten, Jamieson-Higgans, ($0.75).
64. Arnold, F. and Johnston, H., Poker, Routledge, 1929, (3s 6d).
65. Bergholt, E. G. B., Poker, De La Rue, (9d).
66. Browning, H. S., Royal Auction Bridge and Poker, Routledge, 1920, 64 pages.
67. Carcini, Nick, A Course in Professional Poker Playing, Memphis, Tennessee, Edall Publishing Co., Box 12403, 1966 ($1.49), 84 pages.
68. Carleton, Henry Guy, Thompson Street Poker Club, Dick & Fitzgerald, 1888, ($0.25).
69. Coffin, G. S., Poker Game Complete, Faber and Faber, 1950, (12s 6d).
70. Coffin, G.S., Complete Poker Game, Wehman, ($3.95).
71. Crafton, A., Poker: Its Laws and Principles, Wyeil, 1915, ($1.00).
72. Crawford, John R., How to be a Consistent Winner in Most Popular Card Games, New York, Doubleday, 1953, ($2.95), 256 pages.

73. Curtis, D. H., Queer Luck, New York, Brentanos, 1900.

74. Dalton, W., Pocket Guide to Poker Patience, De La Rue, 1909.

75. Davis, A. D., An Analysis of Five and Seven Card Poker, Philadelphia, 1959, 101 pages, (Mimeographed Master's Thesis).

76. Debebian, D., Game of Poker, New York 1889, 25 pages.

77. Decisions on Moot Points of Draw Poker, New York.

78. Diehl, Charles Vidol, Poker Patience and Progressive Poker Patience, London, The Advanced Publishing Co., 1909, 16 pages.

79. Draw Poker, Dick, ($0.15).

80. Draw Poker, Fitzgerald Publishing Corporation ($0.15).

81. Draw Poker, London, 1884, 63 pages.

82. Draw Poker and Spoil Five, London, Routledge & Sons, 1884.

83. Ellinger, M., Poker, Faber, 1934.

84. Erdnase, S. W., The Expert at the Card Table, London, Stationers' Hall, 1902.

85. Fisher, G. H., Stud Poker Blue Book, Los Angeles, Stud Poker Press, 1934, ($1.00).

86. Football Poker, Brentano's, ($0.25).

87. Foster, J. H., Traite du Jeu de Poker, Paris, 1889, 73 pages.

88. Foster, R. F., Pocket Laws of Poker, De La Rue, 1910.

89. Gilbert, Kenneth, Alaskan Poker Stories, Seattle, R. D. Seal, 1958, 46 pages.

90. Guerndale, Richard, Draw Poker Without a Master, Dillingham, ($0.25).

91. Guerndale, Richard, The Poker Book, London, I. Upcott Gill, 1889, 80 pages.

92. Habeythe, Jeu de Poker, Paris, 1886.

93. Hirst, E. deF., Poker as Played by Skilled Professional Gamblers, 2nd ed., 1902, ($1.00).

94. Hoffman, W., Draw Poker, the Standard Game, Dutton, 1913, ($1.00).

95. How to Play Poker, Wehman Bros., ($0.10).

96. How to Win at Draw Poker, Dick, ($0.25).

97. How to Win at Draw Poker, Westbrook, ($0.25).

98. Hoyle (pseud.), How to Play Poker, Ogilvie, 1916, ($0.10).

99. Jackpot, Poker-Patience, International Card Co., 1909, 20 pages.

100. Lamenti, C. E., Il Poker, Milano, A. Corticelli, 1929, 59 pages.

101. La Shelle, Kirbe, Poker Rubaiyat, Phoenix, Arizona, Bunder Log Press, 1903, 28 pages.

102. Laugher, A. B., Poker, C. Goodall, 1913, 28 pages.

103. Laugher, A. B., Poker, London, 1889, 28 pages.

104. Laun, Jeu de Poker, Paris, Watilliaux, 1897.

105. Major, The Poker Primer, New York 1886, 31 pages.

106. Matthews, J. B., Poker Talk (p. 187 of "Penn and Ink"), New York, Longmans, Green & Co., 1888.

107. Meehan, C. H. W., The Rules for Playing Draw Poker (Game of Euchre), Philadelphia, T. B. Peterson, 1877.

108. Morehead, Albert Hodges, New Complete Hoyle, Toronto, Doubleday, 1956, ($4.75), 740 pages.

109. Morehead, Albert Hodges, My Secret: How to Play Winning Poker, Los Angeles, W. R. Mathews and Sons, 1957.

110. Morehead, Albert Hodges, The Complete Guide to Winning Poker, New York, Simon and Schuster, 1967.

111. Moss, John (pseud. for Jack Potter), How to Win at Poker, Doubleday, 1955, (pap. $1.50).

112. Mott, Street Poker Club, Dick, ($0.25).

113. Nabot, Jeu de Poker, Paris, Henri Gautier, 1893, (contains many probability tables).

114. Pardon, C. F. (Raudon Crawley), Poker, London, Chas. Goodhall & Sons, 1889.

115. Percy, Alfred, Poker: Its Laws and Practice, Allahabad, India, Pioneer Press, 1879.

116. Phillips, Hubert, Profitable Poker, Arco Publications, 1960, (18s).

117. Philpots, E. P., A Treatise on Poker, London, 1904, 93 pages.

118. Poker: The Nation's Most Fascinating Card Game, Cincinnati, United States Playing Card Company, 1950.

119. Poker, Heines Publishing Co., Inc., Minneapolis, Minnesota, 33 pages.

120. Poker, How to Play It, London, 1882, 109 pages.

121. Poker Primer, Platt & Nourse, ($0.25).

122. Potter, Jack, How to Win at Poker, Garden City Books, 1955, (pap. $1.00).

123. Primer, Excelsior, ($0.10).

124. Proctor, R. A., Poker Principles and Chance Laws, New York, Dick & Fitzgerald, 1883.

125. Rander, S. H., How to Play Poker and Win, (Key), Assoc. Booksellers, 1965, (pap. $1.00).

126. Reese, Terence and Watkins, Anthony, Poker Game of Skill, Wehman, 1962, ($3.95).

127. Reynolds, A., Poker Probabilities Calculated, Sheffield, 1901, 40 pages.

128. Rules of Poker, London, 1882, 16 pages.

129. Sinclair, E., Poker, Arco Publications, (18s) Ambassador, 1964, ($3.75).

130. Strong, Julian, How to Play Poker, London, New York, W. Foulsham, 1928, 61 pages.

131. "Templar," Poker Manual, Warne, ($1.25).

132. Welsh, Charles, Poker: How to Play It, London, Griffith & Farren, 1882.

133. Virt, L. H., Traite Complet du Jeu de Poker, Paris, 1913, (contains only rules).

ADDENDUM BIBLIOGRAPHY
OF POKER BOOKS PUBLISHED SINCE 1968
(through December 1977)

134. Anno, James N., An Encyclopedia of Draw Poker, New York, Exposition, 1973, ($10.00). Primarily a book showing the mathematical calculations of various poker odds and probabilities. Some errors. Not much value. Interesting history of card playing and poker. 159 pages.

135. Anthony, Ross, Get Rich Playing Poker, Birmingham, Alabama, RAM Enterprises, 1975, ($2.25). A valuable booklet. Author is objective and honest. Betting and card-playing advice is elementary, but sound for low-stake games with poor players. Excellent information on running a profitable house game. No strategy information. 44 pages.

136. Castle J. L., How Not to Lose at Poker, Boston, Little, Brown and Company, 1970, ($4.50). Perpetuates many of the erroneous clichés about poker. Goes deep into probability mathematics. Little value. 150 pages.

137. Dangel, Philip N., Poker Poker, Las Vegas, Nevada, Gambler's Book Club, 1977, ($4.95). Highly technical. Little new information. Limited value. 286 pages.

138. Dowling, Allan ("Jack King"), Play Winning Poker, Las Vegas, Nevada, Gambler's Book Club, 1974, ($2.00). A good history of poker. Some interesting observations about opponents and about table-stake games. But filled with fallacies and invalid clichés about poker. 64 pages.

139. Fox, John, Play Poker, Quit Work, and Sleep Till Noon, Seal Beach, California, Bacchus Press, 1977, ($14.95). Poorly written. Borrows, uses and distorts some of the "Advanced Concepts of Poker". But does contain some original and useful ideas about draw poker in public card clubs. Worthwhile for serious or professional poker players who can sort out the valid information from the misleading material. 394 pages.

140. Gibson, Walter, Poker is the Name of the Game, New York, Barnes & Noble, 1974, ($1.75). Instructions and "rules" for 18 basic variations of poker. Gives some examples of various plays. Little new or useful information. Some erroneous concepts. 143 pages.

141. Jacoby, Oswald, Penny-Ante Poker, New York, Doubleday, 1977, ($2.95). Concentrates on off-beat poker games such as baseball, pass-the-garbage. Available in early 1978.

142. Livingston, A. D., Poker Strategy and Winning Play, Philadelphia, J. B. Lippincott Company, 1971, ($5.95). Little new information except for two tables of odds for widow games such as hold me (hold 'em). Heavy on calculations of odds and descriptions of stud, lowball, and widow variations of poker. 227 pages.

143. Preston, Thomas Austin ("Amarillo Slim"), Play Poker to Win, New York, Grosset & Dunlap, 1973, ($6.95). Interesting book of poker anecdotes with some useful information about hold 'em and lowball poker. A worthwhile book to read. 175 pages.

144. Rubins, J., Win at Poker, New York, Funk & Wagnalls, 1968, ($1.50, paperback). Well written, but

based on many of the fallacious concepts advanced by other poker books. 218 pages.

145. Sklansky, David, Hold 'em Poker, Las Vegas, Nevada, Gambler's Book Club, 1976, ($2.00). The only book that contains detailed information about playing hold 'em poker. Some errors. 64 pages.

146. Smith, Al, Poker to Win, Las Vegas, Nevada, Gambler's Book Club, 1975, ($2.00). Good outline of various methods used in cheating at poker. But holds many erroneous and misguided views about poker. 64 pages.

147. Spanier, David, Total Poker, New York, Simon and Schuster, 1977, ($8.95). Contains history, stories and anecdotes about poker. A dozen pages devoted to Wallace's "Advanced Concepts of Poker." Not a how-to-play book, but interesting reading for poker players. 255 pages.

148. Taetazsch, L., Winning Methods of Bluffing and Betting in Poker, New York, Drake Publishers, 1976 ($8.95). Some value. Attempts to use some of the "Advanced Concepts of Poker." 138 pages.

149. Thackrey, Ted, Jr., Dealer's Choice, Chicago, Henry Regnery Co., 1971, ($5.95). Fairly well organized. Elementary ideas about poker strategy. Some ideas are basically correct; others are in error. 212 pages.

150. Wagner, W., To Gamble or Not to Gamble, New York, World Publishing, 1972, ($9.95). Many interesting anecdotes and facts about casino, club, and private poker games. Spoiled by unsubstantiated assertions and false conclusions. 370 pages.

151. Wallace, F. R., Poker, A Guaranteed Income for Life by using the Advanced Concepts of Poker, New York, Crown Publishers, Inc., 1968, revised in 1972 and 1976. Expanded in 1977, ($10.00). 246 pages.

152. Wallace, F. R., Win $130,000 in Neighborhood Poker, to be published in 1978.

153. Wallace, F. R., The Great American Poker Player, to be published in 1978.

154. Wallace F. R., and Cortine, Max, Neocheating, to be published in 1978.

155. Winfield, T. D., If you Are Going to Play Poker . . . Win, McLean, Virginia, The Kingsway Company, 1971, ($2.00, paperback). Some practical

information, but laced with many fallacious clichés. 93 pages.

156. Zachary, Hugh, Wild-Card Poker, Brattleboro, Vermont, Stephen Greene Press, 1975, ($7.95). Recognizes the added skill needed to play wild-card games. Little new information. Contains erroneous concepts. 118 pages.

157. Zadeh, Norman, Winning Poker Systems, Englewood Cliffs, New Jersey, Prentice-Hall, 1974, ($8.95). Heavily oriented around a mathematical approach. Interesting and moderately useful, but not valid as a total or even as an important approach to poker. 208 pages.

Notes: 1. The most complete source of poker and gambling books, both in and out of print, is Gambler's Book Club, 630 South 11th Street, Dept. PB, Las Vegas, Nevada 89101. Write for free catalog listing over 700 titles on poker and gambling.
　　　　2. The University of Nevada (Las Vegas) Library has a special collection of nearly 2000 gaming books, including more than 83 different titles on poker. A bibliography of these gaming books is available from the University.

APPENDIX C

GLOSSARY

Over a thousand words and phrases used in poker literature and heard in poker games are defined below.

Action — The betting.

Action Spot — The table area where the betting is occurring.

Active Player — A player competing for a pot.

Add-them-up Lowball — Draw poker where the hand with the lowest point total wins.

"Advanced Concepts of Poker" — The concepts used by the good poker player to win maximum money from opponents.

Advertise — To have a bluff called in order to mislead opponents.

A-game — The highest stake game in the house.

Age — First position to the left of the dealer. (A, Able, or Edge).

Alien Card — A card not belonging to the deck in play.

Alive Card — See Live Card.

All Blue, or All Pink — A flush.

All the Way — Cincinnati with a progressive bet.

Alternate Straight — A sequence of every other card, such as 2, 4, 6, 8, 10. (Dutch Straight, Skipper, Skip Straight).

Ambigue — A French card game that influenced the draw variation of poker.

American Brag — A game where the raiser shows the first caller his hand and the worst hand folds.

Anaconda — A seven-card game with bets made on five rolled-up cards.

Announce—To declare high, low, or the moon in high-low poker.

Announced Bet — A verbal bet made by a player before putting his money in the pot.

Ante — Money put in the pot before dealing.

A Priori Odds — The probability that an event will occur.

Arkansas Flush — A four flush.

Around the Corner Straight — A sequence running from the highest to the lowest values, such as Q, K, A, 2, 3.

Âs Nâs — A Persian card game from which poker was directly derived.

Assigned Bettor — The player who bets first.

Australian Poker — Draw

316

poker with a blind opening.

Automatic Bluff — A lowball situation that always requires a bluff.

Back-in — To win by default or unexpectedly.

Backer — A nonplayer who finances an active player.

Backraise — A reraise. To make a minimum raise to avoid a larger raise.

Back-to-back — A pair on the first two cards dealt in stud. (Backed Up).

Bait — A small bet that encourages a raise.

Bank — Where the money from purchased chips is kept.

Banker — The person responsible for selling and cashing chips.

Bank Night — High-low five-card stud with two twists.

Barn — A full house.

Baseball — A stud game involving nines and threes as wild cards.

Beans — Chips.

Bear — A tight player.

Beat the Board (Table) — To have a hand better than all others showing.

Beat Your Neighbor — A five-card game that requires each player in turn to expose his cards until his hand beats the board.

Bedsprings — Similar to Cincinnati except ten cards are dealt faceup for use in everyone's hand.

Belly Hit — When a draw fills an inside straight. (Gut Shot).

Belly Strippers — Cards with slightly trimmed edges that taper from a wider center to the ends. (Humps).

Best Flush — A game in which only flushes win the pot.

Bet — Money wagered and put into the pot.

Bet Into — To bet before another player who apparently has a better hand.

Bet or Get — A rule that one must either bet or fold with no checking allowed. (Bet or Drop, Passout).

Bet the Limit — To bet the maximum amount allowed.

Bet the Pot — To bet an amount equal to the pot.

Bet the Raise — The maximum bet being twice that of the previous bet or raise.

Betting Interval — The period from the first bet to the last call in any given round.

Betting Pace — The degree, extent, and aggressiveness of bets and raises.

Betting Stakes — The dollar limits of all bets and raises permitted.

Betting Ratios — The differences in maximum bets allowed with each round of betting.

Betty Hutton — Seven-card stud with nines and fives wild.

Bicycle — A straight to the five . . . A, 2, 3, 4, 5. (Wheel).

Bid — To declare for high or low in split-pot poker.

Big Bill — A hundred dollars or a thousand dollars.

Big Bobtail — A four-card straight flush.

Big Cat — Five unpaired cards from the king to the eight.

Big Dog — Five unpaired cards from the ace to the nine.

Big Squeeze — Six-card, high-low stud with one twist.

Big Tiger — See Big Cat.

Bill — A dollar or a hundred dollars.

Bird Dog — One who gets players for a game.

Blaze — A five-card hand containing five picture cards.

Blaze Full — A full house in picture cards.

Bleed — To slowly bleed money from a game or a player.

Bleeder — A tight, winning player.

Blind — A bet before the deal by the Age or by the first player to the dealer's left.

Blind Bet — To bet before looking at one's hand.

Blind Low — Five-card stud bet blind all the way to the last bet.

Blind Open — An opening bet made without looking at one's cards.

Blind Shuffle — A cheater's shuffle used to stack cards or to leave stacked cards undisturbed after shuffling. (False Shuffle).

Blind Tiger — Draw poker with a blind open and a blind raise. (Open Blind and Straddle).

Block System — An ante,

open, and first raise automatically done in the blind by the dealer.

Blood Poker — A higher-stake poker game played primarily for money rather than for social reasons.

Blow Back — A raise after previously calling or checking.

Bluff — The attempt to win a pot by making better hands fold.

Blur Intensity — The lightness or darkness of printing visible on partially flashed cards, indicating a high or a low card.

Board — (1) The poker table. (2) All exposed cards in stud.

Bobtail Flush or Straight — A four-card flush or a four-card, open-end straight.

Bolt — To fold.

Bone — A white chip, the lowest denomination chip.

Bonus — A fixed sum established by house rules that is paid by each player to the holder of a very high-value hand such as a straight flush. (Premium, Royalty, Penalties).

Book — A three-card draw.

Boost — To raise.

Border Work — Markings added by cheaters to the printed borderlines of cards to identify their value.

Bottom Deal — To deal cards off the bottom of the deck when cheating.

Bouillotte — A French card game that influenced the open-card stud variation in poker.

318

Boxed Card — A card turned the wrong way in a deck.

Boy — A jack.

Brag — The betting expression in the English game of Bragg.

Bragg — An English three-card game that influenced the use of the full fifty-two-card deck in poker.

Braggers — Jacks and nines as wild cards. Or the ace of diamonds, the jack of clubs, and the nine of diamonds as wild cards.

Brandeln — A card game similar to Commerce.

Breakers — Openers.

Breathe — To pass the first opportunities to bet.

Brelen — (1) A French card game that influenced the use of straights and flushes in poker. (2) Three of a kind.

Brelen Carre — Four of a kind.

Brief — A single stripper card in a deck used to facilitate illegal cuts.

Buck — (1) A marker used to designate the dealer. (2) A marker or a knife used to designate the player permitted to deal a special hand, usually a hand with a dealer advantage such as draw. (3) A dollar.

Buddy Poker — To avoid betting against a friend or a partner.

Buffalo — To fool opponents.

Bug — (1) The joker used in high-hand poker as an ace or as a wild card for filling straights and flushes. A wild card in lowball. Can be used in high-low as both

a high card and a low card in the same hand. (Joker). (2) A device fastened beneath the poker table by a cheater to hold out a card or cards.

Bull or Bullet — An ace.

Bull Montana — Five-card stud with betting, then jacks required to open the final bet.

Bull the Game — To bluff or bet aggressively.

Bump — A raise.

Buried Card — A card randomly inserted in the deck.

Burn — (1) A full house. (2) To lose a hand. (3) Deal a burn card.

Burned, Burnt, or Burn Card — (1) An exposed card put faceup on the bottom of the deck. (2) A card dealt facedown into the discards.

Busted Hand — (1) A worthless hand. (Bust). (2) A hand that failed to fill a straight or a flush on the draw.

Busy Card — Any card that completes a hand.

Butcher Boy — An open-hand form of poker where four of a kind is needed to win.

Buy — (1) To call bets in order to draw cards. (2) To bluff someone out.

Buy In — The stack of chips that a player buys at the start of a game.

By me — An expression meaning to pass.

California — Draw poker, open on anything.

California Lowball — Lowball.

Call — Money put in the pot

to match a bet or raise.

Calling Station — A very loose player. (Telephone Booth).

Carding — Noting of exposed cards during a hand.

Card Odds — The probabilities of being dealt or drawing to various hands.

Cardsharp — A cheater.

Cards Speak — A rule that the value of a hand is based on what the cards are rather than on what a player declares.

Case Card — The last available card of a particular value or suit.

Cash In — To exchange poker chips for cash and then to quit. (Cash Out).

Casino Poker — Public poker played in gambling casinos.

Cat — Any big or little tiger or cat hand.

Catbird Seat — A position in high-low poker that assures a player at least half the pot.

Catch — To be dealt a certain card or hand . . . usually a desirable card or hand.

Chalk Hand — An almost certain winner.

Chase — To stay against a better hand.

Cheater — A player who intentionally violates the rules to gain advantage unavailable to others.

Check — To pass without betting.

Check Blind (Check in the Dark) — To check without looking at one's own cards.

Check Cop — A paste palmed in a cheater's hand and used to steal poker chips or to hold out cards.

Check Copping — To steal poker chips.

Check Raise — To check and then subsequently raise in the same round of betting.

Chicago — Seven-card stud in which the hand with the highest spade wins half the pot.

Chicago Pelter — A kilter.

Chicken Picken — A game with eleven cards — two cards in hand and nine on the table in rows of three.

Chink Ink — A special ink used by cheaters to mark the edge of cards.

Chip — Money represented by a plastic disc.

Chip Along — To bet the smallest amount possible.

Chip Declaration — To use chips in declaring for high or low.

Chip In — To call a small bet.

Chipping — Betting.

Choice Pots — Dealer's choice.

Cinch Hand — A certain winner. (A Lock, an Immortal).

Cincinnati — A ten-card game with five in each hand and five faceup for everyone's use. (Lame Brains).

Cincinnati Liz — Like Cincinnati, except the lowest faceup card is wild.

Clam — A dollar.

Class — Rank of a poker hand.

Closed Card — A concealed card in one's hand.

320

Closed Game — A game barred to newcomers or outsiders.

Closed Hand — The concealed cards in one's hand as in draw poker.

Closed Poker — Any form of poker in which all cards are dealt facedown.

Close to the Chest — To play tight. (Close to the Belly).

Club Poker — Poker played in public card clubs. (See Gardena, California.)

C-Note — A hundred-dollar bill.

Coffee Housing — To act oppositely to one's emotions or situation.

Cold Deck — (1) A deck from which poor hands are being dealt. (2) A pre-stacked deck.

Cold Feet — A description for a player wanting to quit the game early.

Cold Hands — (1) Showdown hands. (2) A run of poor hands.

Cold Turkey — A pair of kings, back to back, on the first two cards in five-card stud.

Collection or Axe — See Time Cut.

Collusion — Two or more players working together to cheat other players.

Come — See On the Come.

Come In — To call.

Come Off — To break up a lower-value hand to draw for a higher-value hand.

Commerce — A three-card game with three cards in the widow.

Common Card (Communal Card) — An exposed card for use in every player's hand.

Consecutive Declaration — A rule for declaring high-low hands in consecutive order.

Contract — To declare for high or low at the conclusion of split-pot poker.

Contract Poker — High-low split-pot poker with oral declarations.

Cop — To steal chips from the pot.

Corner Card — An eight-card game — five cards in hand and three on the table, with last card up and all like it as wild.

Corner Flash — To tear off a corner of a foreign card and to flash it as a real card in one's hand.

Cosmetics — Preparations such as ashes, waxes, abrasives, aniline pencils, and luminous inks used by cheaters for marking cards. (Daub).

Counter — (1) One chip. (2) A player who continuously counts his chips.

Count Cards — The jack, king, and queen. (Court Cards, Face Cards, Picture Cards).

Coup — A brilliant play.

Cowboy — A king.

Crank — To deal.

Crazy Otto — Five-card stud with the lowest card as wild.

Crimp (Bridge) — To bend and hump the upper or lower section of the deck to make a false or an illegal cut. (See Debone.).

321

Crisscross — Same as Southern Cross except five cards are laid out with the center one wild.

Crooked-Honest System (C-H System) — The system of two cheaters in partnership: One catches a strong hand, and he signals the other to raise, thus squeezing all callers. (Cross Life, Crossfire).

Cross (The Cross) — Like Cincinnati, except the five cards are in a cross formation with the center card and all similar cards as wild.

Crosscards — A ten-hand poker solitaire game. (Patience Poker).

Crossfire — See Crooked-Honest System.

Crossover — A combination of draw and stud poker involving wild cards.

Cull — To arrange or cluster good cards together for cheating.

Curfew — The agreed-upon quitting time.

Curse of Mexico — The deuce of spades.

Curse of Scotland — The nine of diamonds.

Customer — An opponent who calls.

Cut the Cards — Putting the bottom cards of a deck on top of the deck.

Cut the Pot — Money withdrawn from pots for a purpose, such as to pay for refreshments.

Dame — A queen.

Daub — See Cosmetics. (Golden Glow brand).

Dark Bet — A blind bet.

Dead Cards — Discarded or folded cards.

Dead Hand — A foul hand that cannot be played.

Dead Man's Hand — Usually aces and eights, two pair. Sometimes aces and eights, full house . . . or jacks and eights, two pair.

Deadwood — Dead cards.

Deal — To distribute cards to the players.

Dealer — (1) A person who deals the cards. (2) The operator of a gambling game in a casino.

Dealer-Advantage Game — Any game where the dealer has an advantage.

Dealer's Choice — The selection by dealer of game to be played.

Dealer's Percentage — Any game offering the dealer a significant advantage. (Dealer's Game, Dealer's Advantage).

Deal Off — To deal the final hand of the game.

Deal Out — To omit a player from a hand.

Debone — A card or portion of a deck that has been crimped lengthwise or crosswise.

Deception — An important and accepted tool of poker.

Deck — All the cards used in the game. (Pack).

Declare — To announce if going for high or low.

Deep Low — The lowest hand for any card (i.e., a deep seven is an A, 2, 3, 4, 7).

Defensive Bet — A bet designed to decrease one's potential loss.

Dent — To mark cards by creasing their corners. (Rounding).

Deuce — A two.

Deuces Wild — Playing all deuces as wild cards.

Devil's Bedposts — A four of clubs.

Dig — To replenish one's stake or money while playing a hand.

Discard — To exchange old cards for new cards during the draw or twist.

Disproportionate Bet — A peculiar bet or a bet much larger or smaller than the normal bet

Doctor Pepper — Seven-card stud with deuces, fours, and tens wild.

Dog — Any big-dog or little-dog hand.

Doghouse Cut — Any cut that divides the deck into more than two stacks.

Double — To raise.

Double-Barreled Shotgun — High-low draw with four rounds of betting after the draw as each card is turned faceup. (Texas Tech).

Double Bluff — A bluff made by making a bluff bet on the final round and then reraising a subsequent raise.

Double-End Straight — See Bobtail.

Double Header — (1) A pot not won that passes to the next deal. (2) A second game that follows an earlier one.

Doubling Up — Betting twice as much as the previous bet.

Down and Dirty — The final hole card dealt in seven-card stud.

Down Cards — Cards dealt facedown.

Down the Chute — To take a heavy loss.

Down the River — Seven-card stud.

Drag (Snatch) — Money separated fro ma pot to signify the amount owed by a player. (Light).

Draw — The exchange of a card or cards for new ones.

Draw Out — To catch the winning hand with the last card or with draw cards.

Draw Poker — One of the two basic forms of poker (the other is stud). Played as a closed five-card hand with a closed draw.

Drib — An inferior player.

Driller — A loose player. A player who bets and raises frequently.

Driver's Seat — The player holding the best advantage.

Drop or Drop Out — To retire from a hand by not calling a bet or raise. (Fold).

Drum — To play tight.

Drummer or Drummer Boy — A tight player.

Dry — To be out of money. (Broke).

DTC Method — The technique of good poker . . . Discipline, Thought, and then Control.

Duck — A deuce.

Duffer — An inexperienced or poor player.

Duke. A hand of cards.

323

Dutch Straight — See Alternate Straight.

Dynamite — A two-card poker game.

Eagles — The cards of a fifth suit in a sixty-five-card deck.

Early Bet — A small bet after the first card in stud or the first two cards in draw.

Edge — (1) An advantageous position. (2) The dealer or sometimes the Age.

Edge Odds — The advantage or disadvantage of a player relative to all other players.

Edge Shot — A bet made from an advantageous position.

Eldest Hand — The first player to the dealer's left.

Elimination — Like Cincinnati, but cards matched with table cards are discarded. (Weary Willie).

End Bet — The last bet of an interval.

End Bets — Last-round bets.

End Strippers — Cards tapered along the ends for cheating.

English Poker — Draw played with a blind opening.

English Stud — A stud game with a draw.

Ethics or Etiquette — The understandings and courtesies of which violations do not constitute cheating.

Exposed Cards — Cards purposely dealt faceup as in stud.

Face Card — Any picture card.

Faced — (1) A faceup card. (2) To receive a face card.

Fall of the Cards — The order in which cards are dealt.

False Cut — A cheater's cut in which the stacked portion of the deck remains intact on top of the deck.

False Openers — A hand that has been opened improperly.

False Riffle — A cheater's riffle used to keep stacked cards undisturbed after riffling.

False Shuffle — See Blind Shuffle.

Family Pot — A pot in which everyone calls the bet.

Farm System — Several poker games at different stakes under control of a good player.

Fast Game — A game with a fast betting pace.

Fatten — To increase the money in the pot. (Sweeten).

Feeble Phoebe — Like Hollywood, except table cards are turned over two at a time and played for high and low.

Feed the Pot — To bet or raise foolishly.

Feeler Bet — A small or nominal bet made to seek out strength or raising tendencies of opponents.

Fever — A five.

Filling — Drawing and then catching a full house, flush, or straight.

Fin — Five dollars.

324

Finger Poker — A game run on credit.

Finn Poker — To play poker with the objective of winning maximum money.

First Jack Deals — A method to determine who has the first deal.

First Hand — The first player allowed to bet a hand.

Fish — An easy or a poor player.

Fish Hook — A seven or a jack.

Five and Dime — A hand containing a five and a ten with three unpaired cards in between.

Five-Card Stud — Stud poker played with one hole card and four exposed cards.

Five of a Kind — Five cards of the same value.

Fix — To prearrange the cards or stack the deck.

Fixed Limit — Betting with agreed-upon limits or maximums.

Flash — (1) To expose concealed cards. (2) To turn up a common card for everyone's use when insufficient cards are available to complete a stud game. (3) Five cards, one of each suit plus the joker.

Flat Limit — A game in which only one consistent amount is allowed for all bets and raises.

Flat Poker — Poker with a blind open.

Flicker Flicker — Five-card, high-low stud.

Flinger — A wild or crazy player.

Flip Stud — Five-card stud

in which the optional hole card and matching hole cards are wild.

Floorman — (1) A cardroom manager. (2) Shift boss in a casino.

Flop — The first three exposed cards in hold 'em poker.

Flush — Five cards of the same suit.

Fluss (Flux) — A flush.

Foiling the Cut — A cheater's method of returning cards to their original position after a cut.

Fold — To drop out of a hand by not calling the bet or raise. (Drop).

Football — A stud game similar to baseball involving sixes and threes as wild cards.

Force-in — A mandatory blind bet, usually with an option to raise.

Foul Hand — A hand containing the wrong number of cards.

Four Flush — Four cards of the same suit.

Four-Flusher — (1) A cheater. (2) One who tries to win pots by purposely miscalling his hand.

Four Forty Four — Eight-card stud with fours wild.

Four of a Kind — Four cards of the same value. (Fours).

Freak — A joker or a wild card.

Freak Hands — Nonstandard poker hands such as Blazers, Dutch Straights, Kilters and Skeets.

Free Ride — Playing without paying.

Free Wheeler — A bankrupt player allowed to play free until he wins a pot.

Freeze Out — A rule requiring player to leave the game after losing a certain amount of cash.

Freezer — A call for less than the amount of the bet in table stakes. (Short Call).

Friend — A card that improves a hand.

Full House, Full Barn, or Full Tub — Three of a kind with another pair. (Full Hand).

Fundamental Position — The value of a player's hand relative to the other players' hands.

Fuzzing — Mixing the cards by continuously stripping off the top and bottom cards. (Milking, Snowing Cards).

Gaff — A cheater's device or technique.

Gallery — Nonplaying spectators.

Gambler — A player who wagers money at unfavorable edge odds.

Gambler's Last Charge — A game played with five hand cards and five table cards with the last card turned up being wild when matched in one's hand. (If).

Gambling — Betting money at unfavorable investment and edge odds.

Game Behavior — Artificial behavior used in a poker game.

Game Pace — Betting done on various hands compared to betting normally done on those hands.

Gang Cheating — Two or more players cheating in collusion.

Gap — The missing space (card) required to fill a straight.

Garbage — The discards.

Gardena, California — The mecca for public club poker.

Ge — A pair.

Ghost Hand — A hand that reappears on the next deal because of inadequate shuffling.

Giant Twist — A twist allowing the exchange of up to all of one's cards.

Gilet (Gillet or Gile) — An old French card game that was the predecessor of Brelan.

Gimmick — See Gaff.

Girl — A queen.

Gi-Till-Satisfy — Unlimited giant twisting with progressively increasing costs for new cards.

Gleek — (1) Three of a kind. (2) An early English card game.

Go — To start dealing.

Go All In — To bet all of one's money in table stakes.

Going Better — A raise.

Going In — A call.

Golden Chairs — Player with four held cards and three table cards with one's low card sometimes played as wild.

Golden Glow — A superior brand of daub. (See Cosmetics.).

Good Hand — A winning hand.

Good Player — A player who extracts maximum money from the game.

Go Out — To drop.

Grand — A thousand dollars.

Gravy — One's winnings.

Greek — A cardsharp. (Grec).

Greek Bottom — The second card from the bottom dealt by a dishonest player.

Grifter — A cheater.

Gut Shot — See Belly Hit.

Guts to Open — To allow any value hand to open.

Half-Pot Limit — A betting limit equal to half the size of the pot.

Hand — The cards dealt to a player.

Hand Cards — Concealed cards that are dealt face-down.

Hand Pace — The extent of betting, calling, raising, and bluffing compared to the size of the pot.

Head to Head — Two people playing poker.

Heavy — A pot with too much money.

Hedge Bet — A side bet to limit possible losses.

Heeler — A kicker.

Heinz — Seven-card stud with fives and sevens wild and also penalty cards.

Help — To improve a hand on receiving additional cards in stud or draw poker.

Hidden Declarations — A rule for declaring high-low hands by concealing different color chips in one's hand.

Highball — Poker in which the highest hand wins.

High-Low — A game in which the highest and lowest hands split the pot.

High Spade in Hole — Seven-card stud in which the hand with the high spade in the hole divides the pot with the high hand.

Hilo Pocalo — Five-card stud in which the up cards can be refused and passed to the player on the left. (Take It or Leave It).

Hit — A draw or catch that improves one's hand.

Hokum — A stud variation providing an option to receive cards faceup or face-down.

Hold 'em (Hold Me Darling) — A seven-card game with two facedown cards for each player and five faceup cards for everyone's use. (Tennessee Hold Me, Texas Hold 'em).

Hold Out — To cheat by concealing a card or cards for future use.

Hold Out Device — A mechanical device used by cheaters to hold out a card or cards. (See Bug, Lizard, Spider).

Hole Cards — Cards dealt facedown in stud.

Hole-Card Stud — Five-card stud in which betting starts on the first hole card.

Hollywood — Fifteen-card Cincinnati with five in each hand and ten table cards.

Holy City — A big hand, usually with aces and picture cards.

Honest Readers — The normal marks or irregularities on any deck of cards.

Honor Card — A ten or higher value card.

Hook — A jack.

Hot Deck — A deck from which good hands are being dealt.

Hot Hands — A run of high-value hands.

Hot Pot — A special pot, usually played for higher stakes. (Pistol Stud).

Hot Streak — A run of good "luck" or winning hands. (Spinner).

House — A person or organization running a poker game for profit.

House Cut — The amount cut from pots for the house, club, or casino.

House Game — A poker game in which admission is charged or the pots are *cut* for the host's profit. Considered illegal in most states.

House Rules — Rules, especially betting, agreed upon by the players.

Hoyles — Any accepted rules for card games.

Humps — See Belly Strippers.

Hurricane — Two-card poker.

Ice — A cold deck.

Ideal Edge Odds — The theoretical maximum edge odds, which are impossible to achieve.

Idle Card — A card that adds no value to a hand.

"If" — See Gambler's Last Charge.

Immortal — (1) The best possible hand. (2) A certain winner.

Improve — To draw cards that improve one's hand.

In — To remain in the pot.

In Action — The time when a player is involved in playing his hand.

In a Row (Line) — A sequence or a straight.

Index — (1) The number or letter printed on the corners of cards. (2) The marks a cheater puts on the edge of cards.

Indirect Bet — An opponent betting or raising for a player sandbagging a strong hand.

Inside Straight — A broken sequence of four cards, such as 3, 5, 6, 7.

Intentional Flashing — Purposely flashing or showing one's closed cards to an opponent.

In the Hole — Cards dealt facedown in stud poker.

In the Middle — The position of the players calling bets between two raising players. (Middle Man).

Investment Odds — The estimated returns on betting investments.

Iron Duke — An unbeatable hand. (Ironclad Hand).

Jack and Back — Jackpot poker that reverts to lowball if no one opens. (Jack and Reverse, Jacks Back, Jackson).

Jackpots — See Jacks to Open.

Jacks to Open — Draw poker in which jacks or better are required to open. (Jackpots).

Jack Up — To raise.

Jinx — A curse of bad luck.

Jog — An unevenly stacked deck used by a cheater to mark where his partner should cut the deck. (Step).

John, Jake, J-Boy — A jack.

Joker — The 53rd card added to a deck. (See Bug.).

Joker Poker — Poker played with the joker as wild.

Jonah — An unlucky player.

Kankakee — Seven-card stud with the joker as wild.

K-Boy — A king.

Key Card — An important card needed to complete a hand.

Key Player — A player with important influence over the game.

Kibitzer — A commenting spectator.

Kicker — An extra card held with a pair, trips, or four of a kind during the draw or twist.

Kick-it — To bump or raise the pot.

Kilter — A five-card hand starting with the ace and alternating values to the nine — A, 3, 5, 7, 9.

King without the Mustache — The king of hearts as wild.

Kitty—Money cut from pots.

Klu Klux Klan — Three kings.

Knave — A jack.

Knock — To check or pass by rapping the table.

Knock Poker — Draw poker with rummy drawing.

Laddie — A fellow poker player.

Lady — A queen.

Lalapolooze — A freak hand allowed to win only once a night.

Lame Brain Pete — Same as Cincinnati, except the lowest exposed card and all cards like it are wild.

Lame Brains — See Cincinnati.

Las Vegas Riffle — A faster, more concealed method of riffling cards. At times used for cheating.

Lay Down — The revealing of hands after the last bet.

Lay Odds — To offer a larger bet against a smaller bet.

Lead — To make the first bet.

Leader — The player who is betting first.

Lid — The top card or the card of a single-card draw.

Light — Money separated from a pot to signify the amount owed by a player.

Limit — The maximum bet or raise allowed.

Limit Stakes — Poker with maximum bets and raises established by the house rules.

Little Bobtail — A three-card straight flush.

Little Cat — Five unpaired cards from the 8 to the 3.

Little Dog — Five unpaired cards from the 7 to the 2.

Little Squeeze — Five-card high-low stud with a twist.

Little Tiger — See Little Cat.

Little Virginia — Six-card stud with one's low hole card as wild.

Live Card — A card that has not been dealt or exposed.

Live Hand — A hand with a good chance to improve.

Lizard — A hold-out device that works up and down a cheater's sleeve.

Lock — A hand that cannot lose.

Long Studs — Stud poker

with more than five cards dealt to each player.

Look — To call.

Looking Down One's Throat — Having an unbeatable hand against an opponent.

Lowball — Poker in which the lowest hand wins, and 5, 4, 3, 2, A is the perfect low.

Low Hole — A stud game in which one's lowest hole card and all matching cards are wild.

Low Poker — Poker in which the lowest hand wins, and 7, 5, 4, 3, 2, is the perfect low.

Luck — An illusion of winning or losing beyond statistical reality.

Luck Out — To outdraw and beat a good hand.

Luminous Readers — Cards marked by cheaters with a special ink so the markings can be seen through special lenses or glasses (See Pink Eye.).

Ma Ferguson — Five-card stud with the low card on board and all like cards as wild.

Main Pot — The first pot apart from side pots.

Major Hand — A straight or better.

Major-League Game — The largest-stake game of several poker games.

Make Good — To pay money owed to the pot.

Make the Pack — To shuffle and prepare the cards for dealing.

Marked Cards — Cards with inconspicuous markings that enable cheaters to read them from the back side.

Marker — (1) See Buck. (2) A promissory note.

Matching Card — A card of the same value or suit as another card.

Match It — Five-card stud with one's hole card becoming wild if matched by an up card.

Match the Pot — To put in the pot an amount equal to that already there.

Mate — A card that matches or pairs another card.

Mechanic — A dishonest dealer that cheats by manipulating the cards.

Mechanic's Grip — A special way to hold a deck for dishonest dealing.

Meet a Bet — To call the full bet.

Mexican Stud — Five-card stud in which cards are dealt down, and the player has an option to choose his hole card.

Mickey Mouse — A worthless hand.

Middle Dealer — A cheater who can deal cards from the middle of the deck.

Middle Man — See In the Middle.

Milker — A tight player.

Milking the Cards — See Fuzzing.

Milking the Game — The slow draining of money from the game by tight playing.

Minnie — The perfect low hand.

Minor-League Game — A smaller-stake game.

Misdeal — A faulty deal resulting in a redeal.

Misère — The English name for low.

Miss — The failure to draw a helpful card.

Mistigris — A wild joker.

Money Flow — The direction, amount, and pattern that money passes among players in a game. Measures the money that can be won or lost per unit of time.

Monkey Flush — A three-card flush.

Monte — A three-card poker game.

Moon — (1) To win both halves of a split-pot game. (2) To declare for both high and low.

Moon Hand — A hand of good high and low value.

Mortgage — Seven-card stud requiring a player to win twice before winning the pot.

Mouth Bet — A bet not backed by money.

Murder — A two-card or a six-card high-low game with several twists.

Mystical Attitude — An irrational, unreasoned attitude.

Nailing (Blistering, Indexing, Jagging, Pegging, Punctuating, Pricking) — A cheater's technique to mark cards with his fingernail or a device.

Natural — A hand without wild cards.

New Guinea Stud — Seven-card stud starting with four down cards, followed by turning up or rolling any two cards.

New York Stud — Five-card stud in which a four-flush beats a pair.

Nickel-Dime — A small-stake game.

Nigger Bet — An unusual bet such as a nine-dollar bet instead of the normal ten-dollar bet.

Nigger Mike — Six-card draw with a bet on each dealt card.

Nits and Lice — (1) Two pair or a full house of deuces and threes. (Mites and Lice). (2) Deuces and threes as wild cards.

No Limit — The allowing of any size bet or raise. (Sky's the Limit).

Northern Flight — Seven-card stud with all hearts wild, unless a spade is in the hand.

Nucleus Players — The dependable, regular players.

Nursing — Fondling cards.

Objective Attitude — A rational attitude based on reality.

Odds — The chances of getting various hands or cards.

Odds Against — The number of failures per success.

Odds For — The number of attempts per success.

Odds On — Odds at less than even money.

Offensive Bet — A bet designed to build the pot.

Office Hours — A straight from a 5 to a 9, or from a 4 to an 8.

Omaha — Seven-card stud with two hole cards in one's hand and five table

331

cards that are rolled up one at a time.

One-End or One-Way Straight — A four-card straight open only on one end, such as J, Q, K, A.

One-Eye Jacks — The jack of hearts as wild cards.

One Eyes — Picture cards with profiles showing only one eye. (Jack of Hearts, Jack of Spades, and the King of Diamonds).

On the Come — To bet before one has made a good hand.

Open — The first bet of the first round.

Open at Both Ends or Open End — A four-card sequence that can be made a straight by two different value cards.

Open Blind — (1) To open without looking at one's cards. (2) A forced open.

Open Blind and Straddle — A forced opening bet followed by a forced raise.

Open Cards — Face-up cards in stud. (Up Cards).

Opener — The player who opens the pot.

Openers — A hand with which the betting can be started.

Open Game — A game in which anyone can play.

Open Pair — An exposed pair in stud.

Open Poker — Stud poker.

Open Seat — A chair available for another player.

Option — Five-card, high-low stud with a twist.

Option Card — (1) A card that may be either kept or exchanged. (Twist). (2) A Stud card that may be either kept in the hole or exposed.

Original Hand — The cards dealt to a player before the draw.

Overcards — Cards that rank higher than a pair.

Overhand Shuffle — A shuffle made by sliding cards from the top of the deck into the other hand.

Overhand Stack — An overhand shuffling technique for stacking cards.

Pace — See Betting Pace, Game Pace, and Hand Pace.

Pack — The deck of cards.

Packet — A portion of the pack.

Pa Ferguson — Five-card stud with high card on board and all cards like it as wild.

Paint — A face card in a lowball hand.

Pair — Two cards of the same value.

Palmed Card — A card concealed for future use by a cheater.

Pan or Panguingue — A form of rummy played in some Nevada casinos and California poker clubs.

Paperwork — Markings added to cards by cheaters.

Partners — Collusion cheaters.

Pass — To check or drop out instead of betting.

Pass and Out — A game in which checking is not allowed on the first round.

Passed Pot — When no one opens the pot.

Pass-Out — To fold when a bet or a fold is required.

Pass the Deal — To relinquish one's turn to deal.

Pass the Trash (Garbage) — A high-low stud game involving the exchanging of cards among players.

Pasteboard — A card.

Pat Hand — A hand in which the player keeps all his cards without drawing or twisting new cards.

Patience Poker — See Crosscards.

Peeker or Peeper — (1) One who looks at an active player's hand. (2) A cheater who peeks at cards yet to be dealt.

Peek Poker — Seven-card stud.

Peep and Turn — See Mexican Stud.

Pelter (Bracket) — A five-card hand containing a 2, 5, 9, and one card either a 3 or a 4, and the other card either a 6, 7 or 8. (Skeet).

Penalties — See Bonus.

Penny Ante — A very low-stake game.

Penultimate Card — The next to the last card in the deck.

Percentage — (1) The house cut. (2) Probabilities expressed as percentages.

Perdue — Cards turned down.

Perfect Low — An unbeatable lowball hand, such as 1(A)2345, or 1(A)2346, or 23457 . . . depending on the game.

Philosopher — A cardsharp.

Pick Up Checks — To allow a player to bet or raise the limit for every check made before his play.

Picture Card — A jack, queen, or king.

Pigeon — (1) An easy player or a sucker. (2) A valuable card for a hand.

Pig in the Poke — See Wild Widow.

Pile — A player's money.

Pinch — Five dollars.

Pink Eye (Red Eye) — A pink-tinted contact lense worn by a cheater to identify marked cards or luminous readers. (See Luminous Readers.).

Pips — The spots or marks on the face of a card.

Piranha — An aggressive bettor.

Pistol Stud — See Hole-Card Stud.

Place and Show Tickets Split Pot with Twist Your Neighbor — A game in which cards are drawn from hands of other players and the pot is split between the second and third best hands.

Place Tickets — (1) The second best hand. (2) Draw poker in which the second best hand wins.

Play — To call or stay in.

Play Back — To declare a false stake in table stakes.

Played Card — A card dealt to a hand.

Poch — The best pair, three of a kind, or four of a kind.

Pochen — A German card game from which the name poker was partly derived.

Point — The value of a card.

Poker — A money-management game that uses cards

for manipulation and deception for winning.

Poker Dice — Cubical dice, each with a nine, ten, jack, queen, king, and ace on its six faces.

Poker Face — A face not showing any emotion or change in expression.

Poker Rules — A loose, flexible framework of traditions for playing poker.

Poker Solitaire — See Crosscards.

Pone — The player on the dealer's right.

Pool — A pot.

Poque — (1) A French card game from which the name of poker was partly derived. (2) A French betting expression.

Position — The relative situation of a player to the other players. (Fundamental Position, Seat Position, Technical Position).

Pot — The area in which antes, bets, and raises are placed.

Pothooks — Nines.

Pot Limit — Poker stakes in which the maximum permitted bet is the size of the pot.

Pot-Limit Dig — Pot-Limit poker with no table-stake restrictions.

Poverty Poker — A game in which a player can lose only a predetermined amount, after which he can play with the winners' money.

Powerhouse — A very strong hand.

Premium — See Bonus.

Primero — An old, betting card game of Spanish origin.

Private Poker — Poker played without money being cut for the house or for the host's profit.

Proctor and Gamble — A game with four cards in each hand and three rolled table cards with the last card and all like it as wild.

Progression of Bets — The increase in betting limits for each round of betting.

Progressive Poker — A game in which the ante, bets, and opener requirements increase after a passed pot.

Public Poker — Poker played in gambling casinos or in public card clubs in which the pots are cut for profit.

Pull Through — A false shuffling technique used by cheaters.

Punching — Marking cards with pin pricks.

Punters — Those who gamble against the banker.

Puppy Feet — Clubs.

Puppy Foot — The ace of clubs.

Push — Passing unwanted cards to players on one's left.

Put Up — To pay money owed to the pot.

Quadruplets — Four of a kind.

Qualifier — The minimum value hand allowed to win the pot.

Quart — A four-card straight flush.

Quint — A straight flush.

Quint Major — A royal straight flush.

Quitting Time — An agreed-

334

upon time to end a poker game. (Curfew).

Quorum — The minimum number of players needed to start a poker game.

Rabbit — A weak player.

Rabbit Hunting — Looking through the undealt deck of cards.

Rags — Worthless cards.

Raise — See Bump.

Raise Blind — (1) To raise without looking at one's cards. (2) A forced raise.

Rake-Off — Money taken from the pot by the house or casino (Rake).

Rangdoodles — A game in which the betting limit is increased after a very good hand such as four of a kind.

Rank — The relative value of hands.

Rat Holer — A player who pockets his money or winnings during the game.

Razz — (1) Seven-card lowball stud. (2) Draw Poker in which the winner of the previous pot bets last.

Readable Pattern — A behavior pattern that reveals the value of a player's hand.

Readers — Marked cards.

Redeal — A new deal after a misdeal.

Redskin — A face card.

Rembrandt — Any game in which all face cards are wild.

Reraise — A raise after having been raised.

Rest Farm — An expression for the whereabouts of a player driven from a game because of heavy losses.

Restraddle — The third blind bet that is twice as much as the straddle or the second blind bet.

Restricted Pot — A rule requiring a minimum-value hand to win the pot. (Qualifier).

Ribbon Clerk — (1) A player unwilling to play poker at higher stakes or at a faster pace. (2) A small-time gambler.

Rickey de Laet — A form of Mexican Stud in which the player's hole cards and all like them are wild for him.

Ride Along — To remain in a hand because no bets are made.

Ride the Pot — To go light.

Riffle — To flip with the thumb through the edge of a deck.

Riffle Cull — A technique for arranging cards in preparation for stacking the deck.

Riffle Shuffle — To shuffle by riffling the cards together.

Riffle Stack — A technique for stacking the deck.

Right to Bet — A rule allowing every player the right to bet or raise at least once per round regardless of the number of raises during that round.

Ring In — Slipping an unfair or stacked deck into play.

Robin Hood Cheater — One who cheats for someone else without benefiting himself.

Roll or Rolled Card (Rolling, Rolling Up) — A face-down table card or cards turned up one at a time, usually with a round of betting after each exposure.

Roll Your Own Baseball — Same as baseball, except one of three original hole cards is turned up, and the low hole card and all like it are wild.

Roodles — A round of play at increased stakes. (Wangdoodle).

Rotation — Movement in the direction of the deal . . . clockwise.

Rough — The highest lowball hand of a given value, such as 7, 6, 5, 4, 3.

Round of Betting — The action sequence in which each player is allowed to check, open, bet, raise, or drop.

Round of Play — The action sequence in which every player deals a poker hand.

Round the World — The same as Cincinnati, except four cards are dealt to each player and four cards are dealt to the widow.

Rounding — See Dent.

Routine — A straight flush.

Rover — One unable to play because the game is full.

Royal — The best possible lowball hand.

Royal Flush — A straight flush to the ace.

Royals — See Eagles.

Royalties — See Bonus.

Rub the Spots Off — To excessively shuffle the cards.

Run — A sequence or a straight.

Run One — An attempt to bluff.

Runt — A hand of mixed suits and no pairs.

Run Up a Hand — To stack a deck during the day, often by culling discards.

Sandbag — (1) To check and then raise the opener. (2) To check to get more money in the pot.

Sanding — A system of marking cards by sanding the edges or ends of cards.

Sawbuck — Ten dollars.

Say — The turn of a player to declare what to do.

Scarne Cut — To cut by pulling cards from the center of the deck and placing them on top of the deck.

Schenck's Rules — First known rules of poker printed in England in 1872.

Schoolboy Draw — An unsound draw.

Scooping — See Shoot the Moon.

Screwy Louie — Similar to Anaconda, except discards are passed to the player on one's left.

Seat Position — The position of a player relative to the other players.

Seat Shot — A bet or raise made from an advantageous seat position.

Second — The second card from the top of the deck being dealt.

Second Best — The best losing hand.

Second Deal — To deal the second card from the top of the deck when cheating.

See — To call in the final round of betting.

Seed — An Ace.

Sequence — Cards of consecutive value as in a straight (e.g., 4, 5, 6, 7, 8).

Sequential Declaration — The last bettor or raiser being required to declare his hand in high-low poker.

Session — The period in which a poker game is held.

Seven-Card Flip — Seven-card stud in which the first four cards are dealt down and then the player turns any two up.

Seven-Card Pete — Seven-card stud with all sevens as wild . . . or one's low-hole card (or one's last card) and all like it as wild.

Seven-Card Stud or Seven-Toed Pete — Stud poker played with three hole cards and four exposed cards.

Sevens Rule — A rule in lowball in which anyone with seven low or better must bet or forfeit further profits from the pot.

Seven-Toed Pete — Seven-card stud.

Sharp, Sharper, or Sharker — A cheater. (Cardsharp).

Sharp Top — An ace.

Shifting Sands — The same as Mexican stud except one's hole card and all matching cards are wild.

Shill — A house man or woman who actively plays in the game for the house, club or casino.

Shiner — A tiny mirror or any reflecting device used by a cheater to see unexposed cards.

Shoe — A device from which cards are dealt.

Shoot the Moon — To declare both high and low in an attempt to win both halves of a high-low pot. (Moon, Scooping, Swinging).

Short — Insufficient money or cards. (Shy).

Short Call — To call part of a bet in table stakes with all the money one has on the table.

Short Pair — A pair lower than openers, such as a pair of tens in jackpots.

Short Stud — Five-card stud.

Shotgun — Draw poker with extra rounds of betting that start after the third card is dealt.

Shove Them Along — Five-card stud in which each player has the choice to keep his first up card dealt to him or to pass it to the player on his left. (Take It or Leave It).

Show — To expose one's cards.

Show Cards — The exposed cards in stud.

Showdown — (1) The showing of cards at the end of a hand. (2) An open hand played for a predetermined amount.

Show Tickets — (1) The third best hand. (2) Draw poker in which the third best hand wins.

Shuffle — To mix the cards prior to dealing.

Shy — See Short.

Side Arms — The second pair of two pair.

Side Bet — Any bet made outside the pot.

Side Cards — Cards that do not influence the value rank of a hand.

Side Money or Side Pot —

The amount set aside from the main pot in table stakes.

Side Strippers — Cards tapered along the sides for cheating.

Sight — To call for a show of hands after tapping out.

Signals — The system that collusion cheaters use to secretly exchange information about their cards and instructions about betting and raising.

Silent Partner — An innocent player used by a cheater as an unwitting partner.

Simultaneous Declaration — High-low poker in which everyone declares his hand at the same time.

Sixty Six — Six-card stud with sixes wild.

Skeet — See Pelter.

Skeet Flush — A skeet in one suit.

Skin — A dollar.

Skin Game — A game having two or more collusion cheaters.

Skinning the Hand — A cheater's technique to get rid of extra cards.

Skip Straight or Skipper — See Alternate Straight.

Skoon — A dollar.

Sky's the Limit — A game in which no maximum is placed on any bets or raises.

Slicked-Aced Deck — A deck with chemically-treated slippery aces that allows a cheater to locate the aces from within a deck.

Smooth — The lowest lowball hand of a given value, such as 7, 4, 3, 2, A, for a seven low.

Snarker — A player who wins a pot and then ridicules the loser.

Snow — To fake or bluff.

Snowing Cards — See Fuzzing.

Sorts — A deck or cards made up of irregular or imperfect cards sorted from many normal decks of cards.

Southern Cross — A variation of Cincinnati with nine up cards arranged in a cross.

Spider — A hold-out device attached to the cheater's coat or vest.

Spike — (1) An ace. (2) A pair in lowball.

Spinner — A winning streak. (Hot Streak).

Spit Card — A card turned up that is used in every player's hand.

Spit in the Ocean — A draw game in which an exposed card and all matching cards are wild.

Split Openers — To break up the hand required to open.

Split Pair — A pair in stud with one card in the hole and the other exposed.

Split Pot — A pot equally divided between two winners.

Spot — An ace.

Spot Card — Any card from the deuce to the ten.

Spots — The printed marks on the face side of a card.

Spread — (1) A hand. (2) An illegal exchange of cards between two collusion cheaters.

Squared Deck — An evenly stacked deck ready for cutting or dealing.

Squeeze — To look at cards by slowly spreading them apart. (Sweat).

Squeeze Bet or Raise — To bet or raise against another strong hand in order to extract more money from a third player holding a weaker hand.

Squeezed Player — A caller who is being bet into and raised by players on both sides of him. (Whipsaw).

Squeezers — Cards with suit and value indicators printed at the corners.

Stack — (1) A pile of chips. (2) To cheat by prearranging cards to be dealt.

Stacked Deck — A deck with prearranged cards for a dishonest deal.

Stake — The money with which a player enters a game.

Stand — To decline a draw.

Stand Pat — To play the original hand without drawing.

Stand-off — A tie.

Stay — To remain in the hand by calling the bet or raise.

Stenographers — Four queens.

Step — See Jog.

Still Pack — The deck not in play when two decks are used.

Stinger — A sequence.

Stock — (1) The cards remaining in the deck after dealing. (2) The stacked portion of a deck.

Stonewall — One who calls to the end with a poor hand.

Stormy Weather — Similar to Spit in the Ocean, except three cards are dealt in the center.

Straddle — (1) A forced or a compulsory raise (Blind Raise). (2) The right to buy the last-bettor position.

Straight — Five cards in sequence, such as 3, 4, 5, 6, 7.

Straight Draw — Draw poker not requiring openers.

Straight Flush — Five cards of the same suit in sequence.

Stranger — A new or unfamiliar card in a hand after the draw.

Streak — A run of winning or losing hands.

String Bet — A hesitating bet made in segments to lure giveaway reactions from other players, especially those on one's left — not allowed in most casinos and poker clubs.

Stringer — A straight.

Stripped Deck — A deck used with certain cards purposely removed, such as the deuces.

Stripper Deck — A dishonest deck with slightly wedge-shaped cards (usually a thirty-second of an inch tripped off the card's edge or side) allowing the cheater to pull certain cards from the deck. (See Belly Strippers, Side Strippers, End Strippers, Brief).

Strip Poker — A game in which the loser of each pot

must remove an article of clothing.

Stud Poker — One of the two basic forms of poker (the other is draw) and played with open or exposed cards (up cards) and with one or more concealed hole cards (down cards).

Substitution — An exchange of a card for one from the deck. (Twist).

Suck — To call when the proper play is to fold.

Sudden Death — High-low five-card stud.

Suicide King — The king of hearts . . . the king with a sword pointed at its head.

Suit — Any of the four sets (clubs, diamonds, hearts, and spades) in a deck of cards.

Super Seven-Card Stud — A game starting with five cards to each player; then after discarding two, the game proceeds as in seven-card stud.

Swann Methods — Simple undetected card-cheating methods used by most professional cheaters today.

Sweeten — To add more money to a pot such as an extra ante.

Swinging — See Shoot the Moon.

Table — See Board.

Table Cards — Cards turned faceup on the table for use in everyone's hand, such as used in Cincinnati.

Table Stakes — Stakes in which the betting and raising is limited to the amount of money a player has in front of him.

Take It or Leave It — See Shove Them Along.

Take Out — The number of chips a player starts with in table stakes.

Take the Lead — To make a bet or raise.

Talon — The remainder of the deck after the deal.

Tap — To bet all one's money in table stakes.

Tap Out — To bet and lose all one's cash, forcing one to leave the game.

Tap You — (1) An expression for a player betting an amount equal to all the money his opponent has on the table in table stakes. (2) A raise.

Technical Position — The strategic and psychological advantage of a player relative to the other players.

Telephone Booth — A very loose player. (Calling Station).

Tells — Characteristics, habits, or actions of a player that give away his hand.

Tennessee — Draw poker in which a bet is made after each round of cards is dealt.

Tennessee Hold Me — See Hold 'em.

Tens High — Poker in which no hand higher than a pair of tens can win.

Ten Ten — High-low five-card stud with ten for low and a pair of tens for high as qualifiers. Usually played with two twists.

Texas Hold 'em — See Hold 'em.

340

Texas Special or Texas Tech — See Double-Barreled Shotgun.

The Diamond — A measurement of the idealness of a poker game for the good player.

Thirty Days or Thirty Miles — Three tens.

Thirty Three — Six-card stud with threes wild.

Three-Card Monte — A three-card game similar to Bragg.

Three of a Kind — Three cards of the same value. (Treys, Triplets, Trips).

Three-Toed Pete — Three-card poker.

Throat Shot — An expression for a player barely losing a big pot.

Throw Off — To discard.

Throw Up a Hand — To fold.

Ticket — A card.

Tie — Two hands of equal value. The pot is usually divided between tied hands that win.

Tierce — A three-card straight flush.

Tiger — A low hand from the 2 to the 7.

Tight Player — A player who seldom bets unless he has a strong hand.

Time Cut — Money charged each player on a time basis by a casino or poker club. Charge is usually on a 30-minute or an hourly basis. (Axe).

Time Game — Poker game in which players are charged by the house, club, or casino a specified amount each hour or half hour for playing privileges.

Toke — A tip, especially to a dealer in a gambling casino.

Top — To beat an opponent.

Tough Player — A superior poker player.

Trey — A three.

Tricon — Three of a kind.

Trio, Triplets, or Trips — Three of a kind.

Trips Eight — Stud or draw split-pot poker with an eight for low and trips for high as qualifiers. Often played with one or two twists.

Tulsa — See Omaha.

Turn — A player's chance to deal, receive cards, or bet.

Turn Down — To fold.

Turnie-Turnie — See Mexican Stud.

Twenty-Deck Poker — Poker played with twenty cards. All cards lower than tens are removed.

Twin Beds — A high-low game involving five cards in each hand and ten turned up on the table.

Twist — A draw in stud or an extra draw in draw poker.

Twist Your Neighbor — To draw cards from the hands of other players.

Two-Card Poker — Any poker game in which the best two cards win.

Two Pair — Two separate pairs of different values in a hand.

Two Pair Nine — Stud or draw split-pot poker with a nine for low and two pair for high as qualifiers. Often

341

played with one or two twists.

Two-Way Hand — A hand having possibilities of winning both high and low halves of a split-pot game.

Uncle Doc — Five-card stud with a single spit or table card and all like it as wild.

Undercut — (1) The final down card being the lowest hole card in low-hole stud. (2) A shuffling technique for preparing a stacked deck. Especially useful for preparing two stacked hands simultaneously.

Under the Gun — The position of the first bettor.

Unlimited Poker — Poker in which no limit is placed on bets or raises.

Up — (1) The act of anteing. (2) The higher of two pair — e.g., queens and tens is queens up.

Up Cards — The face-up cards in stud. (Open Cards).

Up the Creek — A game in which split-whiskered kings are wild.

Utah — See Cincinnati.

Valet — A jack.

V8 Ford Special — Thirteen-card stud with five cards to each player and eight table cards in a V formation, with one side of the V played for high and the other side played for low.

Vigorish — The amount taken by the house for running a game.

Walk the Table — The automatic winning of the entire pot with a certain specific card or hand.

Wash — to Shuffle.

Waving — Coiling or crimping cards by a cheater so the wavy card can be spotted in an opponent's hand or in the deck.

Weary Willie — See Elimination.

Wedges — Certain tapered or shaved cards that can be pulled from a deck when needed by the cheater.

Welcher — A player who fails to pay a debt.

Whangedoodle — A round of jackpots played after a big hand such as four of a kind.

Wheel — See Bicycle.

Whipsaw — To bet and raise aggressively on both sides of a calling player. (Squeezed Player).

Whiskey Poker — Draw poker with widow cards that can be exchanged from one's hand.

Whore — A queen.

Widow — (1) A card or cards common to all hands. (Split Card). (2) The money cut from pots. (Kitty).

Wild Annie — See Double-Barreled Shotgun.

Wild Card — A card changeable to any value or suit desired by its holder.

Wild Game — (1) A game using wild cards. (2) A highly-spirited or fast-paced game.

Wild Widow — A card turned up for use as a wild card (with all similar cards being wild) in every player's hand. (Spit Card).

Window — The card exposed or flashed at the end of a player's closed hand.

Window Dressing — A card purposely flashed from one's closed hand.

Wing — To have a winning streak.

Wired (Back-to-Back) — A pair, trips, or four of a kind dealt consecutively or back-to-back in a hand . . . usually in a stud hand starting with the first card.

Woolworth — A game in which all fives and tens are wild.

World Series of Poker — A Hold 'em tournament with a $10,000 buy-in held every May at Binion's Horseshoe Casino in Las Vegas.

X Marks the Spot — See Crisscross.

You Roll Two — See New Guinea Stud.

Z-Game — The lowest-stake game in the house.

APPENDIX D

POKER ODDS

Appendix D compiles the following *card* odds:

1. Rank of Hands with Odds
2. Draw Odds
3. Pat-Hand Odds
4. Lowball Odds
5. Stud Odds
6. Stud Catch Odds
7. Two-Pair Odds
8. Wild-Card Odds

Card odds can be calculated and expressed as shown on the opposite page:

Now to calculate the number of three-of-a-kind hands possible *on the deal*, simply divide the deals per pat hand (47) into the total number of hands possible with a 52-card deck (2,598,960). That calculation gives a rounded-off answer of 55,300 possible hands of three of a kind on the deal. . . . The precise answer (as shown on page 347) is 54,913 possible hands, which is calculated by using exact figures.

But in calculating the card odds for *drawing* various poker hands (such as tabulated on page 348), a special problem arises: In 1967, the author discovered that the draw odds reported in all poker books were either inaccurate or imprecise. Further investigation by the author revealed that no practical way existed to give *precise* draw odds for certain hands. In 1968, all the odds in this Appendix were defined and then calculated on IBM computers at the University of Delaware. And today, these calculations represent the only *accurately-defined* and *consistently-calculated* odds in the literature. While certain *draw* odds are not precise for every situation, all odds provided in this Appendix can be used with confidence since the additional knowledge of the precise draw odds would seldom, if ever, make a meaningful difference for any poker decision.

Example for Three-of-a-Kind Odds

Odds For	Deals Per Pat Hand	(52-card deck) Before the Draw	Lower Value Hands per Pat Hand	Odds Against
1 in 47	47	(Starting with 5 cards)	46	46 to 1

Odds For	Draws per Catch	After the Draw	Misses per Catch	Odds Against
1 in 8.7	8.7	(Draw 3 cards to a pair)	7.7	7.7 to 1

[Note: All values are rounded off at two figures.]

For those interested in a more detailed explanation of the draw-odds calculations, see the footnote (page 349) for the Draw-Odds Table.

1. Rank of Hands with Odds
(highest to lowest)

Rank	Hand	Example	Number of Hands Possible
*	Five Aces (with Bug)	AAAAB	1†
*	Five of a Kind (with Wild Card)	8888W (joker wild)	13†
		(deuces wild)	672
*	Skeet Flush	2S 4S 5S 8S 9S	24
1	Royal Straight Flush	10H JH QH KH AH	4
1	Straight Flush	4C 5C 6C 7C 8C	40
2	Four Aces	XAAAA	48
2	Four of a Kind	X7777	624
*	Big Bobtail	X 8D 9D JD QD	144
*	Blaze Full	QQKKK	144
3	Full House	66JJJ	3,744
4	Flush	DDDDD	5,108 (n.s.)
*	Big Tiger (Big Cat)	8 - - - K	4,096 (i.f.)
*	Little Tiger (Little Cat)	3 - - - 8	4,096 (i.f.)
*	Big Dog	9 - - - A	4,096 (i.f.)
*	Little Dog	2 - - - 7	4,096 (i.f.)
5	Straight	78910J	10,200 (n.f.)
*	Round the Corner Straight	32AKQ	3,060 (n.f.)
*	Skip Straight (Dutch Straight)	579JK	6,120 (n.f.)
*	Kilter	A - - - 9	35,840 (i.f.)
*	Five and Dime	5 - - - 10	4,096
*	Skeet (Pelter, Bracket)	2 - 5 - 9	6,144 (i.f.)
6	Three of a Kind	XX10 10 10	54,912
*	Little Bobtail	XX6C 7C 8C	3,120
*	Flash	HDSCB	685,464†
*	Blaze	PPPPP	792
7	Two Pair	X3399	123,552
*	Four Flush with a Pair	DDD 5D 5	34,320
*	Four Flush	XHHHH	111,540
8	Pair	XXX88	1,098,240
9	No Pair (+)	XXXXX	1,302,540
9	Ace High (+)	- - - - A	502,860
9	King High (+)	- - - - K	335,580
9	Queen High (+)	- - - - Q	213,180
9	Jack High (+)	- - - - J	127,500
9	Ten High (+)	- - - - 10	70,360
10	Nine Low (++)	- - - - 9	71,860
10	Eight Low (++)	- - - - 8	35,840
10	Seven Low (++)	- - - - 7	15,360
10	Six Low (++)	- - - - 6	5,120
10	Five Low (++)	A2345	1,024

Rank	Hand	Example	Number of Hands Possible
Total hands possible with a 52-card deck			2,598,960
† Total hands possible with a 53-card deck (with a joker)			2,869,685

Code:
- * = Not a normal hand (freak hand)
- B = Bug card (joker)
- W = Wild card
- P = Any picture card
- H = Heart; D = Diamond; S = Spade; C = Club
- A = Ace; K = King; Q = Queen; J = Jack
- X = Any nonpaired side card
- - = A specific nonpaired side card
- (+) = No straights or flushes, ace is high
- (++) = Including straights and flushes, ace is low
- i.f. = Including flushes, n.f. = no flushes; n.s. = no straights

2. Draw Odds

Original Hand	Cards Drawn	Final Hand	Approximate* Draws per Catch
Ace	4	Two pair or better	14
Ace-King, same suit	3	Two pair or better	14
Pair	3	Any improvement	4
	3	Two pair	6
	3	Trips	9
	3	Full	100
	3	Four	380
Two-card flush	3	Flush	100
Pair + kicker	2	Any improvement	4
	2	Two pair	6
	2	Trips	13
	2	Full	125
	2	Four	1100
Pair + ace	2	Aces up	9
	2	Two pair (lower)	18
Trips	2	Any improvement	10
	2	Full	16
	2	Four	24
Three-card straight flush, double open	2	Straight or better	12
	2	Straight flush	1100

Three-card straight flush, KQJ or 432	2	Straight or better	14
Three-card straight flush, AKQ or 32A	2	Straight or better	21
Three-card straight, double open	2	Straight	24
Three-card flush	2	Flush	25
Two pair	1	Full	12
Trips + kicker	1	Any improvement	12
	1	Full	16
	1	Four	48
Four-card straight, open both ends	1	Straight	6
Four-card straight, inside or one end	1	Straight	12
Four-card flush	1	Flush	5
Four-card straight flush, open both ends	1	Straight or better	3
	1	Straight flush	24
Four-card straight flush, inside or one end	1	Straight or better	4
	1	Straight flush	48

* *Approximate values rather than precise values must be reported for the following reason: Consider an extreme example —the odds on a four-card draw to an ace. . . . Does one assume a blind draw into a 47-card deck that would give a precise value of 12.8 draws per catch of two pair or better? Or does one assume a draw into a 51-card deck (a deck with one ace missing) that would give a precise value of 15.6 draws per catch of two pair or better? Now there is a twenty percent difference between those two precise values, and no basis for selecting one assumption over the other (47-card deck versus 51-card deck). Furthermore, neither assumption represents the actual situation . . . the draw is not blind from a 47-card deck; and the draw is not from a 51-card deck. An accurate and precise value is obtained only by defining each of the four discarded cards and then drawing from a 47-card deck. But that would not be practical because a complete table of draw odds to the ace alone would consist of hundreds of thousands of values. All those values do, however, lie somewhere between the values for a blind draw into the 47-card deck and a draw into the 51-card deck. So where necessary, draw odds are calculated at the midway value between the two extreme precise values and then rounded off to a whole number. That is the most practical way to report such draw odds in a consistent and accurately defined manner.*

349

3. Pat-Hand Odds

Hand	Hands Possible	Pat Hands per 100,000 Deals	Deals per Pat Hand	Deals per Pat Hand or Better
A. VARIOUS HANDS				
Royal straight flush	4	.15	649,740	649,740
Straight flush	36	1.4	72,193	64,974
Four of a kind	624	22	4,165	3,914
Full house	3,744	144	694	590
Flush	5,108	196	509	273
Straight	10,200	392	255	132
Three of a kind	54,912	2,113	47	35
Two pair	123,552	4,754	21	13
One pair	1,098,240	42,257	2.4	2
No pair	1,302,540	50,118	2	1
Total	2,598,960	100,000		
B. HIGH PAIRS				
Aces	84,480	3,250	31	9
Kings	84,480	3,250	31	7
Queens	84,480	3,250	31	6
Jacks	84,480	3,250	31	5
C. DRAW HANDS				
Four-card straight,* any	408,576	15,625	6.4	—
Four-card straight,* inside	332,800	12,821	7.8	—
Four-card straight,* outside	92,160	3,571	28	—
Four-card flush*	111,540	4,347	23	—
Four-card straight flush	144	5.5	18,048	—
Three-card straight flush	3,120	120	833	—
Pair with an ace	253,440	10,000	10	—

* Including four-card straight flushes.

4. Lowball Odds

A. PAT CARD ODDS ON THE DEAL

Highest Card in five cards	Including Straights and Flushes, Ace is Low	No Straights and Flushes, Ace is Low	No Straights and Flushes, Ace is High
	Pairless Hands Possible		
Ace	0	0	502,860
King	506,880	502,860	335,580
Queen	337,920	335,580	213,180
Jack	215,040	213,180	127,500
Ten	129,024	127,500	70,360
Nine	71,680	70,360	34,680
Eight	35,840	34,680	14,280
Seven	15,360	14,280	4,080
Six	5,120	4,080	0
Five	1,024	0	0

B. DRAW ODDS

Highest Card in four cards →	five cards	One-Card Draws per Catch		
Ten	Ten	2	2.03	2.45
Nine	Nine	2.4	2.45	3.10
Eight	Eight	3	3.10	4.30
Seven	Seven	4	4.30	7.53
Six	Six	6	7.53	—
Five	Five	12	—	—

Highest Card in three cards →	five cards	Two-Card Draws Per Catch		
Eight	Eight	7.35	7.59	13.44
Seven	Seven	12.50	13.44	30.75
Six	Six	24.50	30.75	—
Five	Five	73.50	—	—

351

| Highest Card in | | Three-Card Draws per Catch | | |
two	five			
cards	cards			
Seven	Seven	30.63	31.91	95.15
Six	Six	76.56	95.15	—
Five	Five	306.25	—	—

| Highest Card in | | Four-Card Draws per Catch | | |
one	five			
card	cards			
Seven	Seven	65.08	70.02	244.96
Six	Six	195.24	244.96	—
Five	Five	976.17	—	—

5. Seven-Card-Stud Odds

Hand	Hands Possible	Approximate Hands per 100,000 Deals
Straight flush	37,444	28
Four of a kind	224,848	168
Full house	3,473,184	2,590
Flush	4,051,784	3,030
Straight	8,466,876	6,330
Three of a kind	6,374,520	4,760
Two pair	30,834,000	23,050
One pair	56,851,296	42,500
No pair	23,470,608	17,500
Total Hands	133,784,560	

6. Seven-Card-Stud Catch Odds

	Misses per Catch of a		
Start With	Straight (outside)	Flush	Full House or Fours
FFX	66	31	13
FFXX	106	275	19
FFXXX	—	—	38
FFGG	53	137	4
FFGGX	—	—	7
FFGGXX	—	—	11
FFF	4	4.5	1.5 (11 for fours)
FFFX	8	9	1.7
FFFXX	22	23	2
FFFXXX	—	—	4
FFFF	1.5	1	—
FFFFX	2	2	—
FFFFXX	5	4	—

F or G = a flush, straight (outside) or a paired card
X = a nonhelping card

7. Two-Pair Odds

Hand	Hands Possible	Hands Higher	Hands Lower
Aces up	19,008	0	104,544
Kings up	17,424	19,008	87,120
Queens up	15,840	36,432	71,280
Jacks up	14,256	52,272	57,024
- 50%			
Tens up	12,672	66,528	44,352
Nines up	11,088	79,200	33,264
Eights up	9,504	90,288	23,760
Sevens up	7,920	99,792	15,840
Sixes up	6,336	107,712	9,504
Fives up	4,752	114,048	4,752
Fours up	3,168	118,800	1,582
Threes up	1,584	121,968	0
Total	123,552		

353

8. Wild-Card Odds

VARIOUS HANDS

	Deals to Get on First Five Cards			
Hand	*No Wild Cards*	*Joker Wild*	*Deuces Wild*	*Deuces Wild, Hands Possible*
Five of a kind	—	220,745	3,868*	672
Royal straight flush	649,740	119,570	5,370	484
Straight flush	72,193	14,666	575	4,072
Four of a kind	4,165	920	81*	30,816
Full house	694	438	205	12,672
Flush	509	362	159	13,204
Straight	255	221	38	66,236
Trips	47	21*	8*	355,056
Two pair	21	23	27	95,040
One pair	2.4	2.4	2.4	1,222,048
No pair	2	2.2	3.4	798,660
Total				2,598,960

* *With deuces wild, five of a kind is easier to get than a straight flush, four of a kind is much easier to get than a flush or a full house, and three of a kind is easier to get than two pair.*

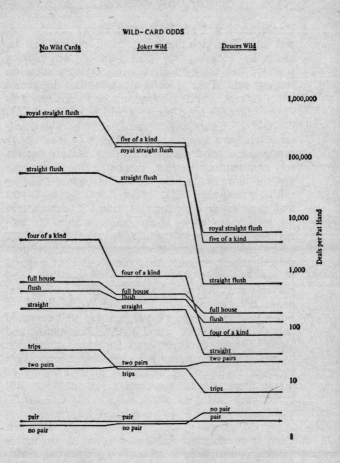

WILD-CARD ODDS

No Wild Cards	Joker Wild	Deuces Wild

royal straight flush

five of a kind
royal straight flush

1,000,000

100,000

straight flush

straight flush

four of a kind

royal straight flush
five of a kind

10,000

four of a kind

straight flush

1,000

full house
flush

full house
flush

straight

straight

full house
flush
four of a kind

100

trips

straight
two pairs

two pairs

two pairs

trips

trips

10

no pair
pair

pair

no pair

pair

no pair

Deals per Pat Hand

1

Various Hands

355

1. Concepts 38 and 126 imply that, except for the special situations described, the good player benefits more by focusing his concentration on playing sound poker than by diluting his concentration on staging acts. That is certainly true. But in games with several good players or top professionals (games that the good player would normally avoid), the faking of carefully planned *tells* (behavior patterns that give away a player's hands or intentions) can make a good player almost unbeatable against any competition. In fact, the better his opponents are, the more easily they can be drawn into traps by subtle, preplanned tells. Because both good players and experienced professionals look for, detect, and use tells projected by each opponent, they are vulnerable to fake or set-up tells. A variety of effective set-up tells also distracts observant opponents from detecting unintentional tells projected by the good player. Indeed, a good player can beat other good players and dramatically win major professional poker tournaments (including the World Series of Poker) with a series of preplanned, well-executed tells that "give away" good hands, poor hands, and bluffs. The good player beats superior competition by systematically *training* his observant opponents to react to his set-up tells and then reversing or faking those tells for the crucial, big pots. . . . But again, such faking or acting is generally not worthwhile against poor or average poker players.

    J.F., Nv.

2. Ever since the Poker Manual revealed the card-flashing collusion by a cadre of skilled lowball cheaters in Gardena, card flashing seems to have either diminished or become more sophisticated. But other forms of collusion seem to be increasing. *W.W., Ca.*

INDEX

357

358

362

363